OXFORD ENGLISH FOR CAREERS

NURSING

Tony Grice

with additional material by Antoinette Meehan

Student's Book

OXFORD
UNIVERSITY PRESS

Contents

1 The hospital team

Scrub up

1 Work with a partner to match each job with a person in the picture.

13	anaesthetist	___	pharmacist
___	cardiologist	___	physiotherapist
___	consultant	___	porter
___	lab technician	___	radiologist
___	midwife	___	receptionist
___	paediatrician	___	scrub nurse
___	paramedic	___	surgeon

2 Match each phonetic spelling to one of the jobs. Try to say them with your partner.

a	/ˈskrʌb nɜːs/	___	f	/ˌreɪdiˈɒlədʒɪst/	___
b	/kaːdiˈɒlədʒɪst/	___	g	/kənˈsʌltənt/	___
c	/rɪˈsepʃənɪst/	*12*	h	/əˈniːsθətɪst/	___
d	/ˈsɜːdʒən/	___	i	/ˌpiːdiəˈtrɪʃn/	___
e	/ˌfɪziəʊˈθerəpɪst/	___	j	/ˈpɔːtə/	___

3 Listen and repeat. How is stress marked in phonetic spelling?

Listening 1

An admission

1 Mrs Benson is admitted to hospital. Listen to the five short conversations, and decide who is speaking to her in each one. Write 1–5.

___ a a receptionist
___ b a consultant
___ c a paramedic
___ d a sister
___ e a radiologist

2 Listen again and decide if these sentences are true (T) or false (F).

1 Mrs Benson has had a fall. ___
2 This is not Mrs Benson's first x-ray. ___
3 Mrs Benson can't find the toilet. ___
4 She has a heart problem. ___
5 The consultant sends her home. ___
6 Mrs Benson's appointment is next week. ___

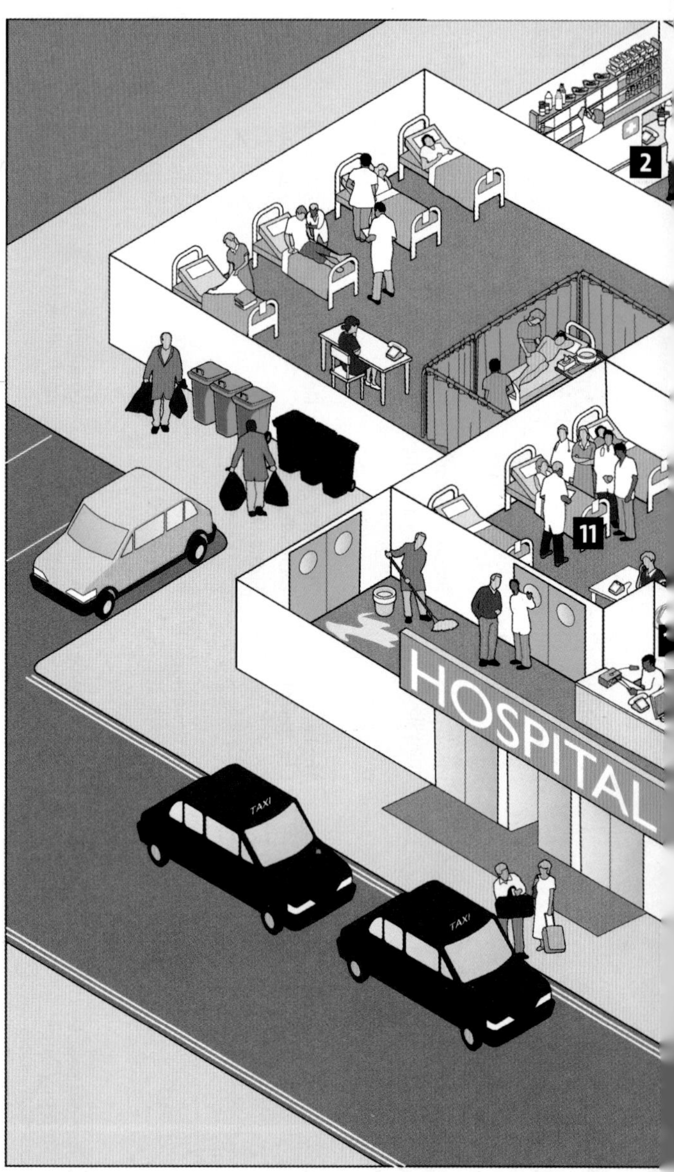

Vocabulary

Verbs for describing jobs

Complete descriptions 1–10 with a job from *Scrub up* and the verbs below.

moves	performs	specializes
gives	examines	prepares
supports	~~treats~~	takes
delivers		

In this unit

- hospital jobs
- describing what people in a hospital do
- describing routines and current activities
- the nursing profession

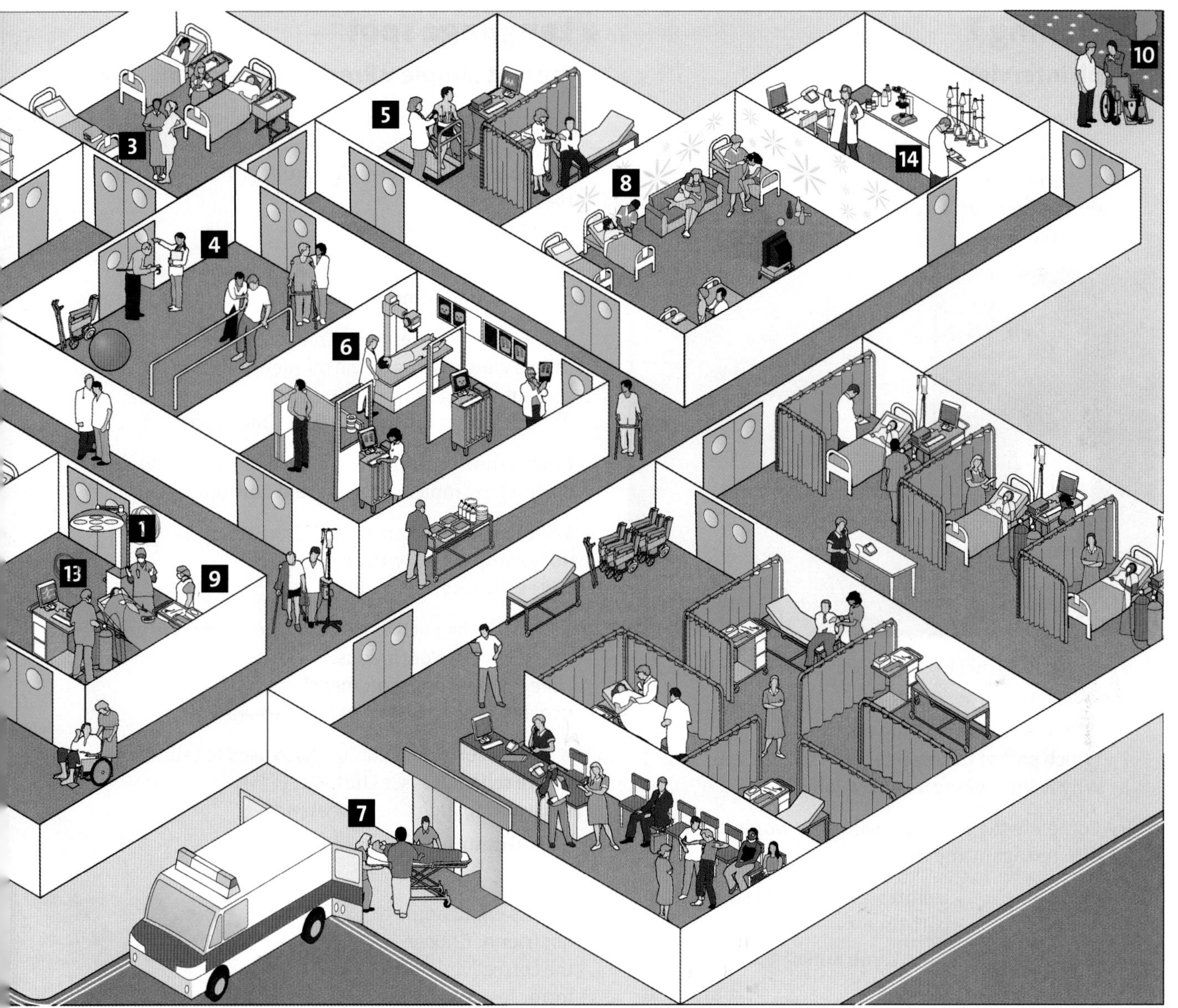

1 A paediatrician *treats* children.

2 A ______ attends births and ______ babies.

3 A ______ ______ in illnesses of the heart and blood vessels.

4 A ______ ______ equipment, furniture, patients, etc. around the hospital.

5 A ______ ______ x-rays and other images.

6 A ______ ______ surgeons in the operating theatre.

7 A ______ ______ medicines to give to medical staff or patients.

8 A ______ responds to emergencies and ______ first aid.

9 A ______ ______ operations.

10 A ______ ______ samples and tissues under a microscope.

Listening 2

A job interview

1 Before you listen, answer the questions.

- How do you feel about interviews? Are you good at them?
- When was your last interview? What was it for? How did it go?

2 Listen to Rachel having a job interview, and answer the questions.

1 Where is Rachel working now?
2 Which part of the hospital does she work in?
3 Why is she looking for a new job?

3 Complete the sentences using the words below. Then listen again and check.

applying for lectures night shift
fully-qualified part-time rewarding

1 Are you a __________ scrub nurse?
2 At the moment I'm doing a __________ course and working at the same time.
3 It's hard, especially when I'm working a __________ and going to __________ next day.
4 ... it's the contact with the patients that's most __________
5 Why are you __________ a new job?

• Language spot

Present Simple v Present Continuous

- We use the Present Simple to talk about routines, duties, and things that happen all the time.
*I **prepare** the instruments for surgery and **help** with the operations.*
*A midwife **delivers** babies.*

Look at the listening script of Rachel's interview on p.125, and underline all examples of the Present Simple.

- We use the Present Continuous to talk about things we are doing at the moment, or things that are happening now.
*At the moment I'**m doing** a part-time course.*

Look at the listening script of Rachel's interview, and circle all examples of the Present Continuous.

- We can use certain verbs in the Present Simple (for example *like*) with an *-ing* form.
*I **like** watch**ing** operations.*

- Some verbs, such as *like*, *want*, *know*, etc., are not used in the Present Continuous.
*I **like** my work at the moment!*
NOT ~~*I'm liking my work at the moment!*~~

- The Present Continuous is also used to talk about future schedules (see Unit 14).
*I'**m working** nights next weekend.*

» Go to **Grammar reference** p.116

1 Read this student nurse's email home to her friend. Choose the correct verb forms to complete it.

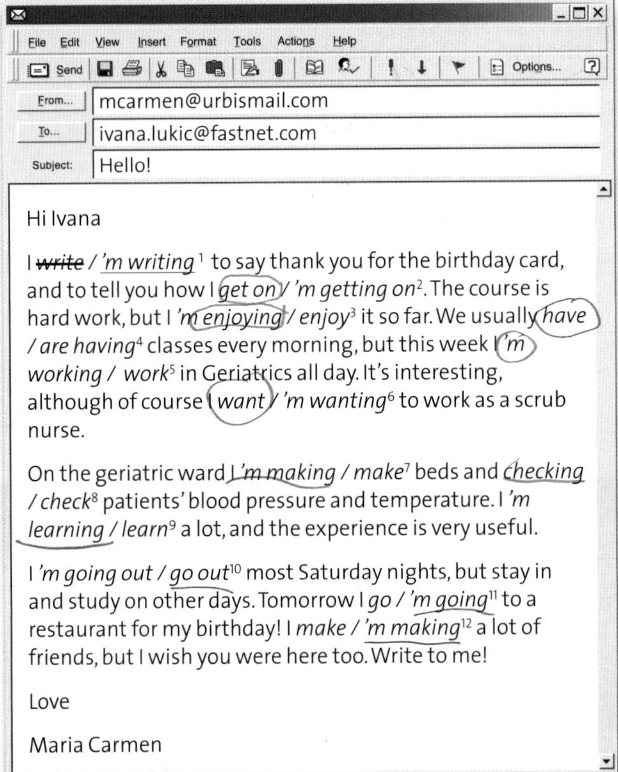

File Edit View Insert Format Tools Actions Help

Send Options...

From... mcarmen@urbismail.com

To... ivana.lukic@fastnet.com

Subject: Hello!

Hi Ivana

I *write / 'm writing*[1] to say thank you for the birthday card, and to tell you how I *get on / 'm getting on*[2]. The course is hard work, but I *'m enjoying / enjoy*[3] it so far. We usually *have / are having*[4] classes every morning, but this week I *'m working / work*[5] in Geriatrics all day. It's interesting, although of course I *want / 'm wanting*[6] to work as a scrub nurse.

On the geriatric ward *I'm making / make*[7] beds and *checking / check*[8] patients' blood pressure and temperature. I *'m learning / learn*[9] a lot, and the experience is very useful.

I *'m going out / go out*[10] most Saturday nights, but stay in and study on other days. Tomorrow I *go / 'm going*[11] to a restaurant for my birthday! I *make / 'm making*[12] a lot of friends, but I wish you were here too. Write to me!

Love

Maria Carmen

2 Choose three jobs from *Scrub up*. Write a sentence to describe what the person does, and a sentence to describe what the person is doing in the picture on p. 4 and p. 5. Then read your sentences to your partner. They must name the job.

EXAMPLE

A *He moves patients from one part of the hospital to another. In the picture, he's pushing a trolley.*

B *Is it a porter?*

A *Yes.*

Speaking

Work in pairs. Take turns to choose one of the sentence heads in the box for your partner to talk about. Ask questions to make them talk as much as possible, and note down the main information. Keep going until you have both used all the sentence heads.

EXAMPLE

A *One day, I hope to work in another country.*

B *Really? Where?*

A *Maybe Australia.*

B *Why do you want to work in Australia?*

A *It's an interesting place and nurse's pay is not bad!*

B *How much ...*

I'm interested in ...
I've worked ...
I'd like to work ...
One day, I hope to ...
In my free time, I ...
At the moment, ...
I really enjoy ...
I'm studying ...
I really don't like ...
I'm very ...
I'm good at ...
I want to be a nurse because ...
Next year, I ...

Writing

Profile of a student nurse

1 Read this profile of a student nurse. Do you have anything in common with her?

Rossitza Bontcheva is nineteen years old. She's studying for a diploma in nursing at Vazov Nursing College. She has exams next month, so at the moment she's studying hard. She wants to be a nurse because she likes working with people and she's interested in science, but she really doesn't like doing paperwork.

She'd like to be a paediatric nurse because she really enjoys working with children. She's worked on a children's ward for three months as a work placement. One day, she hopes to work in a children's hospital in India, which she saw on television.

She's good at talking to people and making them feel comfortable, and she's very organized. In her free time she plays the guitar, and goes out dancing most weekends.

2 Write a text about your partner using the information you got in *Speaking*.

Florence Nightingale (1820–1910) was the founder of modern nursing. She dramatically improved conditions for soldiers in field hospitals, and educated people about the importance of hygiene. She saved thousands of lives and became very famous. She later started her own training college for nurses, and wrote many books on nursing.

Reading

1 Read the article and decide if these sentences are true (T) or false (F).

1. The more responsibility you have, the higher your grade. ___
2. Nursing officers are the same as auxiliary nurses. ___
3. Students are paid less than auxiliary nurses. ___
4. A charge nurse is a man. ___
5. There are not many opportunities for British nurses to specialize. ___
6. Many nurses say that the job is rewarding, but the pay is low. ___

2 Number these jobs from the highest grade (1) to the lowest (4). Two of them are equal.

a charge nurse ___
b nursing officer ___
c auxiliary nurse ___
d sister ___
e staff nurse ___

THE NURSING PROFESSION

One hundred and fifty years ago, nurses were unpaid, untrained, and unpopular, but then Florence Nightingale made nursing into a profession. The methods she introduced in the 1850s were copied all over the world, and now nursing is a career with a three- or four-year training, qualifications, grades, unions, and pensions.

In Britain, every nurse is on a grade. The grade depends on experience and skills, and each grade has different responsibilities and pay. On the bottom grades are unqualified auxiliary nurses, who do the routine work on hospital wards. On the top grades are nursing officers, who are usually administrators.

Auxiliary nurses are on the bottom grades, but student nurses get the lowest pay. However, students don't stay at the bottom of the pay scale forever. When they qualify, they start working on a middle grade. As they get experience, they can get promotion and move up the ranks to become staff nurse, then sister (charge nurse if a man), and perhaps eventually nursing officer.

Many nurses work shifts, and often they work overtime to earn more money. After basic training, many nurses choose to do further study and become specialists. Nurses can specialize in many different fields – there are triage nurses working in Casualty, and psychiatric nurses who treat the mentally ill. There are health visitors who visit patients in their own homes, practice nurses working in GPs' surgeries, and midwives who deliver babies.

Many of them say they do not get enough pay and respect for the work they do. They say that the work is physically and mentally hard, that they work long hours and get very tired. But they also say that there are many great rewards which have nothing to do with money.

3 Find words in the article with these meanings.

1 exams and courses that you have taken
q__________
2 money that you will receive when you are old
p__________
3 similar work that you have done before
e__________
4 special abilities
s__________
5 levels of pay
p__________ s__________
6 extra hours you can work to earn more money
o__________
7 study and practice to learn how to do a job
b__________ t__________
8 more advanced learning
f__________ s__________

Project

1 Go online and try to find the answers to the questions.

1 What is the NHS?
2 What's the starting salary for a qualified nurse in the UK?
3 How much annual leave does a grade B nurse get?
4 How many hours a week does a nurse work?
5 What English language exam do you need to pass to work in the UK?
6 What grades can a staff nurse be?
7 What is the salary range for a staff nurse in the UK?
8 Search the word 'nursing' at the bookstore www.amazon.co.uk. What's the first book that comes up?

2 Find a site that advertises nursing jobs. Find a job that would interest you in the future and find these details if possible.

- job title
- grade
- location
- duties
- salary and benefits
- qualifications and experience
- how to apply
- closing date for applications

3 In the next class, compare your answers.

Checklist

Assess your progress in this unit. Tick (✔) the statements which are true.

I can name and describe hospital jobs
I can talk about duties and regular activities
I can describe what is happening at the moment.
I can understand an article about nursing
I can talk about my work and training

Key words

Work and training
apply for a job
fully-qualified
lecture
night shift
part-time
promotion
qualifications
rank
responsibility
rewarding
specialize

Jobs
auxiliary nurse
consultant
nursing officer
physiotherapist

Look back through this unit. Find five more words or expressions that you think are useful.

2 In and around the hospital

Scrub up

Work with a partner. Look at these pieces of equipment. Do you know, or can you guess, what they are for?

EXAMPLE

A *I think this one is for measuring a patient's heart rate.*

B *Or maybe it's for monitoring brain activity.*

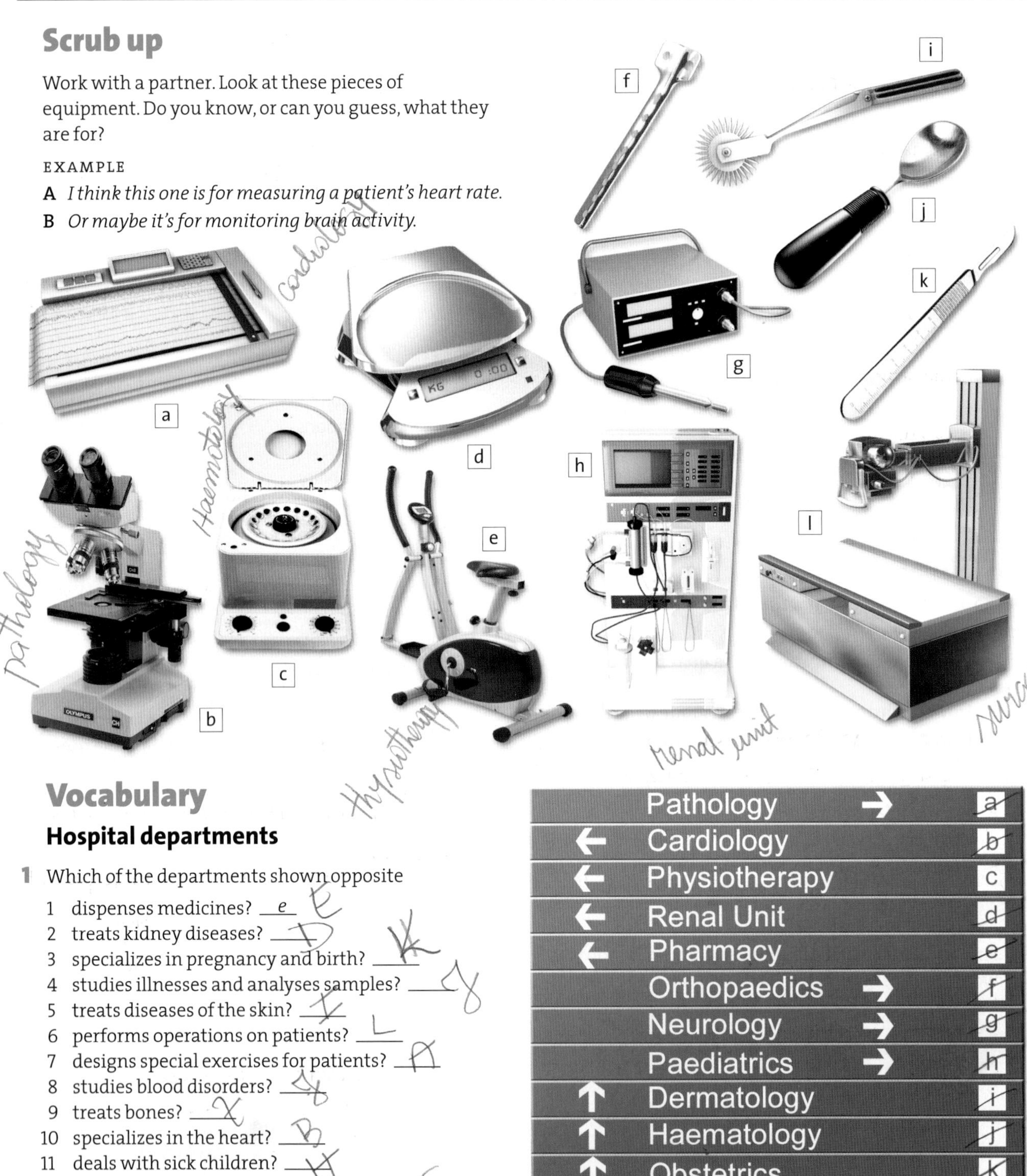

Vocabulary

Hospital departments

1 Which of the departments shown opposite

1. dispenses medicines? ___
2. treats kidney diseases? ___
3. specializes in pregnancy and birth? ___
4. studies illnesses and analyses samples? ___
5. treats diseases of the skin? ___
6. performs operations on patients? ___
7. designs special exercises for patients? ___
8. studies blood disorders? ___
9. treats bones? ___
10. specializes in the heart? ___
11. deals with sick children? ___
12. treats disorders of the nervous system? ___

2 Match each department to one of the pieces of equipment in *Scrub up*.

In this unit

- describing what different hospital departments do
- prepositions of place and of movement
- describing where things are
- giving directions in a hospital

Pronunciation

Where is the stress?

1 Match each of the words below to a stress pattern.

1 Cardiology
2 Pharmacy
3 Gynaecology
4 Neurology
5 Obstetrics
6 Orthopaedics
7 Paediatrics
8 Pathology
9 Dermatology
10 Physiotherapy
11 Renal Unit
12 Surgery

a ●●●⬤●●
b ⬤●●●
c ⬤●●
d ●●⬤●●
e ●⬤●●
f ●●⬤●
g ●⬤●

2 Listen and check, then listen again and repeat.

3 Work in small groups. Tell the group what department you would like to work in. Which ones would you not like to work in?

Language spot

Prepositions of place and movement

- To describe the place where something is, we use prepositions such as *in, on, on top of, at the top / bottom of, inside / outside, near, next to, by, in front of, behind, opposite, under, over, at, on the left / right.*
The shop's ***near*** *the entrance,* ***on the right*** *of reception.*
The toilets are ***at the bottom of*** *the stairs,* ***on the left****.*

- To talk about movement, we use prepositions such as *up, down, into, out of, away, from, to, through, across, along, past, back to, around, left / right.*
Go ***through*** *the swing doors, turn* ***left*** *along the corridor, and the coffee bar's* ***in front of*** *you.*

- Prepositions of movement are used with verbs of movement such as *go, come, take, push, carry.*
Can you take these files ***back to*** *the office, please?*
To get ***from*** *here* ***to*** *surgery, you have to wheel the trolley* ***through*** *three wards.*

» Go to **Grammar reference** p.116

1 Complete the sentences with the prepositions below.

at by in next to on outside over under

1 The toilets are __________ the ground floor, __________ reception.
2 I always keep a pen __________ my pocket.
3 Press the button __________ your bed if you need the nurse.
4 I'll put your bag __________ your bed, out of the way.
5 The restaurant's __________ the top of the building, so take the lift!
6 Reception is __________ the main entrance, __________ the left.
7 See that door over there? The car park is just __________.
8 He's __________ Ward 3, __________ the end of this corridor.

2 Underline the correct prepositions in these sentences.

1 Walk *through / near* reception, and take the lift *to / at / in* the third floor.
2 Go *around / along / past* this corridor, and it's the third door *on / at* the left.
3 If you go *past / through / behind* the swing doors, you'll see the waiting room.
4 The toilets are *at the bottom of / over* the stairs.
5 Physiotherapy is *in front of / opposite* this department, so just *go across / out of* the corridor.
6 *Go past / down* the restaurant, take the stairs *up to / along / on* the second floor, and the ward is *out of / opposite* the lift.

3 Choose five prepositions, and write five sentences with them about the building you are in now.

EXAMPLE
Cardiology is on the first floor, next to Neurology.

Speaking

Work in pairs. Student A go to p.14. Student B go to p.112.

Listening 1

Directions

1 Listen to these people giving directions. Match each dialogue with a picture.

1 ______ 2 ______ 3 ______

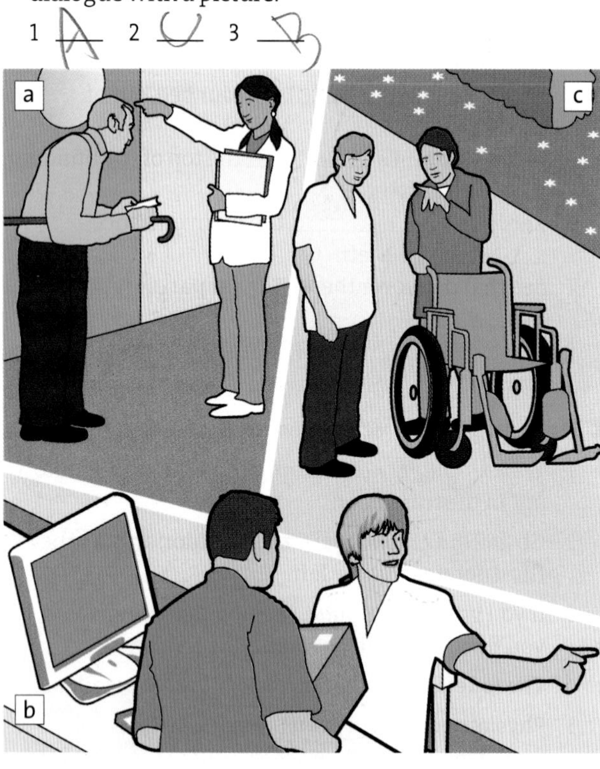

2 Listen again. Look at the picture on p.4 and p.5 at the same time. Where is the person giving directions to?

1 ______ 2 ______ 3 ______

3 Try to fill in the missing words. Then listen again to check.

1 ______ out of here and the door you want is just opposite.

2 So it's ______ outside ______?

3 Go ______ the hospital ______ these swing doors.

4 ... ______ the first right, and it's the second door ______.

5 ... take the second left and go ______ along that corridor.

4 Work in pairs. Study the picture on p.4 and p.5 for one minute, then Student B closes the book. Student A asks for directions from reception, and B tries to give them from memory.

EXAMPLE

A *How do you get from Physiotherapy to Surgery?*

B *You go along the corridor, and ...*

Writing

Giving directions via email

1 Use the map and complete the spaces in the email.

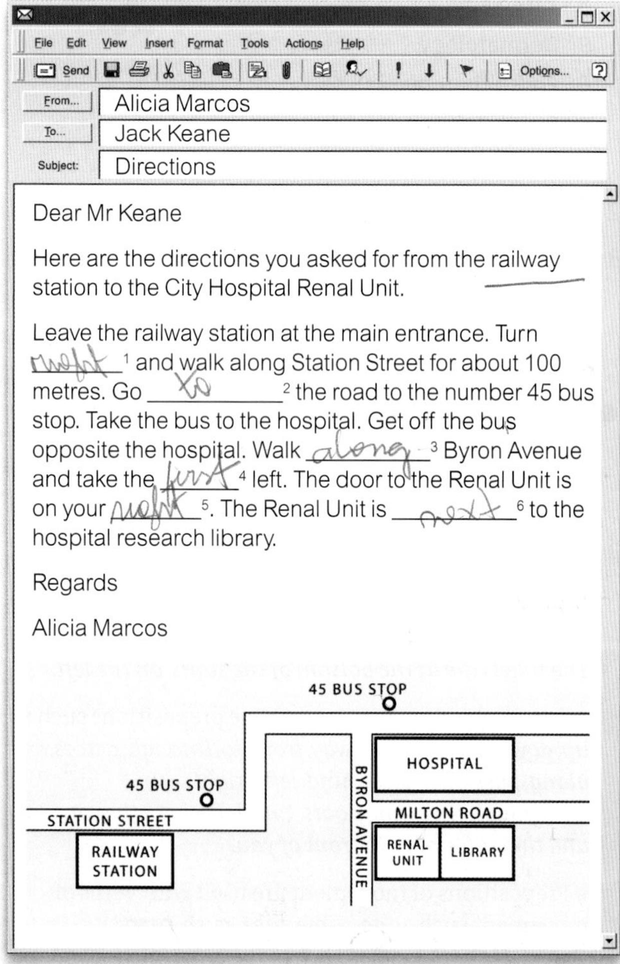
File Edit View Insert Format Tools Actions Help

Send Options...

From... Alicia Marcos

To... Jack Keane

Subject: Directions

Dear Mr Keane

Here are the directions you asked for from the railway station to the City Hospital Renal Unit.

Leave the railway station at the main entrance. Turn ______ 1 and walk along Station Street for about 100 metres. Go ______ 2 the road to the number 45 bus stop. Take the bus to the hospital. Get off the bus opposite the hospital. Walk ______ 3 Byron Avenue and take the ______ 4 left. The door to the Renal Unit is on your ______ 5. The Renal Unit is ______ 6 to the hospital research library.

Regards

Alicia Marcos

2 Write an email giving a friend directions to where you work or study from the bus or railway station.

It's my job

1 Before you read, make a list with a partner of the things you think a hospital porter does. Read about William O'Neill. Does he mention any of the same things as you?

William O'Neill

I'm the Head Porter in this hospital. What do I do? Well, I run the place.

Porters do more than just push food trolleys around the hospital. We transport patients by wheelchair or stretcher from the wards to Radiology or Physiotherapy and back again. We remove dead bodies to the mortuary, we lift and carry heavy equipment and furniture, and we dispose of all the waste. Each hospital bed produces 4.5 kilos of waste every day. We collect it each day and take it away for recycling.

We deliver the post all over the hospital and bring letters for patients – that's a very important thing. As we move around the place, we take files, samples, and specimens from here to there and back again. Last year I walked 1,800 kilometres!

To do all these things a porter must be fit, be able to think clearly in an emergency, and be polite and friendly. Next time you are waiting for a porter to answer your call, please be patient. He will be with you as soon as he can.

2 Decide if these sentences are true (T) or false (F).

1 Porters only push food trolleys around. ____
2 They move patients around the hospital. ____
3 Porters take dead patients from the wards. ____
4 Each ward makes 4.5 kilos of waste a day. ____
5 The porters destroy all the waste. ____
6 Porters give the patients their mail. ____

3 Try to remember the verbs in the text about William O'Neill and complete these sentences.

1 We t________ patients by wheelchair or stretcher ...
2 We l________ and c________ heavy equipment ...
3 ... and we d________ of all the waste.
4 We c________ it each day and t________ it away for recycling.
5 Each hospital bed p________ 4.5 kilos of waste every day.
6 We d________ the post ... and b________ letters for patients ...

4 Now read the text again and check your answers.

Listening 2

The porter's office

🎧 Listen to William O'Neill answering telephone calls and directing operations. Complete these notes that he makes of the phone calls.

The Pathology lab wants ________ [1] and ________ [2].

Take ________ [3] to the waste bins. They are outside ________ [4], near the ________ [5] on the ________ [6].

Ward 4 needs a ________ [7] to take a patient to ________ [8].

Jedrzej Jaxa-Rozen from Poland has designed a **flying wheelchair**.

Speaking

Student A (Speaking p.11)

Describe your picture, and listen to student B describe their picture.
Without looking at each other's pictures, find ten differences between them.

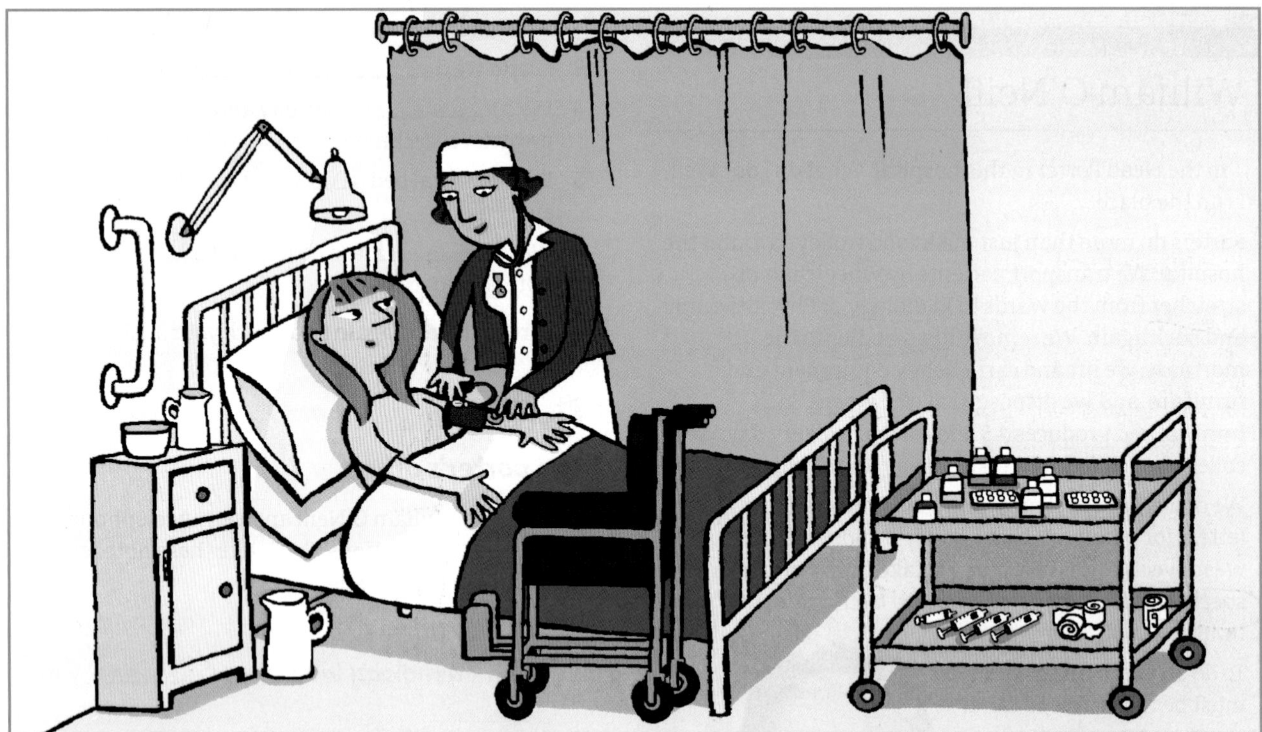

Reading

Wheelchairs

1 Read the article on p.15 quickly. Tick the things that are mentioned.

1 ☐ computer programs
2 ☐ hospitals
3 ☐ problems getting around buildings
4 ☐ sport
5 ☐ what wheelchairs are made of
6 ☐ children
7 ☐ history of wheelchairs
8 ☐ high-speed wheelchairs

2 Read the text again and answer the questions.

1 What material was the first wheelchair made of?
2 What are modern wheelchairs made of?
3 What difference does an electric engine make?
4 Apart from your arms, what can you use to control a wheelchair?
5 What three things can an iBOT do that an ordinary wheelchair can't?

3 Find words in the text with these meanings.

1 the place you put your arms __________
2 orders __________
3 not disabled __________
4 moved by the user's own power __________
5 how easy it is to move around __________
6 that does everything __________

Modern wheelchairs are a big improvement on the first wheelchairs, which were just wheelbarrows like the ones we use in the garden. Professor Stephen Hawking's wheelchair, for example, is a vehicle, an office, and a domestic servant, all in one.

The first real wheelchair was owned by King Philip of Spain in the sixteenth century. It had the latest technology – removable arm rests and leg rests – and was made of wood. Modern wheelchairs are made from the same strong, light metal as aircraft, and electric engines mean that users don't need to use their arms or have someone to push.

Wheelchair design made a big jump forward with the invention of a computer program that responds to voice commands. For users who cannot speak, computer technology also makes it possible to manoeuvre a machine by small movements of the head, hand, tongue, and breath.

Some things that able-bodied people do without thinking can be a major problem for disabled people, for example climbing stairs, entering and leaving buildings, and using toilets. A wheelchair can either help or make the problems worse. So before choosing a wheelchair there are many questions you have to ask: Will the wheelchair be self-propelled or manual? Which is more important, manoeuvrability or stability? How do you get in and out of it?

The iBOT claims to solve many of the problems of standard wheelchairs. It is a highly advanced, all-purpose wheelchair that can travel up stairs, raise the user to reach high shelves, and balance on two wheels in the shower. It is great fun to use, but beware the price – the iBOT costs as much as a luxury car.

Checklist

Assess your progress in this unit. Tick (✔) the statements which are true.

- I can name the main departments in a hospital
- I can describe what departments do
- I can understand and give directions
- I can describe where things are
- I can understand an article about wheelchairs

Key words

Parts of a hospital
corridor
floor
lift
mortuary
reception
ward

Nouns
disorder
nervous system
sample
specimen
stretcher
waste

Verbs
dispense
dispose of

Adjective
disabled

Look back through this unit. Find five more words or expressions that you think are useful.

3 Hospital admissions

Scrub up

1 Work in pairs. These patients have arrived in hospital and are waiting in reception. Discuss why you think each one is there.

2 Listen to the patients describe their problems, and decide which one is speaking.

1 ______ 3 ______ 5 ______
2 ______ 4 ______

3 Decide the order, 1–5, in which the patients should be seen.

Vocabulary

The admissions procedure

1 Complete the sentences with the words below.

a triage nurse	treatment
an initial assessment	a priority
life-threatening	waiting room
registration	cubicle

1 Take a seat in the ______.
2 The first nurse you meet will be a specialist called ______.
3 This nurse will make ______ of your problem.
4 This helps decide who is ______.
5 A patient with a ______ condition will see a doctor immediately.
6 A nurse will get personal details from you and fill in a hospital ______ form.
7 When there is a free ______, a doctor will see you.
8 The doctor will decide on the ______.

2 Have you ever been admitted to hospital? Do you have any stories of unusual hospital admissions? Describe exactly what happened.

In this unit

- describing the hospital admissions procedure
- describing what happened
- filling in a patient record card
- Past Simple v Past Continuous
- writing a summary of a patient

It's my job

1 Work in pairs. Discuss the question.

- What are the main responsibilities of a hospital receptionist?

2 Read about Carmen and answer the questions.

1. What qualities does Carmen need in her job?
2. How do medical staff cause Carmen problems?
3. What does she know about medicine?

Carmen Dornan

I'm a hospital receptionist. If you need to find somebody, or if you need to know anything about the hospital – ask me. If you want new paper towels, or you need to speak to a surgeon – ask me.

I often meet people when they are frightened, angry, or drunk, so it's important to be diplomatic and strong. I often need to reassure people, so it's important to be calm.

My normal work is to greet and assist patients when they arrive, make appointments for patients, record patients' information, and organize and file patient records. I also keep the accounts. You need to be very organized to do this job.

Of course, I have to operate a computer, a fax machine, and other office equipment, but I also have to know first aid, and understand medical terminology and abbreviations. My biggest problems are with the handwriting of medical staff. It wastes a lot of time when I don't understand reports and forms because of handwriting or abbreviations.

I believe that without me and the other receptionists the whole hospital would come to a stop.

Vocabulary

Patient record

1 Which *Scrub up* patient is recorded on this form?

PATIENT RECORD

Surname	Grady	First name	Jim
DOB	2.3.50	Gender	M F
Occupation		retired	
Marital status		widowed	
Next of kin		son	
Contact no.		07765 432178	
Smoking intake		n/a	
Alcohol intake		30 units per week	
Reason for admission		snake bite	
Medical history		high blood pressure	
Allergies		none	
GP		Dr Parkinson, Central Surgery	

2 Find words and abbreviations in the patient record with these meanings.

1. job *occupation*
2. bad reactions, for example to certain medications ______
3. family doctor ______
4. closest relative ______
5. the amount of something you eat, drink, etc. regularly ______
6. date of birth ______
7. male / female ______
8. past illnesses and injuries ______
9. married / single / divorced / widowed ______
10. not applicable (= not a question for this patient) ______
11. in each (day, week, etc.) ______
12. number ______

Research shows that **hospital admissions increase** when there is a full moon, and in the two days following a World Cup defeat.

Listening

A patient record form

1 Listen to the nurse get personal details from a patient. As you listen, complete the form.

PATIENT RECORD

Surname ....
First name ....
Gender M F
DOB ....
Place of birth ....
Occupation ....
Marital status ....
Next of kin ....
Contact no. ....
Smoking intake ....
Alcohol intake ....
Reason for admission ....
Family history
☐ mental illness ☐ tuberculosis
☐ diabetes ☐ HIV/AIDS

2 Listen again and complete these questions that the nurse asks.

1 What ________ you?
2 ________ date of birth?
3 ________ you born?
4 ________ married?
5 ________ smoke?
6 ________ do you smoke a ________?
7 ________ allergic to ________?
8 Do any of your ________ family ________ from any of the following ... ?

Speaking

1 Student As work together in pairs. Student Bs work together in pairs. You are going to play the role of a patient admitted to hospital. Invent the following details.

- full name
- allergies
- occupation
- next of kin
- family history
- date and place of birth
- smoking and alcohol intake
- marital status
- reason for admission
- medical history

2 Student A – you are the nurse. Ask Student B, the patient, questions to complete the patient record below.

3 Now change roles.

PATIENT RECORD

Surname ....
First name ....
Gender M F
DOB ....
Place of birth ....
Occupation ....
Marital status ....
Next of kin ....
Contact no. ....
Smoking intake ....
Alcohol intake ....
Reason for admission ....
Medical history ....
Family history ....

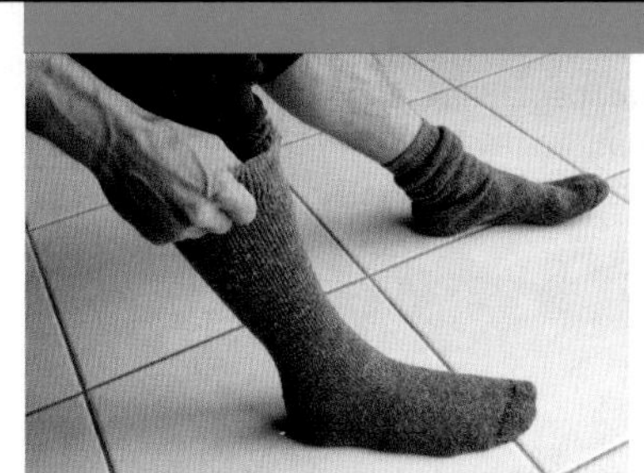

In one year in the UK, 10,733 **people** were admitted to hospital because of accidents with **socks and tights**.

• Language spot

Past Simple v Past Continuous

- We use the Past Simple to talk about things which happened in the past.

*I **felt** terrible when I **got** home last night.*
*I **slipped** on ice and **hurt** my knee.*

- Some verbs have a regular Past Simple, ending in *-ed*.

ask – asked *arrive – arrived*

- The Past Simple of some verbs is irregular.

go – went *come – came* *take – took*

Find examples of the Past Simple in the Listening script for *Scrub up* on p.125. Write the base form for each one.

EXAMPLE *had (have)*

- When we are telling a story, we often use a verb in the Past Continuous to give a background to what happened.

*I **was riding** my bike. A cat ran in front of me and I fell off.*
*She cut her finger when she **was preparing** food.*

Underline examples of the Past Continuous in the Listening script for *Scrub up* on p.125.

» Go to **Grammar reference** p.117

1 Complete the sentences using the verbs in brackets in the Past Simple and Past Continuous tenses. Decide the order of the verbs first.

1. When he was working, he broke his arm. (break, work)
2. My son ________ a firework when it ________ and ________ his hand. (explode, hold, burn)
3. I ________ of the car. My dad ________ the door and ________ my fingers. (get out, break, close)
4. My mum ________ in the bathroom. She ________ and ________ her head. (hit, fall, get dressed)
5. I ________ to music, when suddenly I ________ a whistling in my ear and I ________ deaf. (hear, go, listen)
6. I ________ in the park, and a man ________ me and ________ me. (punch, chase, run)

2 Write at least three sentences about these people, inventing details about what happened to them.

3 Describe an accident that happened to you. What were you doing and what happened?

Every minute spent filling in forms is a minute spent NOT with patients.
Elena Kneip
Nurse

Reading

Bad handwriting

1 What do people say about your handwriting? Is it clear and easy to read?

2 As fast as you can, write down three types of medicine and three diseases. Show it to your partner. Can they read what you have written? Have you made any mistakes?

3 Read the article and decide if these sentences are true (T) or false (F).

1. Nurses study doctors' handwriting at school. ___
2. Doctors generally write numbers more carefully than words. ___
3. Methimazole and Metolazone are used for different conditions. ___
4. Ramachandra Kolluru is a pharmacist. ___
5. Researchers could understand 84% of doctors' notes. ___
6. Many hospitals use abbreviations in order to avoid mistakes. ___
7. At Charing Cross Hospital, staff carry computers around. ___

4 Find words in the article to match these definitions.

1. non-medical people who work in hospital offices ___
2. written instructions on what drug to give a patient ___
3. made somebody pay money as a punishment ___
4. to cut off part of the body ___
5. an arm or leg ___
6. mistakes that result in death ___

There is an old joke that doctors go to school to learn how to write badly, and nurses go to school to learn how to read doctors' handwriting. There is truth in the joke – computer analysis of the handwriting of medical staff shows that doctors' writing is a lot worse than that of nurses and administrative staff. Maybe it's because doctors are always under pressure of time that they write very fast. The habit starts when they are medical students and gets worse as time passes.

Computer analysis shows that generally, medical staff are careful with numbers. However, they tend to form letters of the alphabet badly. When drug names look very similar, bad handwriting can mean patients get the wrong medicine. A young girl nearly died when she was given Methimazole instead of Metolazone (one is for high blood pressure and the other is for thyroid problems). And in 1999, an American cardiologist, Ramachandra Kolluru, wrote a prescription so badly that the pharmacist gave a patient the wrong medicine. This time the patient did die and a court fined the doctor 225,000 US dollars.

Recently, researchers studied 50 patient progress notes. They found that they could not read 16% of the words. The misunderstandings that this causes can mean that a patient is given the wrong blood, or that a surgeon amputates the wrong limb. Fatal errors, of course, make news, but studies show that every year hundreds of thousands of mistakes are made in hospitals around the world, and a lot of them are because of bad handwriting or abbreviations which nobody understands. Bad handwriting also causes delays, which are expensive and wasteful.

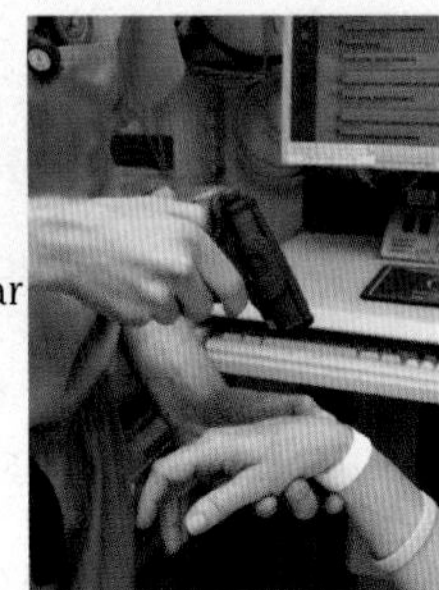

There are many technological solutions for the problem, and though digital technology can't improve handwriting, it can improve the situation. At London's Charing Cross Hospital, for example, patients wear bar codes (the same as in a supermarket) on their wrists or ankles. Staff use the bar codes along with hand-held computers to get accurate, clear, and easy-to-read information.

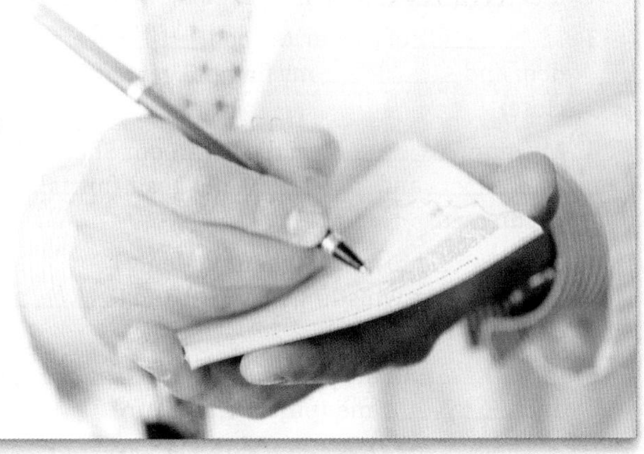

Checklist

Assess your progress in this unit. Tick (✔) the statements which are true.

- I can describe the admissions procedure
- I can understand and complete patient records
- I can ask somebody for their personal details
- I can describe events in the past
- I can understand an article about handwriting

Key words

Adjectives
allergic
fatal

Nouns
accounts
appointment
cubicle
first aid
initial assessment
life-threatening condition
limb
prescription
priority
progress notes
registration
treatment
triage nurse

Look back through this unit. Find five more words or expressions that you think are useful.

Writing

Patient summary

1 Read this summary about Mustapha Hussein, the patient in *Listening*. Find three mistakes in it.

Mustapha Hussein was admitted with possible concussion after falling from a ladder and hitting his head. Mr Hussein was born in 1982. He is divorced, and works as a painter. His next of kin is his brother, Yusuf. He can be contacted on 07709-401229. Mr Hussein smokes 40 cigarettes a day. He does not drink alcohol. He is not allergic to anything. There is a family history of diabetes on his father's side.

2 Write a similar summary about Sarah Behr using the information on the patient record below.

PATIENT RECORD

Surname	Behr	First name	Sarah
DOB	2/1/84	Gender	M F
Occupation	teacher		
Marital status	married		
Next of kin	father Ian		
Contact no.	01792-793456		
Smoking intake	n/a		
Alcohol intake	10 units per week		
Reason for admission	suspected fractured arm		
Family history	heart disease (father's side)		
Allergies	nuts		

Mr Behr was born on second of one eighty-four. He's a teacher, married, and his next of kin is Ian, his father. Mr Behr intakes 10 un of alcohol per week and was admission for suspected fractured arm. Hes allergic of nuts and his father's side had heart disease.

4 Accidents and emergencies

Scrub up

You are in a light aircraft when it crashes into the jungle. Your radio is broken so you can't call for help. There are two of you and you must get ready to walk 100 kilometres to safety. You already have clothes, food, and water.

You can take only ten more things with you – five from each list. Discuss what to take with your partner and explain your reasons.

Medical	General
bandages	a torch
a scalpel	a box of matches
a snake bite kit	soap
Morphine	a mirror
Aspirin	a compass
disposable gloves	a knife
a thermometer	scissors
tweezers	fish hooks
a first aid manual	large plastic bags
hypodermic needles	a cooking pot
adhesive tape	a mosquito net

Vocabulary

First aid

1 Work in pairs. Discuss the questions.

- Have you ever experienced a patient with
  blisters?
  third-degree burns?
  severe bleeding?
- How should you treat them?

2 Complete each sentence with a word from the box.

apply	keep	squeeze
check for	make sure	sterilize
immerse	puncture	swab
immobilize	remove	treat

1 ______ a clean, sharp needle with alcohol.
2 ______ there is no glass or other foreign body in the wound.
3 Use the needle to ______ the blister.
4 Don't ______ burnt clothing.
5 ______ a main artery if necessary.
6 ______ the injured person lying down.
7 ______ the injured body part once the bleeding has stopped.
8 ______ the person for shock.
9 Don't ______ severe large burns in cold water.
10 ______ signs of circulation.
11 ______ with Iodine or rubbing alcohol.
12 ______ antibiotic ointment and cover with a bandage.

3 Compare your answers with a partner. Working together, decide which of the above instructions belong with each of these conditions.

a blisters ______
b third-degree burns ______
c bleeding ______

4 Add an instruction of your own for each condition.

In this unit
- talking about first aid
- understanding and giving instructions
- the symptoms of shock
- describing how to deal with an emergency

• Language spot

Instructions

- To tell somebody what to do, you can use the Imperative.
  Check *for signs of circulation.*
  Apply *the pads to his chest.*
- To tell somebody what not to do, add *Don't …*
  Don't remove *burnt clothing.*
- To emphasize what is important, you can use *Make sure …*
  Make sure *the wound is clean.*
  Make sure *you don't touch his body.*
- When asking for instructions, you can use the Present Simple, *have to, shall,* and *should.*
  What ***do I do*** *now?*
  Do I ***have to immobilize*** *his leg?*
  Shall I take off *the dressing now?*
  What dosage ***should I give*** *him?*

» Go to **Grammar reference** p.117

1 Match the beginnings and endings of the sentences.

1 Check that
2 Make sure you
3 What do
4 Don't let
5 Should I
6 Shall I bandage
7 Don't
8 What dosage shall
9 Take
10 Where do I

a I count up to between breaths?
b I give her?
c have to apply the pads?
d the patient is breathing.
e the patient try to stand up.
f put the burnt area under running water?
g the patient's pulse again.
h tie the bandage too tight!
i the wound now?
j use a sterile needle.

2 Work in pairs. Think of three emergencies a member of the public might have to deal with. For each one, write three instructions to help them. Tell your instructions to another pair. They must guess the emergency.

EXAMPLE
(a patient is unconscious)
Don't move the person.
Make sure they are still breathing.
Keep the person warm until medical help arrives.

Speaking

Work in pairs. Student A look at this page. Student B go to p.112.

Student A

1 You are a parent. Five minutes ago a poisonous snake bit your child. You phone an emergency helpline. Explain the situation to the helpline nurse, then listen and use these notes to find out what to do. Note down the instructions that you are given.

EXAMPLE
What shall I do with the wound?
Should I put it on ice? Should I … ?

- wound – ice? bandage?
- child thirsty – milk OK?
- walk around?
- doctor?

2 You are a nurse working on a telephone helpline. Listen to your caller explain the emergency, then use these notes to tell the caller what to do and to answer any questions.

EXAMPLE
Make sure he gets fresh air! Open windows and doors, and …

- fresh air ✓✓ (windows / doors ✓, carry if necessary ✓, walk ✗)
- mouth – wash out ✓ (water)
- milk ✓ (alcohol ✗)
- skin – remove clothes if covered in pesticide ✓
  – wash ✓ (running water, soap)
- eyes – wash ✓ (running water, 15 minutes+, chemicals ✗)
- touch pesticide ✗✗ (gloves ✓✓)

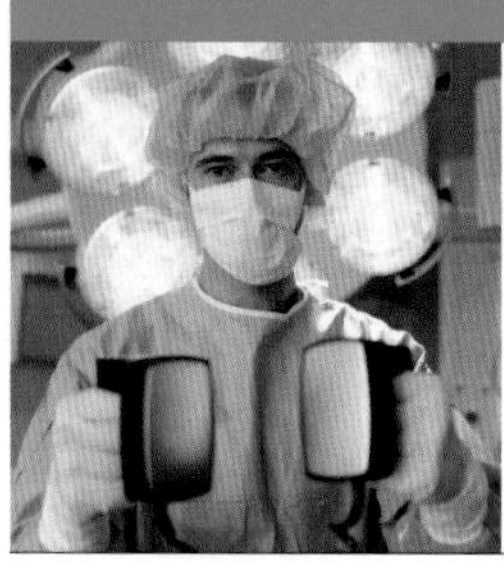

A **defibrillator** is used to make the heart start beating correctly after it has stopped or become irregular. It works by sending an electric shock through paddles or electrodes placed on the patient's chest.

paddle

Listening

Instructions

1 Work with a partner to put these pictures in a logical order. Describe what is happening in each one.

1 D
2 E
3 B
4 A
5 C

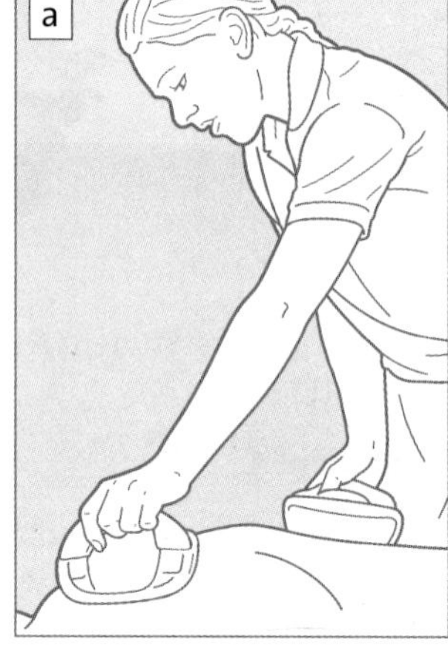

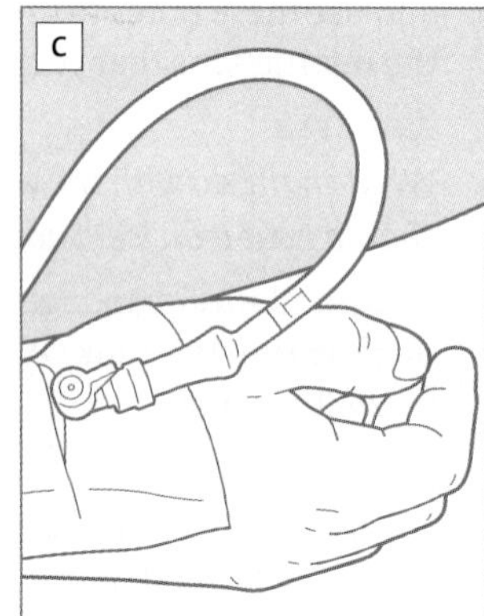

2 Listen to the student nurse receiving instructions from a paramedic, and check your order.

3 Listen again. Underline the correct option in italics.

EXAMPLE

The patient has had a stroke / a cardiac arrest.

1 The nurse gives *two / three* breaths into the patient's mouth.
2 The paramedic counts up to *three / four* after each push down on the chest.
3 The nurse pushes down on the chest *fifteen / sixteen* times.
4 They set the charge on the defibrillator at *100 / 200*.
5 The nurse applies the pads *on each side of / above and below* the heart.
6 The patient starts to respond after the *first / second* charge from the defibrillator.
7 The patient is given *Lidocaine / Atropine*.
8 The dosage is *200 ml over one minute / 100 ml over two minutes*.

4 Complete each sentence with a verb from the list, then listen again to check.

check	hold	repeat	stand
give	press	set up	support
give	put		

1 give him CPR.
2 give him mouth-to-mouth first.
3 hold his head. support
4 Right, press his nose closed, then ... hold
5 put your hand on his chest.
6 stand clear of his body.
7 ... then press the buttons and hold for two seconds.
8 check his pulse again.
9 OK – repeat the procedure.
10 Well done. Now set up an IV and give ...

set up

Taxi drivers in Bangkok are now being trained to help women give birth. An estimated 300–400 **women** in the city give birth in taxis or tuk-tuks on the way to hospital each year.

Reading

1 Look at the pictures. What do you think the article is about?

2 Discuss these questions with a partner.

- Have you ever helped with a birth? How was it?
- Were you born in hospital, at home, or somewhere else?
- Have you heard of any births that happened in an unusual place?

3 Read the text and answer the questions.

1 Was this Clive's first experience of a birth?
2 Who gave instructions to Clive?
3 Who is Mohammed Clive?
4 How is the baby now?

4 Work in pairs. Cover the article. Can you remember the midwife's instructions? Look at the words below to help you remember.

blanket	medical help	mother's chest
head		nose and mouth
umbilical cord	back	towel

A surprise passenger

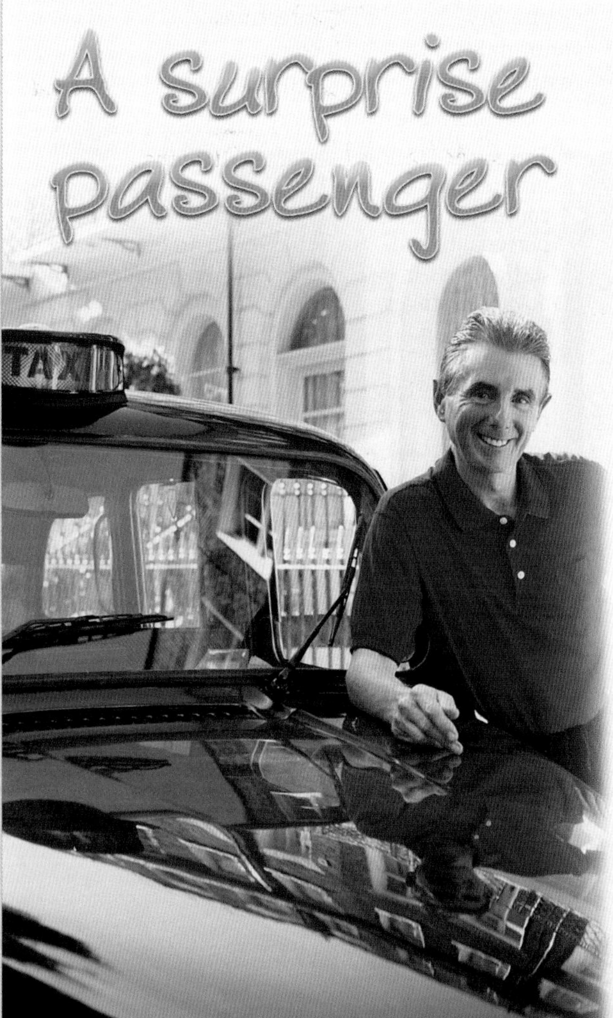

British taxi driver, Clive Lawrence, became a midwife for an hour when a passenger gave birth to a baby in the back of his taxi.

Asha Gemechu's baby was due in a month, but when her contractions started she called for a taxi to take her to hospital. Mr Lawrence answered the call.

The expectant mum was in the taxi for ten minutes when she realized that things were happening too fast. The baby was not going to wait. Its head appeared, and Mr Lawrence stopped the taxi to help with the birth.

Mr Lawrence said, 'I was there when my kids were born, so this was not completely new for me. I spoke to a nurse on the taxi radio and she gave me instructions – I only did what she told me. There's nothing special about that. One minute I had one passenger, then I had two, but there's no extra charge!'

A midwife at the hospital said, 'Giving birth on the way to hospital doesn't happen often, but if you're there when it does, just support the baby's head and guide it out – don't pull. Then clean the baby's nose and mouth, but don't cut the umbilical cord – just lay the baby on the mother's chest, cord and all. Dry the baby with a clean towel or cloth, gently rub its back, then cover mum and baby with a dry blanket to keep them both warm, and wait for medical help to arrive.'

'Clive was wonderful,' the mother said later, 'he did everything right.' Asha is naming the baby Mohammed Clive. Mother and baby are both doing well.

Worldwide, somebody is killed in a car accident **every 30 seconds**.
(World Health Organisation statistics)

It's my job

1 Read about Jeff Oliver and answer the questions.

1 When did Jeff decide to become a paramedic?
2 How long did he train for the job?
3 What things do you have to be good at do Jeff's job?
4 Who makes Jeff's job difficult?

Jeff Oliver

I'm Jeff Oliver. I'm 24 years old. I decided to become a paramedic when I saw two of them treating a driver at the scene of an accident when I was a boy.

I started as a trainee ambulance technician, and trained for two and a half years to become a qualified paramedic. Now I administer life-saving procedures myself. It's part of my everyday work to defibrillate the heart of a cardiac arrest, to apply splints to limbs and dress wounds, and to set up drips.

I have to make quick decisions – it's an important part of giving emergency treatment. So is communicating clearly and keeping a clear head in some difficult situations. And situations are often *very* difficult, especially when we have to deal with people under the influence of drugs and alcohol. But paramedics don't think twice – we are always first at the scene when there is a suicide, a road accident, or a fire. When you save a life, it's the best job in the world.

2 Join these word combinations used in the text.

1	become	a	a life
2	deal with	b	as a trainee
3	give	c	a qualified paramedic
4	make	d	treatment
5	save	e	people
6	start	f	decisions

3 Would you like to do Jeff's job?

Signs and symptoms

Shock

Paramedics often have to deal with shock, a condition that is often caused by major trauma such as a traffic accident. Shock occurs when the heart is unable to supply enough blood to the organs. This results in a slowing-down of the vital functions, and can cause death. Shock is difficult to diagnose in its early stages, which makes it hard to treat. Read about the signs and symptoms of shock, and complete them with words below.

dangerously	blood pressure
abdominal	cardiovascular
respiratory	intestines
abnormally	coma
gastrointestinal	central nervous system

The ___[1] is affected. This can cause changes in personality, and restlessness. In advanced stages, confusion and ultimately ___[2] can result.

___[4] problems may develop. The patient's heart often beats abnormally fast, but heavy bleeding may cause it to beat too slowly.

Their temperature may be ___[3] low (hypothermia) or high (hyperthermia).

Checklist

Assess your progress in this unit. Tick (✔) the statements which are true.

- I can talk about first aid procedures
- I can understand instructions for CPR
- I can instruct somebody how to give first aid
- I can understand a description of the symptoms of shock
- I can write instructions for dealing with an emergency

Key words

Medical problems
blister
cardiac arrest
circulation
foreign body
stroke
trauma
wound

Treatment
CPR
disposable
dressing
hypodermic needle
sterile
sterilize
swab
tweezers

Look back through this unit. Find five more words or expressions that you think are useful.

Writing

Information poster

You have been asked to produce a poster telling motorists what to do in an emergency. Write a list of instructions for the following situation. Give reasons where it will help people to understand.

FIRST AID FOR MOTORISTS 

A car has crashed. You are the first to arrive on the scene. The driver is unconscious.

What do you do?

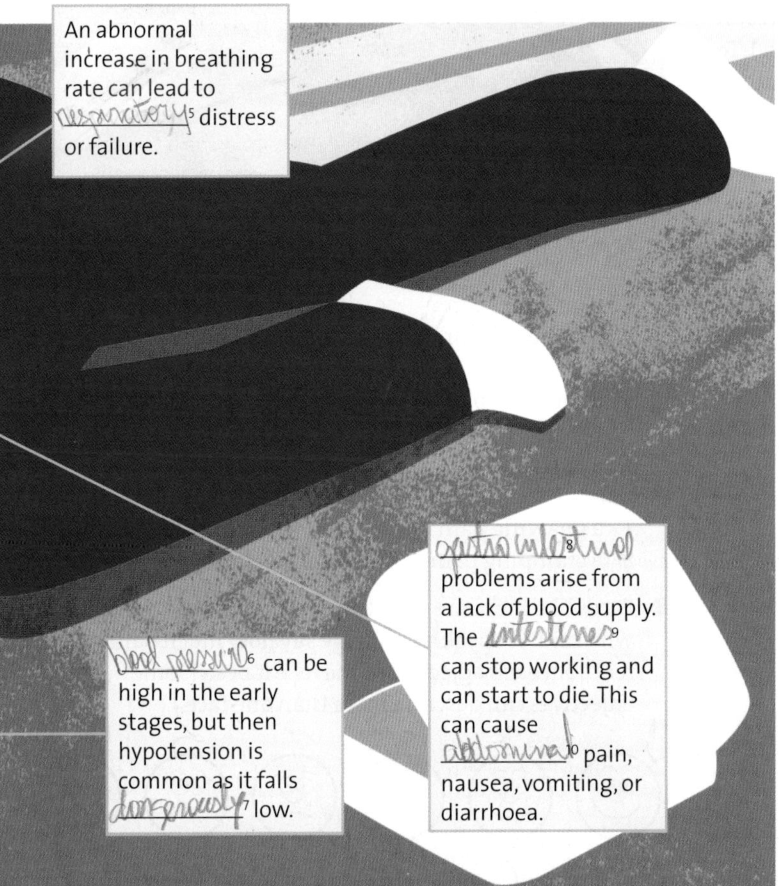

An abnormal increase in breathing rate can lead to respiratory 5 distress or failure.
blood pressure 6 can be high in the early stages, but then hypotension is common as it falls dangerously 7 low.
gastrointestinal 8 problems arise from a lack of blood supply. The intestines 9 can stop working and can start to die. This can cause abdominal 10 pain, nausea, vomiting, or diarrhoea.

5 Pain

Scrub up

1 Work with a partner. Which of these parts of the body do you think is the most sensitive to pain? Number them from 1 (the most sensitive) to 10 (the least sensitive).

_____ back of hand	_____ forehead
_____ cheek	_____ nose
_____ fingertip	_____ palm
_____ foot	_____ upper arm
_____ forearm	_____ upper lip

2 You need a paperclip and a ruler. Bend the paperclip into a U shape. With the points of the U about 10mm apart, touch your partner on the back of the hand with both points at the same time. Can they feel one or two points? Adjust the distance between the points and do the test again until you find the shortest distance where they can feel two points. Write down the result and repeat on the other parts of the body listed in 1. To make it more difficult, sometimes touch your partner with just one point.

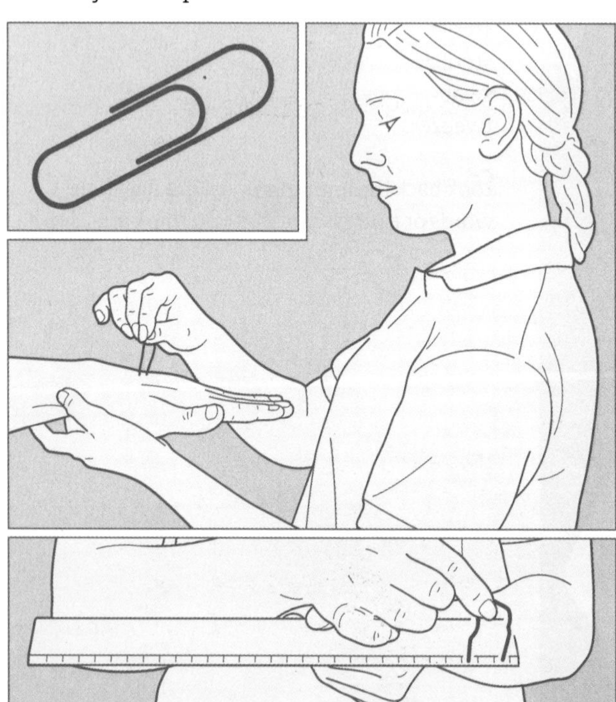

3 Look at your answers for 1. Did the experiment give the same results?

Vocabulary

Describing pain

1 Discuss these questions with a partner.

- Are you good at dealing with pain?
- Do you have any special techniques to help you deal with pain?
- What is your experience of looking after people in severe pain?

2 Match these words for types of pain with their descriptions.

1 a throbbing pain
2 a sharp pain
3 a burning pain
4 a stabbing pain
5 a shooting pain
6 a dull ache
7 a gnawing pain
8 a cramping pain

a feels like it is eating you
b travels fast along part of your body
c is steady and not too painful
d feels like a muscle is being squeezed
e feels like something sharp is stuck into you
f comes and goes rhythmically
g feels like fire
h is strong and sudden

3 Faces like these are used to help children and people who cannot speak a language say how much pain they feel. Join each adjective to the face it best. (Some adjectives can describe more than one face.)

agonizing moderate quite bad slight
mild not bad severe unbearable

In this unit

- describing types of pain
- describing degrees of pain
- comparing things
- asking about pain
- referred pain

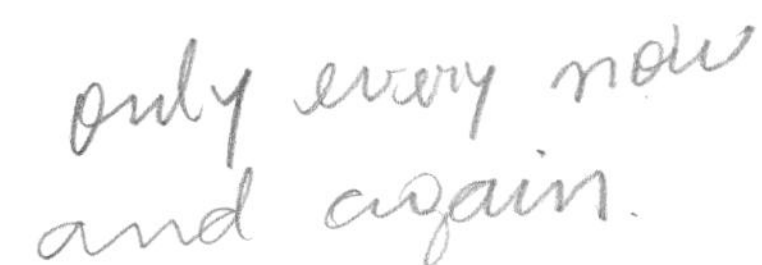

Listening 1

A pain chart

1 Listen to four patients describing their pain. Tick (✓) the boxes that describe the pain, and mark the position on the body.

	Patient 1	Patient 2	Patient 3	Patient 4
burning	☐	☐	☐	☐
stabbing	☐	☐	☐	☐
throbbing	☐	☐	☐	☐
shooting	☐	☐	☐	☐
constant	☐	☐	☐	☐
frequent	☐	☐	☐	☐
occasional	☐	☐	☐	☐
mild	☐	☐	☐	☐
moderate	☐	☐	☐	☐
severe	☐	☐	☐	☐
getting better	☐	☐	☐	☐
getting worse	☐	☐	☐	☐
staying the same	☐	☐	☐	☐

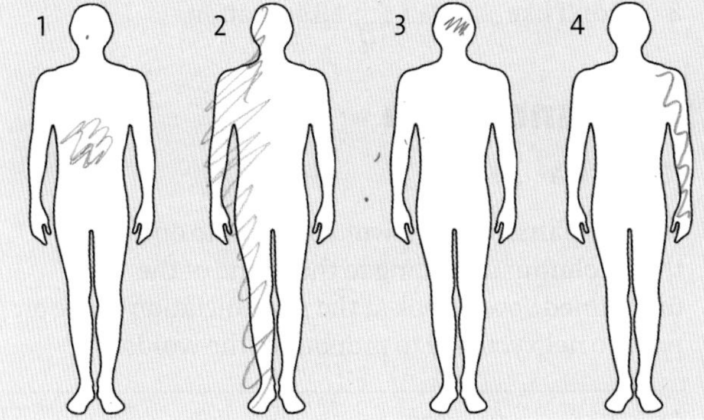

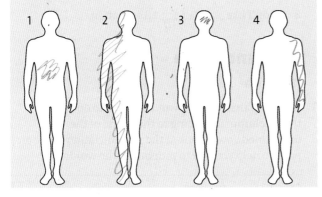

2 Work with a partner. Try to complete these phrases, then listen again and check.

1 Are you still ________ pain?
2 Well, ________ pain around my stomach.
3 I ________ a slight pain, just here ________ my right side.
4 I've ________ this throbbing pain ________ my head.
5 I ________ getting this terrible pain ________ my left arm.

3 What kind of pain do you think these conditions might cause? Discuss your thoughts with a partner.

- a deep cut
- migraine
- a tumour
- labour
- a stomach ulcer
- kidney stones
- a broken ankle
- a severed finger

Language spot

Making comparisons

1 Match these examples with the rules below.

a *It's much **less sore** than it was yesterday, thanks.*
b *They have **more beds** in the City Hospital.*
c *This is **the strongest** painkiller available without a prescription.*
d ***Most women** choose to have pain relief when giving birth.*
e *Last night the pain was **more severe** than it was this morning.*

- We use comparatives to say how things are different.
*These painkillers are **milder than** those.*

1 ________________________________

- To make a comparative stronger, we often use *much* or *a lot*.
*You look **much better** today.*

- The opposite of *more* is *less*.

2 ________________________________

- We can use *more* and *less* with a noun to talk about quantity.

3 ________________________________

- We use superlatives to compare something to all other things of the same type.

4 ________________________________

- The opposite of *the most* is *the least*.
*This is **the least** serious type of fracture.*

- We can use *most* with a noun to talk about a large proportion of something.

5 ________________________________

» Go to **Grammar reference** p.118

2 Look at the information about these three painkillers. Complete the sentences, then write three more of your own.

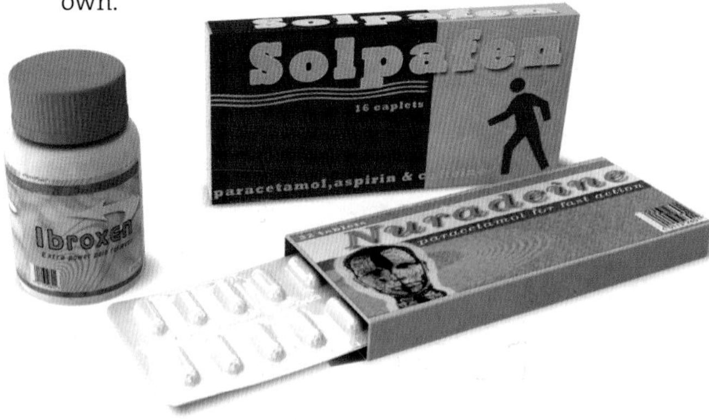

	Effective	Cost	Side effects
Nuradeine	✓✓✓✓	€€	✓
Ibroxen	✓	€	✓✓✓
Solpafen	✓✓	€€€€	✓✓

1 Nuradeine is much ________ (effective) than Ibroxen.
2 Ibroxen is ________ (cheap) than Nuradeine.
3 Ibroxen has ________ (side effects) than Nuradeine.
4 Nuradeine is ________ (effective).
5 ________
6 ________
7 ________

» Go to **Grammar reference** p.118

Listening 2

Pain relief

1 Listen to Janice and Karen talking about their experiences of pain relief in labour. Underline the part of the sentence in italics that is true.

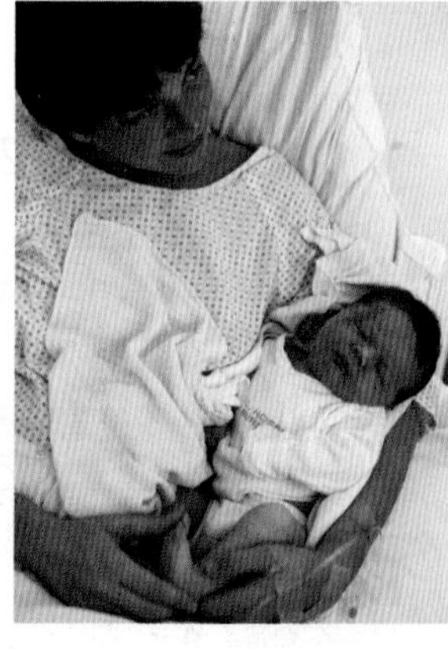

1 Their babies are *different sexes / the same sex.*
2 Karen started with *gas and air / Pethidine.*
3 Gas and air *made / didn't make* her feel good.
4 The epidural relieved *all / some* of the pain.
5 Janice *had / didn't have* gas and air.
6 Janice lost *no / all* feeling during her previous birth.

2 Complete these sentences with the verbs below, then listen again to check.

became, got, took away, cope with, losing, wears off, feel, relieve

1 It does ________ the pain a bit …
2 … the effect ________ very quickly.
3 It made me ________ sick too.
4 … when the pain ________ unbearable, I had an epidural.
5 Did that help you ________ the pain?
6 It ________ the pain completely!
7 I decided to have gas and air if the pain ________ worse …
8 I didn't like ________ all sensation.

Pronunciation

/ɜː/, /eə/ , /ə/

1 Work in pairs. Put each word below into one of the three columns according to the sound of the underlined vowel. Look at the pronunciation guide on p.132 to help you. Try to pronounce the words.

/ɜː/	/eə/	/ə/
		ulcer

air	hurt	doctor
care	nurse	appointment
first	hair	tumour
~~ulcer~~	worse	where

2 Listen to the words and repeat them.

Reading

1 Before you read the article, discuss these questions with a partner.

- Can you give a definition of 'pain'?
- Why do we feel pain?
- What would happen if you could feel no pain?

2 Read the article, and decide if these statements are true (T) or false (F).

1 People who are born unable to feel pain are unlucky. ____
2 Pain starts in the brain. ____
3 Chronic pain lasts longer than acute pain. ____
4 All drugs which stop pain work directly on the brain. ____
5 'Phantom limb' pain is felt by people who have lost an arm or leg. ____

3 Complete the gaps using verbs from the article. You may need to change the tense.

1 She wears a mask to p__________ the area of burnt skin.
2 The pain in your legs should go when we t__________ your back problem.
3 She used breathing exercises and gas and air to m__________ the pain of childbirth.
4 A local anaesthetic will p__________ you feeling any pain during the operation.
5 Breathing exercises help c__________ the pain to some extent.
6 When you s__________ a serious injury, you may not feel pain immediately.

Pain is a vital part of our body's defences, and without it we could not survive.

Pain warns us what things are dangerous, and so helps us avoid damage to our body. If the body is already damaged, pain helps with healing because it makes us protect our injuries. Some babies are born with a rare condition that makes them unable to feel pain. They do not learn the lessons that pain teaches, and as a result suffer many fractures and infections.

Pain happens when nerve endings in our skin and our internal organs send messages through the central nervous system to our brain. The brain itself cannot feel pain. There are two types of pain – acute pain, which lasts a short time and is removed when the cause is cured, and chronic pain, which can last a lifetime and cannot usually be treated. Chronic pain must be managed using drugs or other methods.

Drugs relieve pain in two ways. Some block the nerves' messages and prevent them getting to the brain. Others change the way the brain receives the messages, reducing their effect. Many methods of controlling chronic pain without drugs have been developed. These include hypnosis, acupuncture, massage, and electronic stimulation of nerves.

Pain sometimes works in strange ways. It is possible, for example, to suffer a serious injury but not feel any pain – soldiers in battle may not feel pain from wounds until after the battle. The opposite can happen too – patients who lose a limb can continue to feel pain in the limb long afterwards, even though it is missing. This 'phantom limb' pain is an example of neuropathic pain, caused by damage to the remaining nerves.

referred pain (n)
pain that is felt in a different part of the body from where the pain is caused

Patient care

Questions to assess pain

Here are some basic questions to ask a patient when assessing pain. Match the beginnings of the sentences with the endings.

1 Where does
2 Does it
3 When did it start
4 Does the pain
5 How much
6 Can you
7 Does anything make
8 What makes it

a worse?
b it hurt?
c does it hurt?
d describe the pain?
e hurting?
f hurt all the time?
g stay in one place or move around?
h the pain feel better?

Speaking

Work in pairs. Student A look at this page. Student B go to p.111.

Student A

1 You have a problem with your liver which is causing you pain. Imagine the pain you might feel, and be ready to answer the nurse's questions in a lot of detail. Think about the following details.

- where?
- when?
- how bad?
- type of pain?
- same place or moving?
- getting better / worse?
- what helps / makes it worse?

2 You are the nurse. Ask Student B about the pain they are experiencing, and fill in the chart at the top of the next column.

3 Change roles. Answer the nurse's questions.

	1	2	3	4
burning	☐	☐	☐	☐
stabbing	☐	☐	☐	☐
throbbing	☐	☐	☐	☐
shooting	☐	☐	☐	☐
constant	☐	☐	☐	☐
frequent	☐	☐	☐	☐
occasional	☐	☐	☐	☐
mild	☐	☐	☐	☐
moderate	☐	☐	☐	☐
severe	☐	☐	☐	☐
getting better	☐	☐	☐	☐
getting worse	☐	☐	☐	☐
staying the same	☐	☐	☐	☐

Writing

A pain report

1 Read this report on a patient's pain. Can you find and correct five mistakes in it?

> The patient has abdominal pain. It begin suddenly last night as mild but constant pain all over abdomen. Now it is more bad, and is on the right-hand side to the abdomen. The pain has worse when he coughs.

2 Write a report about the pain your partner described in *Speaking*. Use the chart you filled in to help you remember the details.

Body bits

Areas of referred pain

Look at the diagrams showing areas of **referred pain**. Work with a partner. Discuss which colour you think refers to each of the following parts of the body.

a kidney
b appendix
c ovary
d liver and gallbladder
e small intestine
f pancreas
g stomach
h colon
i bladder
j lung and diaphragm
k heart

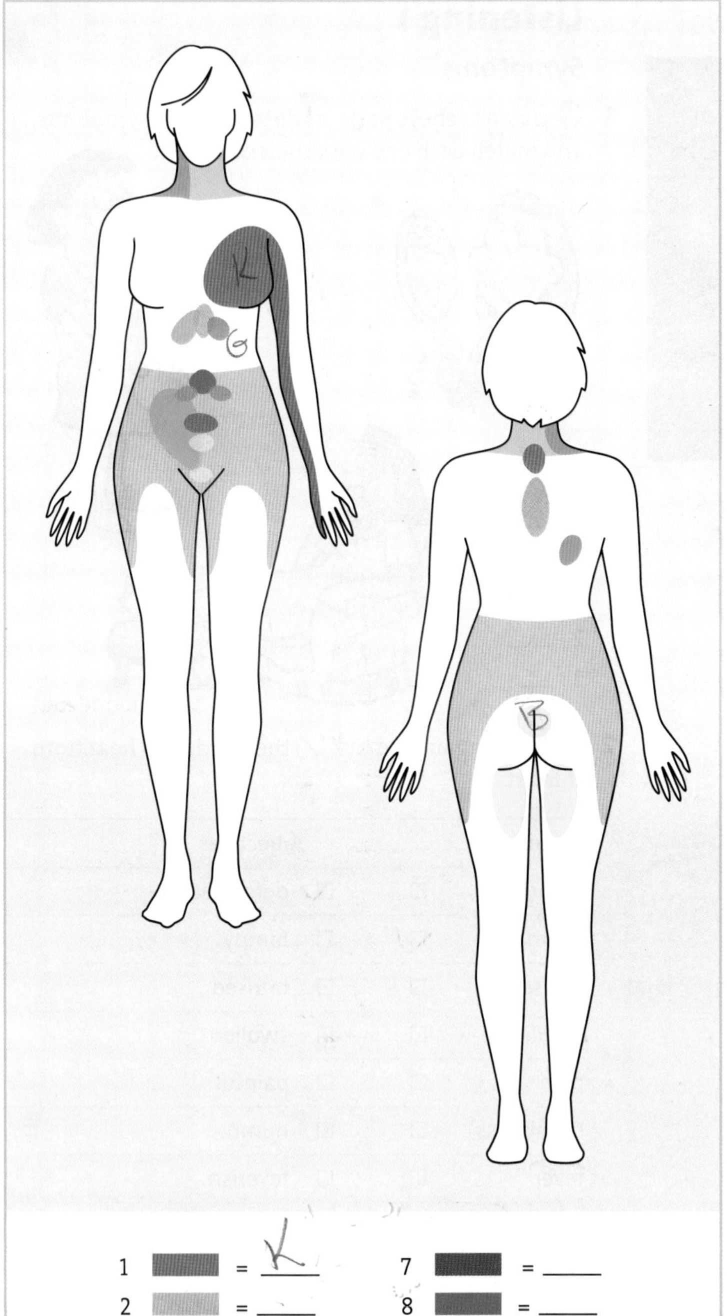

Checklist

Assess your progress in this unit. Tick (✔) the statements which are true.

- I can understand a patient describing pain
- I can ask a patient about their pain
- I can understand an article about pain
- I can write a report on a patient's pain
- I can name the main internal organs

Key words

Adjectives
agonizing
mild
severe
severed
slight
sore
unbearable

Nouns
cough
gas and air
labour
local anaesthetic
migraine
pain relief
stomach ulcer
tumour

Look back through this unit. Find five more words or expressions that you think are useful.

6 Symptoms

Scrub up

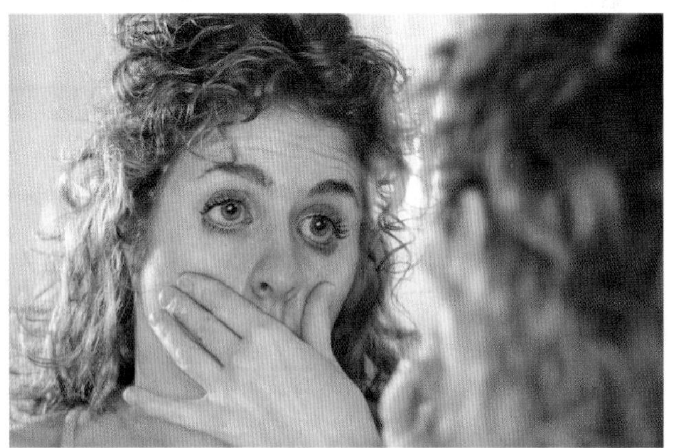

1 Work with a partner. Match each phonetic spelling to one of the words on the list. How do you say those seven words?

1 /ˌdaɪəˈrɪə/	a rash *O*
	bruising ____
	consti**pa**tion ____
2 /ˈnɔːzɪə/	a **cough** ____
	cramp ____
	de**form**ity ____
	dizziness ____
3 /kɒf/	**fe**ver ____
	itching ____
	diar**rhoe**a ____
4 /ˈnʌmnəs/	a **lump** ____
	nausea ____
	numbness ____
	vomiting ____
5 /ˈeɪkɪŋ/	a runny **nose** ____
	sickness ____
	sneezing ____
6 /ˈbruːzɪŋ/	a sore **throat** ____
	spots ____
	swelling ____
	tiredness ____
7 /ˈtaɪədnəs/	**ach**ing ____

2 Listen and repeat the seven words.

3 Work in pairs. Decide if each of the symptoms on the list affect the inside of the body, the outside of the body, or both. Write *I* (= inside), *O* (= outside), or *B* (= both) next to each one. Say the words as you decide together (the bold parts of the words are stressed).

Listening 1

Symptoms

1 Listen to these patients describe their symptoms, and match each one with their condition.

1 ____
2 ____
3 ____

2 Listen again and tick (✓) the words you hear from this list.

Nouns			Adjectives
deformity	☐	☐	deformed
a lump	☐	☐	lumpy
bruising	☐	☐	bruised
swelling	☐	☐	swollen
pain	☐	☐	painful
numbness	☐	☐	numb
fever	☐	☐	feverish
redness	☐	☐	red
tiredness	☐	☐	tired
		☐	tiring
ache	☐	☐	achy
dizziness	☐	☐	dizzy
sickness	☐	☐	sick
constipation	☐	☐	constipated

In this unit

- describing symptoms
- asking about symptoms
- how to form questions
- syndromes
- tongue diagnosis

3 Can you remember the questions that the nurse asked? Work in pairs to try to complete them from memory, then listen again to check.

1 How ________ it feel?
2 A little deformed, ________?
3 ________ it painful when you move it?
4 ________ move your toes?
5 How ________ feeling?
6 ________ a sore throat?
7 ________ redness?
8 ________ going?
9 ________ dizzy at all?
10 When ________ sick, mostly?
11 ________ pain?

• Language spot

Question forms

- We change the word order to form a question with *be*, with tenses that are formed with *be* and *have*, and with modal verbs such as *can, will, should*, etc.
Are you all right? (NOT ~~*You are all right?*~~)
*What **is she** doing?*
*Where **have they** put that wheelchair?*
***Can you** move your toes?*

- We use the verb *do* to make questions with the Present and Past Simple.
*What side effects **does** this drug **have**?*
***Did** you **take** your medication last night?*

- If *what, who*, etc. asks about the **subject** of the verb, *do* is not necessary.
*What **happened**? (not ~~What did happen?~~)*
*Who **said** that? (not ~~Who did say that?~~)*

- We often use question tags to check information, to express surprise, to be friendly, etc.
*This **is** your first time on this ward, **isn't it**?*
*You **don't** eat meat, **do you**?*

- We sometimes leave out the verb, if it is easily understood.
Any pain? (= Do you have any pain?)
Comfortable? (= Are you comfortable?)

» Go to **Grammar reference** p.118

1 Match the beginnings of the questions with the endings.

1	OK,	a	it hurt?
2	What	b	Mrs Hales?
3	Where does	c	are you?
4	What about	d	broken?
5	Let's have a look – swollen,	e	happened to you?
6	You've had an x-ray,	f	haven't you?
7	Anything	g	your shoulder?
8	You aren't on any other medication,	h	isn't it!

2 Listen and check your answers.

3 Work in pairs. Close your books and try to remember as much of the conversation as you can.

4 Write questions to go with these answers.

Nurse ________
Patient Not bad, thanks – a bit sore.
Nurse ________
Patient I fell off my bike.
Nurse ________
Patient Here, around my wrist.
Nurse ________
Patient Yes, I can, slowly.
Nurse ________
Patient Yes, *very*! I've also got a cut on my leg – look.
Nurse ________
Patient Yes, it *is* deep. Will I need stitches?
Nurse ________
Patient No, never – and I don't want any!
Nurse ________
Patient No, I haven't seen him yet.

5 Now listen to the conversation. Were any of your questions exactly the same?

In the UK, the most common reason given for taking time off work is **'flu-like symptoms'**, which are typically a fever and aches and pains in the body.

It's my job

Read about Sandy McGuire and decide if these sentences are true (T) or false (F).

1 Sandy works at night. ____
2 Her shift is a quiet one. ____
3 Some people phone because they are lonely. ____
4 Sandy only gives information – not advice. ____
5 Helpline nurses have to speak foreign languages. ____

Sandy McGuire

I operate the telephone helpline on the graveyard shift – that's the one from midnight through to the morning. Although it's quiet and still in the streets outside, it's not so quiet in the office. The early hours of the morning are sometimes the busiest time, when the telephone never stops ringing.

People call the helpline for information or advice, or sometimes they just need to hear a friendly voice. We talk to people who are depressed and worried, and sometimes in pain. Sometimes we get some funny enquiries – yesterday, a teenager phoned because he had swallowed some chewing gum and he was afraid he was going to die!

We can't see our patients, so we have to be very good on the phone. We have to learn how to do it, because it doesn't come naturally. We have to know how to ask the right questions so that we get clear and accurate answers, and we have to be able to speak in language anyone can understand.

Signs and symptoms

Night coughing

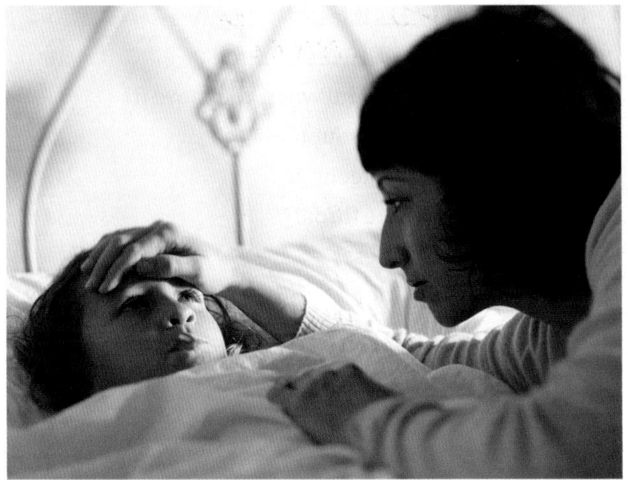

Here are descriptions of four possible conditions that can cause a child to cough in the night. Complete them with the words below.

coughing up	occurs	make	sounds
accompanied	get	are	wheeze
breathe	has		

Asthma
Children with asthma cough, and ________[1] when they breathe out. They become very short of breath when an attack ________[2].

A cold
Sometimes a child ________[3] a cough and a fever with a cold. A bad cough can ________[4] a child vomit.

Croup
Children under three years old sometimes ________[5] croup. They have a sore throat and they wheeze when they ________[6] in. When they cough, it often ________[7] like a dog barking.

Pneumonia
The symptoms of pneumonia ________[8] a temperature of over 102°F (39°C), fast breathing, sometimes ________[9] by vomiting and sometimes ________[10] blood.

Listening 2

A helpline call

1 Listen to Sandy McGuire taking a call on the helpline. As you listen, fill in the information about the patient.

1 age of patient ______
2 wheezes breathing in ☐ breathing out ☐
3 coughs up blood yes ☐ no ☐
4 vomits yes ☐ no ☐
5 allergies yes ☐ no ☐
6 fever yes ☐ no ☐

2 Which of the conditions in *Signs and symptoms* do you think the child has? Discuss your idea with a partner.

Speaking

Student A look at this page. Student B go to p.112.

Student A

1 You have hurt your wrist. Memorize these symptoms. You will describe them to the helpline nurse later.

You fell off your bicycle. It happened five days ago. Your right wrist is very painful. The skin feels hot, and is red and sore. The shape of the wrist seems normal, but it's a bit swollen, and it hurts when you touch it. You can move it without making the pain worse. You can also hold heavy bags, and put weight on it.

2 1 You are the helpline nurse. Ask the caller questions to find out exactly what the problem is. Use the notes below to help you, and make notes as you listen to the answers.

- aches?
- nausea?
- vomiting? (blood?)
- fever?
- diarrhoea? (blood?)
- cramps?
- bloating?

2 When you have all the answers you need, look at the diagnosis table on p.111. What do you think Student B's problem is?

3 Now change roles. You are the patient. Call the helpline and tell the nurse about your injured wrist.

Writing

Symptom report

1 Read this report about a patient with appendicitis and find three mistakes.

Two days ago Miss Jabarti had a mild fever and complained of a loss appetite. Later she suffered nausea and vomiting with an occasional pain in the centre of her stomach. She was admitted hospital yesterday. Today her abdomen is swollen and she is suffering a constant sharp pain her lower right side.

2 Write a report on this patient who has food poisoning using these notes.

Patient name: Ivan Abashev
History:
Yesterday – vomiting with headaches, diarrhoea
On admission – severe abdominal pain, high fever
This morning – weakness, shivering. Pain in left abdomen – constant, stabbing

Project

Research the symptoms of one these illnesses and give a short presentation describing them to the class.

- AIDS
- tuberculosis
- malaria
- gangrene
- rabies
- leprosy

I used to have complete faith in doctors. Now I'm fighting to make them understand that they don't have all the answers.
Dave Harries
Gulf War veteran

Reading

1 Discuss the question with a partner.

- Have you ever had symptoms with an unknown cause? What did the doctor say?

2 Read the article and decide if the sentences are true (T) or false (F).

1 CFS is caused by a virus. ____
2 CFS sufferers cannot lead a normal life. ____
3 Some doctors believe CFS sufferers are not really ill. ____
4 Gulf War Syndrome sufferers were attacked with chemicals. ____
5 They were vaccinated against the syndrome. ____
6 The army officially says that stress caused their illness. ____

3 Tick (✓) the things that each syndrome affects.

	Chronic Fatigue Syndrome	Gulf War Syndrome
appetite		
arms		
head		
mood		
muscles		
neck		
skin		
sleep		
throat		

4 Work with a partner. Try to match the words without looking back at the text, then look back and check.

1 a recurrent	a sleep
2 an overwhelming	b glands
3 chronic	c swings
4 loss of	d aches and pains
5 mood	e appetite
6 muscle	f sore throat
7 poor	g feeling of tiredness
8 swollen	h illnesses

MYSTERY SYNDROMES

When you are ill, you expect your doctor to tell you what you have, and then to treat you. But sometimes people have symptoms whose cause is not understood, and for these people it can be difficult or impossible to get treatment.

The main symptom of Chronic Fatigue Syndrome (CFS) is an overwhelming feeling of tiredness. The tiredness is so disabling that it is impossible for the sufferer to continue normal physical and mental activities. Other symptoms include muscle aches and pains, poor sleep, loss of appetite, a recurrent sore throat, and swollen glands in the neck. Sufferers often undergo many tests for known diseases, which prove negative, and many feel that doctors see them as hypochondriacs.

After the Gulf War of 1991, tens of thousands of ex-soldiers suffered chronic illnesses which doctors still cannot explain. Symptoms include dizziness, numbness in the arms, rashes, severe headaches, mood swings, and persistent, extreme tiredness. The cause remains a mystery, but the symptoms have been given the name Gulf War Syndrome. Some soldiers believe they may have been exposed to chemical weapons without knowing, and others blame the vaccinations they were given before they went to war. Military officials say that Gulf War Syndrome is not a real illness. There is no doubt the ex-soldiers are ill, they say, but their symptoms are simply the result of stress.

Maybe one day the cause of these syndromes will be known and will be treatable. But for people like ex-soldier Dave Harries, the first step is for their condition to be recognized by the medical profession. Then people will believe that their symptoms are not imaginary.

Body bits

Tongue diagnosis

1 *Zetsu shin* is used in traditional Chinese medicine. Practitioners examine the tongue in order to diagnose illness and to find out about the personality of the patient. Complete the text about *zetsu shin* using the words below.

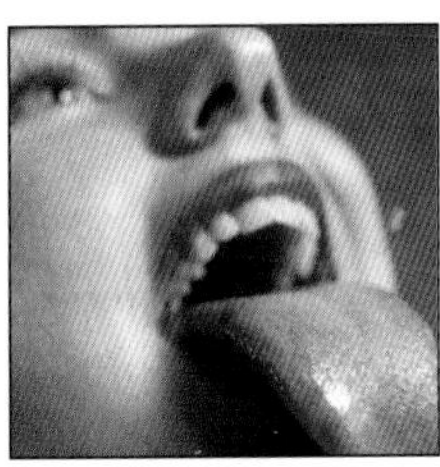

disorder	balance	sign	state
condition	problems	effectively	indicates
thinking	aggressive		

Colour

Blood ___________[1] are associated with a white tongue. Yellow ___________[2] a disordered liver and gallbladder. Blue or purple shows up a ___________[3] in the digestive system. Purple on the underside shows the immune system is not working ___________[4]. A dark red tongue can be a ___________[5] of inflammation or ulcers in the body.

Movement

The flexibility of the tongue shows the general ___________[6] of the digestive system.

Width

A wide tongue is good, for it shows a physical and psychological ___________[7]. A narrow tongue indicates sharp ___________[8].

Tip

A rounded tip shows a ___________[9] of good physical and mental health. People whose tongues have a pointed tip have ___________[10] personalities.

2 Examine your partner's tongue and make notes. Tell them what their tongue indicates about them according to *zetsu shin*.

3 Discuss what you told each other. Do you think there is any truth in *zetsu shin*?

Checklist

Assess your progress in this unit. Tick (✔) the statements which are true.

I can describe symptoms

I can ask a patient about their symptoms

I can form questions in all main tenses

I can understand an article about syndromes

Key words

aching
bruising
cramp
deformity
dizziness
itching
lump
mood swings
nausea
numbness
rash
spot
stitches
swelling
swollen

Look back through this unit. Find five more words or expressions that you think are useful.

7 Caring for the elderly

Scrub up

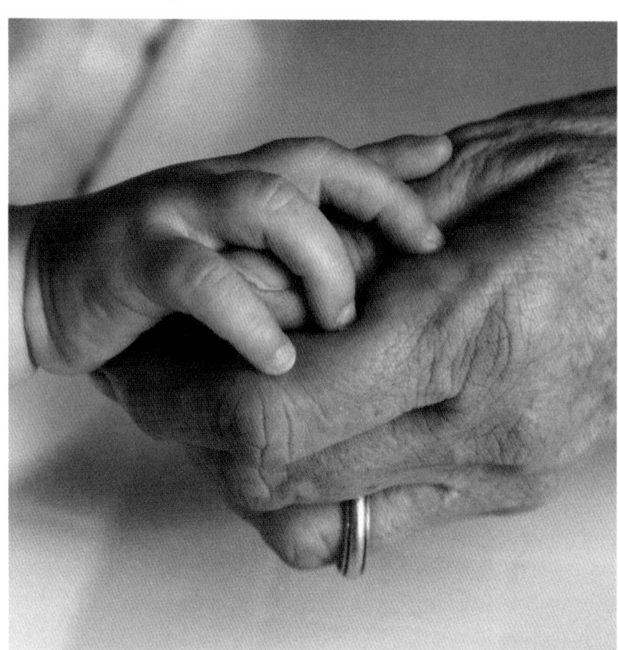

1 Think of an elderly person you know well and how ageing has affected them. Think about the answers to these questions. Then talk to your partner about the person.

- What daily tasks does he / she need help with?
- How does he / she keep mentally fit?
- How does he / she keep physically fit?
- What worries him / her?
- How happy is he / she?
- How healthy is he / she?

2 Discuss what special difficulties are faced by elderly patients and the staff who are caring for them. Use the words below to help you, and write sentences.

EXAMPLE

They may have more side effects from drugs.

medication	getting around	
diagnosis	daily tasks	food
home	attitude of staff	
recovery	mind	complications

Listening 1

A care home

1 Discuss the questions with a partner.

- Would you like to live in a care home when you are old? Why / Why not?
- In your notebook, make a list of the advantages and disadvantages of care homes.

EXAMPLE

+	–
You always have company.	*You don't live with your family.*

2 Listen to two elderly people in a care home talking. Do they mention any of the points in your list?

3 Listen again and tick (✓) the things that Edith (the first speaker) mentions.

Edith doesn't like ...	Edith wants ...
☐ the staff	☐ respect
☐ Barbara	☐ friends
☐ her own name	☐ privacy
☐ bingo	☐ to play bingo
☐ coach trips	☐ more stimulation
☐ her own home	☐ less stimulation
☐ her old life	☐ to go to the seaside
☐ the food	☐ independence
☐ washing up	☐ more food
	☐ to go home

In this unit
- care homes
- the ageing brain
- Alzheimer's disease
- *will*
- describing the problems of the elderly
- aids used by the elderly

Reading

1 Write your name as fast as you can with your right hand, then do the same with your left hand. Was one easier? Does it look better? Discuss the reason why with a partner.

2 Read the article, and decide if these sentences are true (T) or false (F).

1. You can learn to write with the wrong hand. ____
2. Learning makes new nerve cells grow. ____
3. As we get older, large numbers of brain cells die. ____
4. If our brain is healthy, it continues to develop when we are old. ____
5. Mental stimulation keeps your memory good. ____

Old age and the brain

If you hold a pen in your 'wrong' hand, writing becomes uncomfortable and difficult. But keep doing it and you will get better at it – you learn. This is because connections between neurons in your brain get stronger, and your brain grows.

In our early years our brains grow very fast as we learn language, writing, numbers, music, and how to coordinate movement. By the time we are teenagers, each neuron in our brain has connected to tens of thousands of other neurons, and every time we have a new thought or memory, our brains make new connections. Just as muscles get stronger by using them, the brain develops when it is stimulated. Without stimulation, it gradually dies.

A healthy brain does not lose huge numbers of brain cells as it ages. It continues to rewire itself and grow new neurons. However, degenerative brain diseases are very common in old age, and so we associate ageing with diseases such as Alzheimer's disease.

Even though these diseases are very common in the elderly, it is a mistake to think that old age automatically equals mental decline. When elderly people who do not have Alzheimer's disease suffer age-related losses of memory and motor skills, it is often not because of ageing, but because of inactivity and lack of mental stimulation.

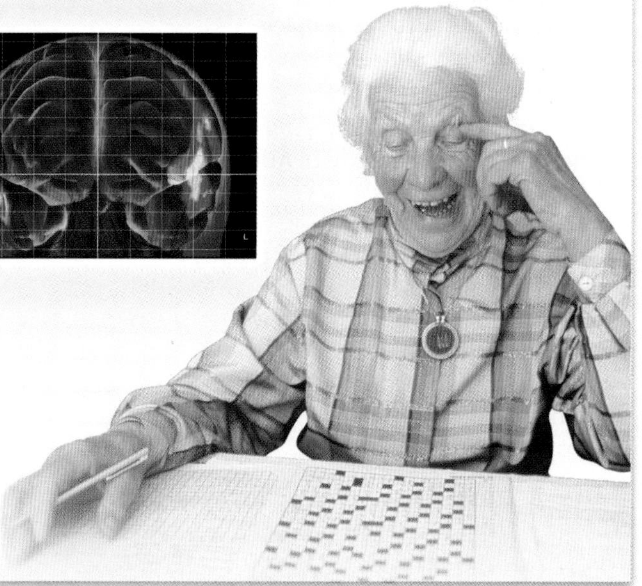

3 Find words in the text with these meanings.

1. to make things happen at the same time
   c__________
2. to change the electrical connections
   r__________
3. conditions that kill brain cells
   d__________ __________ __________
4. loss of the ability to use your brain well
   m__________ d__________
5. connected to getting old
   a__________-r__________
6. the ability to control your body's movement
   m__________ s__________

4 Try these brain exercises. Do you know any others?

- Name the colours of the following words as fast as you can. Don't read the words but say what colour they are.

BLUE BROWN PURPLE YELLOW
GREEN MULTICOLOURED ORANGE
RED BLACK PINK WHITE GREY

- Read a page of writing upside-down.

ADLs (n)
Activities of Daily Living. These include eating, bathing, dressing, toileting, and walking. A person's ability to perform these activities without help is used when assessing how much care they need.

If you see a little less spring in my step, if your name fails to leap to my lips, you'll know why. And if I tell you a funny story for the second time, please laugh anyway.
Charlton Heston
Film star and Alzheimer's sufferer

Signs and symptoms

Alzheimer's disease

1 Discuss with a partner what you know about Alzheimer's disease. How does it affect the following things?

- the memory
- behaviour
- speech
- walking
- daily life

2 Read the text. Which effects did you mention?

3 Decide if each symptom is more connected with movement (M), thought (T), or behaviour (B). Then compare your ideas with your partner.

Alzheimer's disease damages the brain, destroying memory and reason. People with Alzheimer's disease suffer confusion and loss of cognitive function. They need more and more nursing care as they become progressively more helpless, and finally die. The illness has three stages:

early stage
- forgetting recent conversations or events ___*T*___
- minor changes in abilities and behaviour ______
- repetition ______

middle stage
- needing some help with **ADLs** ______
- wandering ______
- loss of interest in other people ______
- unusual behaviour ______
- shuffling gait ______

later stage
- needing constant help with **ADLs** ______
- forgetting names ______
- complete loss of memory ______
- inability to recognize familiar people, objects, or places ______
- getting easily upset or aggressive ______
- confusing night and day ______
- confinement to bed or a wheelchair ______
- difficulty in swallowing ______
- loss of speech ______

• Language spot

will

We use *will*

- to talk about future facts.
In twenty years' time, there ***will be*** *more old people and fewer young people.*

- to make predictions and express hopes about the future. We often use words such as *I think …*, *I hope …*, and *probably* when we do this.
I think *I'll* ***die*** *when I'm 90!*
I don't think *I'll* *play sport when I'm 80.*
I hope I won't *live in a care home.*
*With family around, you'****ll probably have*** *a long and healthy old age.*

- when we decide what to do, have, etc.
Tea or coffee? Er … ***I'll have*** *coffee, please.*

- to make offers, requests, and promises. We can also use *Shall I …?* for offers.
I'll get *you a drink.*
Shall I get *you something to eat?*
Will you do *me a favour?*
I won't be *back late, so don't worry.*

» Go to **Grammar reference** p.119

1 Complete the sentences with the words below. Then decide if each one is a future fact (F), a prediction (P), or a decision you're making (D).

'll be able　'll have　'll probably
'll sleep　Shall I　will open

1 The new hospital __________ in 2010. ___*F*___
2 I don't think you __________ tonight if you have a nap now. ______
3 __________ go out tonight? Er … no, I think I'll stay at home. ______
4 You __________ to go home a week after your operation. ______
5 I __________ chicken curry with rice, please. ______
6 I'm working tonight, so I __________ be tired tomorrow. ______

geriatrics (n)
the medical care of old people
gerontology (n)
the scientific study of old age and ageing

'Elderly' and 'older' are acceptable words to use about the elderly. 'Old' is considered rude by many people.

2 Complete this dialogue of offers and requests. Use *'ll*, *will*, or *won't* and one of the verbs below.

fall ~~pass~~ stand do see

A *Will* [1] you *pass* [2] me my glasses? Then I __________ [3] be able to __________ [4] the television.

B Here you are.

A Thanks. Oh and __________ [5] you __________ [6] me another favour?

B What now?

A __________ [7] you help me __________ [8] up? I want to switch it on.

B You __________ [9] probably __________ [10] over. I __________ [11] do it.

A Thank you. I __________ [12] trouble you again.

3 Listen and check. Then practise the dialogue with your partner.

4 How do you imagine yourself at 75 years old? Discuss it with your partner. Talk about these topics.

family	home	friends	health
sport	hobbies	routine	travel

EXAMPLE

A *Where do you think you'll live when you're 75?*

B *I hope I'll live at home with my family.*

Vocabulary

Problems and aids

1 Work in pairs. Match the adjectives with the cases. Say the adjectives as you do the exercise. The stressed part of each word is in **bold**.

An elderly person who ...

1 can not leave her bed	a frail
2 often wets himself	b im**mo**bile
3 breaks a bone easily	c **bed**ridden
4 can't hear very well	d con**fused**
5 cannot move around freely	e inde**pen**dent
6 often can't remember things	f for**get**ful
7 wears his pyjamas in the street	g in**con**tinent
8 can't see very well	h short**sigh**ted
9 likes to be free	i deaf

2 Match each vocabulary item with a picture.

a b c d e f g h i j k l

1 hearing aid ____	7 power chair ____
2 walking stick ____	8 helping hand ____
3 glasses ____	9 false teeth ____
4 pressure pad ____	10 artificial hip ____
5 incontinence pad ____	11 walking frame ____
6 bath lift ____	12 commode ____

3 Work in pairs. Take turns to choose a vocabulary item from above and explain what it is used for. The other student must guess the item.

EXAMPLE

A *It's for helping people who are immobile to get around.*

B *Is it an artificial hip*

A *No, try again.*

If I'd known how old I was going to be, I'd have taken better care of myself.
Adoph Zukor
Film producer
(just before his 100th birthday)

Listening 2

Assessing a patient

1 An elderly patient is admitted to hospital after a fall. Listen as a nurse talks to the patient's daughter, and complete the table.

0 = none ✓ = mild ✓✓ = moderate ✓✓✓ = severe

deafness	✓✓✓
loss of sight	
restricted movement	
sleep disorders	
problems feeding self	
incontinence	
signs of confusion	

2 Listen again and make notes.

EXAMPLE

deafness ✓✓✓ *very deaf, hearing aid*

Speaking

1 An elderly patient who you are nursing is going to be transferred from your ward to a care home. With a partner, invent details about the patient and make notes. Include details about these topics.

- state of health
- medication
- other treatment
- help needed
- hearing and sight
- mental state
- mobility
- personality

2 Now work with a different partner to exchange information.
Student A – You are the patient's nurse. Tell Student B, a hospital transfer specialist, about your patient.
Student B – You are the hospital transfer specialist. Find out as many details as possible about the patient, and make notes.

3 Now change roles.

Writing

Letter of introduction to a care home

You are a hospital transfer specialist. Using the notes you made when listening to the patient's nurse in the *Speaking* exercise, write a letter of introduction to the care home.

Body bits

The effects of ageing

Complete the labels for the picture on p.45 using the words below.

wrinkled	focus	constipation
growth rate	impairment	sensitivity
fragile	discoloured	leakage
restrict	grey	

a Hair loses pigmentation and turns ________[1]. It becomes thinner and its ________[2] slows down.

b The lenses of the eyes become stiffer and thicker. It becomes harder to ________[3] on near objects.

c Deterioration of the inner ear causes hearing ________[4]

d Teeth become ________[5] and fragile, and fall out.

e Skin loses elasticity and becomes dry and ________[6]. It also becomes thinner, causing increased ________[7] to the cold.

f Digestion slows down, causing ________[8].

g Fatty deposits ________[9] the blood flow and cause high blood pressure.

h The bladder can't hold as much urine, and there is some ________[10].

i Bones become ________[11].

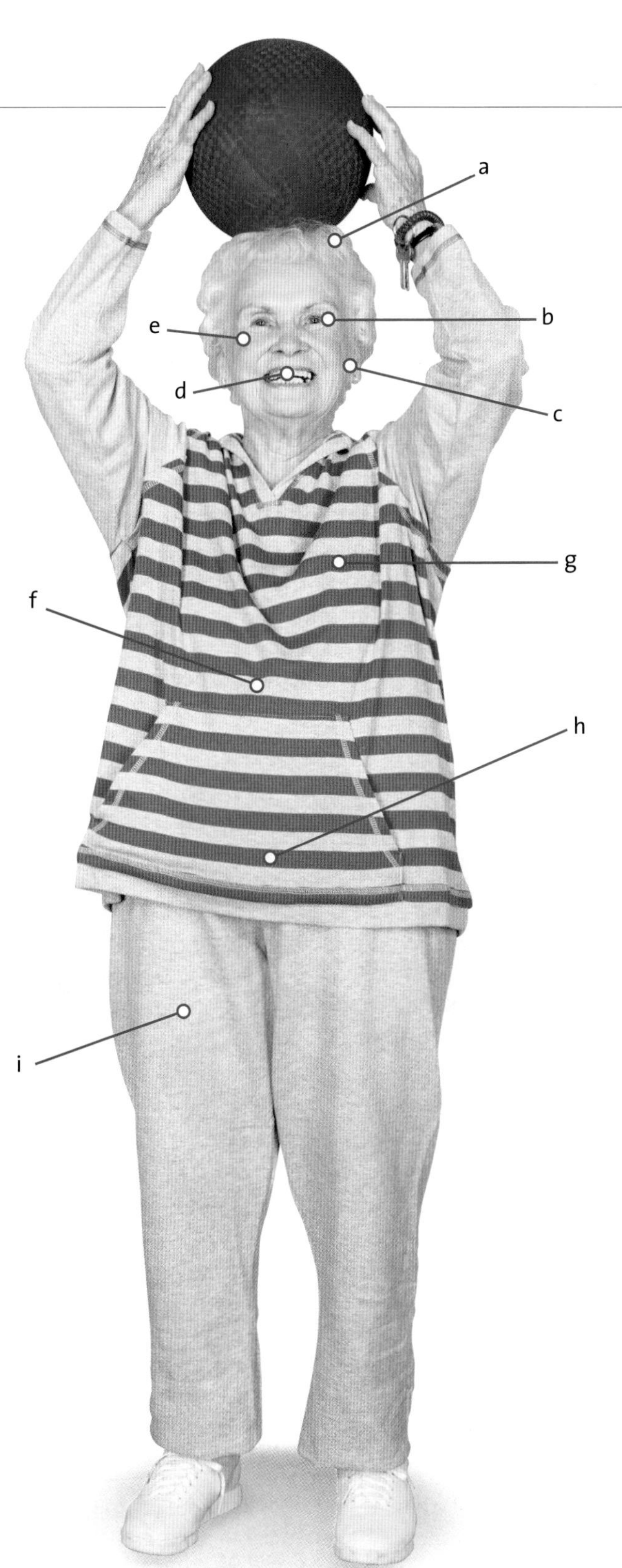

Checklist

Assess your progress in this unit. Tick (✔) the statements which are true.

- I can talk about some of the main issues of geriatric care
- I can understand an article about the brain
- I can use *will* to talk about the future
- I can use *will* to express decisions, and to make offers and requests
- I can talk about the physical problems and aids of the elderly
- I can understand a description of the physical effects of ageing

Key words

Nouns
care home
cognitive function
confinement
confusion
gait
independence
mobility
nap
stimulation

Adjectives
deaf
degenerative
frail
immobile
incontinent
shuffling

Look back through this unit. Find five more words or expressions that you think are useful.

8 Nutrition and obesity

Scrub up

1 Work with a partner. How many of these foods can you name? Can you find them in the lists below?

2 Look at the lists, and answer the questions.

- Find two good sources of protein.
- Find two good sources of carbohydrate.
- Find two dairy products.
- Find two pulses.
- Find seven ways of cooking food.
- Which foods on the list are high in fat?
- Which foods contain high levels of vitamin C?
- Which foods are low in vitamins?
- Which items on the list are junk foods?
- Which food do you think is highest in calories?

3 With your partner, use the lists to create

- the most nutritious meal possible
- the most unhealthy meal
- a meal for an athlete
- a meal for a diabetic
- a meal for somebody who needs to lose weight.

Main course

A (choose one)

two grilled burgers
tuna fish pie
a cheese pizza
lentil soup
egg noodles
two slices of roast beef
two fried eggs
tofu curry
a lamb kebab

+B (choose two)

fried rice
boiled potatoes
salad
baked beans in tomato sauce
tinned tomatoes
stir-fried mushrooms
fried onion rings
steamed broccoli

Dessert

chocolate pudding
a banana
a doughnut
yoghurt

Drink

a bottle of cola
a glass of orange juice
a glass of wine
a glass of milk

In this unit

- nutritional value of different foods
- vitamins and minerals
- diabetes
- body measurements and bmi
- giving advice
- eating disorders

Body bits

Nutrition

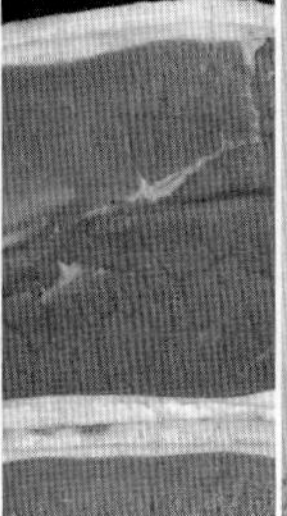
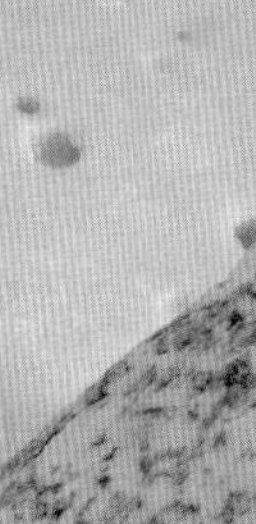
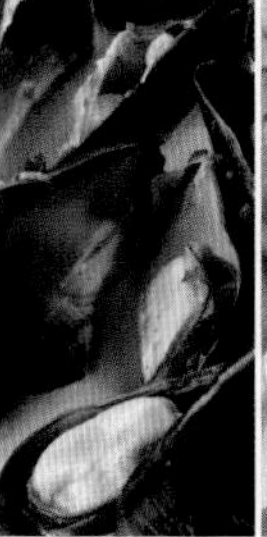

1 Work in pairs. Look at the pictures above. Talk about why our body needs the things shown. What does each one contain? Which part of the body is each one especially good for?

2 Complete the descriptions of vitamins, minerals, and oils with the words below. Some words are used more than once.

teeth	organs	enzymes	nervous system
brain	eyes	skin	immune system
blood	muscles	bones	cardiovascular system
cells			

Vitamin C is needed to help the __________[1] repair itself when it is cut or damaged. It is found in fruit, especially citrus fruit like oranges and grapefruit.

The B-vitamins keep the __________[2] healthy and help reduce stress. They are found in foods like wholegrain bread and cereals.

Vitamin A keeps the __________[3] healthy and is important for good vision. It is found in fatty foods like butter, cheese, whole milk, and yoghurt.

Vitamin D is needed for healthy bones and __________[4] because it helps the body absorb calcium. Our body makes Vitamin D when our __________[5] is exposed to sunlight.

Calcium is needed for children's __________[6] and teeth to grow. It is found in foods like milk, cheese, and yoghurt.

Iron helps your __________[7] carry oxygen. If you do not get enough iron, you will be pale and tired and you may get anaemia. Iron is found in red meats, especially liver.

Zinc makes your __________[8] stronger so that you can fight colds and infections. It is found in shellfish, nuts, and seeds.

Omega-3 is an essential fatty acid which helps your __________[9] function well. It is found in oily fish like mackerel, sardines, salmon, and tuna.

Protein builds up, maintains, and replaces the tissues in your body. Your __________[10], your __________[11], and your immune system are made up mostly of protein.

Carbohydrates are sugars which are broken down by __________[12] then stored in the __________[13] as a source of energy. Grain products such as rice, bread, and pasta are sources of carbohydrate.

Fats fuel the body and help absorb some vitamins. They are also the building blocks of hormones, and they insulate nervous system tissue in the body. Unsaturated fats, found in oils and nuts, for example, are believed to protect the __________[14].

Project

Research two of the following substances, and write about why our body needs them, and what they are found in. Try to use some of the language in *Body bits*.

- Vitamin E
- Vitamin K
- Potassium
- Selenium
- Folic acid

194 million people worldwide suffer from diabetes. In the USA, it is the sixth most common cause of death.

Vocabulary

Diabetes

1 Discuss with a partner what you know about diabetes.

2 Match these words with their definitions.

1 balance	a taking regular exercise
2 childhood	b small amounts of food that you eat between meals
3 diet	c sugar that the body uses for energy
4 glucose	d the time of your life when you are a child
5 active	e the correct amount of different things
6 obesity	f the type of foods that you usually eat
7 overweight	g the condition of being very fat, in a way that is not healthy
8 snacks	h too heavy and fat

3 Put the words into the spaces in this text about diabetes.

Diabetes occurs when your body does not produce enough insulin, a hormone that controls the level of ________[1] in the blood. One type of diabetes appears in ________[2], and the other type appears after the age of eighteen.

It is very common for very ________[3] people to get diabetes, so the illness is linked to ________[4].

For this reason, it is important to get the right ________[5] between food and exercise. It is important to be ________[6], and to eat a healthy ________[7], containing plenty of fruit and vegetables. Nutritionists say ________[8] are better than big meals.

Listening 1

A diabetic patient

1 Listen to a student nurse discussing a patient with a hospital nutritionist, and answer the questions.

1 How long has the patient had diabetes?
2 Which type of diabetes does the patient have?
3 Is the patient obese?
4 What does the patient's 'special machine' do?
5 Can the patient eat sugar?
6 Why should the patient not have big meals?
7 What is hypoglycaemia?

2 Try to complete the missing verbs. Then listen again to check.

1 Does he i________ himself with insulin?
2 He's o________ a special diet, is he?
3 Type one diabetes is not l________ to obesity.
4 This patient has a special machine to ch________ levels of glucose ...
5 He needs to c________ the calories in his meals ...
6 ... he should h________ snacks, not big meals ...

Reading

1 Do you like fast food? How often do you eat it? Do you think it is addictive?

2 Read the article and decide if these sentences are true (T) or false (F).

1 The two girls in the article said fast food is 'nutritious and good for you'. ____
2 Fast food changed Morgan Spurlock psychologically. ____
3 The film proved that fast food is good for you. ____
4 Morgan Spurlock was overweight when he started filming. ____
5 Morgan Spurlock became a fast food addict. ____
6 Morgan Spurlock died from liver failure. ____

BMI (n) BMI means **Body Mass Index**. It is used to assess whether a person's weight is healthy or not. To calculate a patient's BMI you use the formula:

$$\frac{\textbf{weight in kilograms}}{\textbf{height in metres}^2}$$

- BMI of 18.5 to 24.9 is the right weight
- BMI of below 18.5 is underweight
- BMI of 25 to 29.9 is overweight
- BMI of over 30 is obese

Eat yourself to death

3 Discuss these questions with a partner or in a group.

- Is obesity a choice or an illness?
- Do you think fast foods should be limited like cigarettes (for example health warnings, high price, special places for eating, etc.)?
- Should overweight people pay more for health care, plane tickets, etc.?

In 2003, American film maker Morgan Spurlock made a film about the effects of eating only hamburgers, pizzas, and fries for a month. The idea came to him when two overweight American girls took legal action against a famous fast-food company. The girls accused the company of making them fat. The company said that it was not the food that made them fat, but eating too much. The company also said their food was 'nutritious and good for you'.

The girls' legal action failed, but Morgan Spurlock decided to test what the company said about their food. For a month he ate only fast food, three times a day, and took the daily exercise of an average American. He filmed himself during this month and the film he made records the changes that happened to him.

When Spurlock started making the film, he was healthy and slim. On the second day, he had his first 'fast-food stomach ache', and vomited. Over the following thirty days, he gained 24.5 lb (11.1 kg). He also had other problems – depression, headaches, and lethargy. He had cravings for a fast-food meal – only this would relieve the symptoms. A doctor told Spurlock he was addicted.

Towards the end of the month, doctors warned him that the food was causing life-threatening liver damage, and said he should stop. It took five months on a vegetarian diet to get back to a normal weight.

The film he made is called *Super size me*. It was nominated for an Academy Award for best documentary in 2005. The film's message was that the fast-food industry was probably as bad as the tobacco industry – it made a lot of money by encouraging illness.

Speaking

1 Work in pairs. Which person on the right do you think these statistics refer to?

1 1.80 m
2 95.7 kg
3 5'11"
4 211 lbs
5 1.8 x 1.8 = 3.24
6 95.7 ÷ 3.24 = 29.54

2 How do you say them? Listen and check.

3 Work in pairs. You are going to exchange information about the other three pictured people. Student A go to p.110. Student B go to p.113.

4 Calculate the **BMI** of the three people.

Walter Hudson

Heidi Klum

Robert Wadlow

George Clooney

The idea of human beauty changes over time. At the beginning of the 20th century, **Lillian Russell**, a Hollywood star, weighed over 200 pounds (91 kilos).

Obesity now contributes to the death of more than 360,000 Americans a year. The incidence of childhood obesity is now at epidemic levels.
Tom Harkin
American politician

• Language spot

should / shouldn't

- We use *should / shouldn't* to give advice and to say what would be correct.
  *You **should give up** smoking.*
  *Your blood sugar **shouldn't go** over 240 mg/dl.*
- *Should* is weaker than *must*.
  *I **should stop** eating sweets – but I'm not going to!*
- Here are some other ways of giving advice.
  ***It would be a good idea to** lose some weight.*
  ***I'd** see a nutritionist **if I were you**.*

>> Go to **Grammar reference** p.120

Complete these sentences using *should* or *shouldn't* + verb.

1 You <u>should</u> <u>drink</u> some water before you go running.
2 I'm getting fat. I __________ __________ more exercise.
3 You __________ __________ breakfast – it wakes up the body and provides fuel for the day.
4 People with high blood pressure __________ __________ too much salt on their food.
5 You __________ __________ plenty of vitamin C in your diet.
6 People with diabetes __________ __________ large meals.
7 A person with an eating disorder __________ __________ help from a psychologist.
8 Children __________ __________ too many sweets.

Writing

Advice to a friend via email

1 A close friend has written you an email asking for advice. She is worried about her eating habits. Complete the email with the words below.

addicted to	feel depressed
bad for you	fills my stomach
cut down	get cravings
cut out	losing weight
skip meals	

File Edit View Insert Format Tools Actions Help
Send Options...

and that's terrible because I should be only 65 kilos! I'm really shocked. Every time I look in a mirror I __________[1], but that just makes me eat more. I am so busy these days, and I don't have any time for exercise. Of course, I know fast food is __________[2], but every time I stop eating it I __________[3] for a burger. I suppose I must be __________[4] fast foods. Nothing __________[5] in the same way.

I am trying hard to lose a kilo a week. Sometimes I __________[6], but it doesn't work. I just feel hungry and then I give in and have spaghetti or a steak – they're better for me than burgers, aren't they? I will stop eating fast foods, I promise – but don't say I should do without cola, because I have __________[7] on chocolate and even __________[8] sugar from hot drinks completely.

I thought, being a nurse, you should know about __________[9] and diet, and you could give me some advice.

Love

Hesta

2 Discuss with a partner what advice to give Hesta to help her lose weight successfully and in a healthy way. Think about these topics.

- exercise
- how much weight to lose
- how quickly to lose weight
- what to eat
- what not to eat
- when to eat
- what to drink
- other good habits

3 Write an email replying to Hesta.

Listening 2

An eating disorder

1 Eating too much is not the only eating disorder. What other kinds do you know?

2 Listen to a staff nurse pass on information about a new patient at a shift handover. Answer the questions about the patient.

1 How old is the patient?
2 How long is she in for observation?
3 What is her weight?
4 What illness does her mother think Anita has?
5 What is Anita obsessed with?

3 Complete these symptoms that the staff nurse mentions.

1 abnormal	a changes
2 attacks of	b constipation
3 difficulty	c dizziness
4 feeling	d loss
5 frequent	e miserable
6 hair	f weight loss
7 mood	g periods
8 personality	h sleeping
9 stomach	i swings
10 stopped having	j pains

Project

Interview a person about their food intake, and write a report. Include information about these topics.

- what they typically eat in a day
- their calorie intake
- how active they are
- how balanced their diet is
- their bad habits
- their general health
- your recommendations

Checklist

Assess your progress in this unit. Tick (✔) the statements which are true.

I can talk about food groups

I can describe the nutritional value of food

I can talk about diabetes

I can use *should / shouldn't* to give advice

I can understand a text about the effects of fast food

I can make calculations about people's size

Key words

Adjectives
addicted
diabetic
obese
overweight

Nouns
calorie
craving
diet
intake
junk food
mineral
nutritionist
protein
snack
source
vitamin

Look back through this unit. Find five more words or expressions that you think are useful.

Reading bank

1 Pet visits

1 Read the article and decide if the sentences are true (T) or false (F).

1 Pet visits can help patients in hospital feel better. _____

2 Pets are nervous when they see their owners in hospital. _____

3 Pet visits help children make a link with their life outside the hospital. _____

4 Pets often transmit diseases to patients. _____

5 It is easy to set up a pet visiting programme in a hospital. _____

2 What guidelines or rules would you make for a pet visiting programme in a hospital? Make a list.

Pets come to visit

When Patricia Stevens, a nurse, was in hospital for the birth of her twins, she was scared and uncomfortable. She didn't want to see her family or friends, but she wanted to see her dog. 'I persuaded my doctor to let me see my dog. I was taken in a wheelchair to the hospital entrance, where my husband was waiting. I was so excited and happy when my dog ran towards me, wagging her tail,' said Stevens. 'It was better than any medication.'

Pet power

In recent years, more and more hospitals have found that pet visits can help to calm, reassure, and motivate patients. Studies show that petting animals can reduce anxiety, lower blood pressure, and help patients to heal faster. Patients are sometimes happier to see their pets than they are to see people – their dog doesn't care if they smell funny or look terrible.

Impressive results

Lea Ann Matura, an advanced practice nurse at the Methodist Hospital in Houston, Texas, remembers the time a pet visited her owner, a woman with lung cancer. 'This patient hardly ever woke up or spoke. She never got out of bed and she rarely ate anything,' says Matura, 'but after a visit from her dog, she sat up, looked happier, and started talking. She was a different person.'

Not all results are as impressive as Matura's, but pet visits can make a difference. When 31 pet visits were observed at The Hospital for Sick Children in Toronto, Canada, researchers found that pet visits helped to improve patient and parent morale. Pet visits are also allowed on the paediatric ward at Sutter Medical Center in Sacramento, California. 'Many children have a strong connection to their pets,' explains Amy Medovoy, child life programme co-ordinator. 'If the pets can visit them on the ward, we can bring the child's normal, everyday life into the hospital, and we feel this helps the child to heal better.'

Breaking down barriers

People may be concerned that pets will transmit diseases to patients, but hospitals report that they have had no cases of patients being infected by animals. Some hospital staff may feel that pet visiting is not a good idea. Lea Ann Matura comments, 'I thought the doctors wouldn't agree, but all of our doctors think it's a good idea. However, it is important to have a clear policy and a list of rules or guidelines before pets are allowed to visit. It can take a lot of time and effort to make sure that the programme is successful.'

2 Mobile medical units

1 Before you read the text, answer the question.

After a natural disaster (earthquake, flood, hurricane, etc.) what kinds of problems might affect hospitals and hospital staff?

2 Now read the text and answer the questions.

1 Apart from its use in disasters, in what two other situations can NorHosp be used?
2 Describe two ways in which NorHosp is flexible.
3 Does the surgical module contain lighting equipment?
4 How many weeks' supply of disposables does the nursing module have?
5 Which module provides outpatient services?
6 Are disinfectants or insecticides supplied with the hygiene module?

3 Match the green words in the text with the meanings below.

1 experienced or suffered __________
2 likely to last for a long time __________
3 ready to use __________
4 machines for sterilizing equipment __________
5 items that are thrown away after use __________
6 a system of assessing illness or injury and treating the most serious cases first __________

File Edit View Insert Format Tools Actions Help

NorHosp

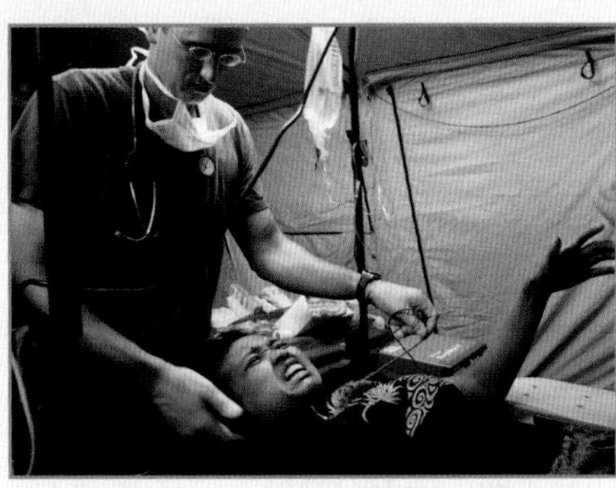

The Norwegian Mobile Hospital and Disaster Unit (NorHosp) is a flexible medical emergency unit composed of different modules. It is specially designed for the surgical treatment of injuries **sustained** in natural disasters and wars. But it can also be used for other purposes, such as the introduction of health services to rural areas.

The NorHosp modules can be used in one place, packed up, and used again in other places. Most of the equipment can be packed in lightweight, **durable** cases. It can therefore easily be transported on jeeps, trucks, boats, and aircraft.

The module system makes it possible to split up the complete unit and use the various modules in different combinations. In this way, NorHosp can be tailored to meet particular needs. NorHosp contains all the instruments and equipment necessary for the treatment of adults and children.

NorHosp modules can be transported quickly and efficiently to the site, and facilities can be **operational** within 72 hours.

Each **surgical module** contains sufficient medical equipment to establish an operating theatre with two operating tables. Two operation and examination lamps are included. Two **autoclaves** allow for continuous sterilization of instruments and textiles.

Each **nursing module** contains all the necessary nursing equipment to establish and maintain a surgical ward with 50 inpatients, and has sufficient **disposables** for fourteen days.

The **x-ray module** contains a complete x-ray department including x-ray machine, manual developing equipment, darkroom equipment, chemicals, films, light boxes, and protection equipment.

The **medicament module** contains medicines and infusion fluids sufficient for the treatment of 300 surgical patients (intravenously and orally), half of them with abdomen / chest injuries.

Each **Medical Officer module** contains equipment for establishing a simple outpatient department for diagnosis, and where **triage** and emergency treatment can be provided.

The **hygiene module** contains equipment for gathering, heating, storing, testing, and distributing water. Disinfectants or insecticides must be ordered separately.

3 Hospital error

1 Read the text and decide if the sentences are true (T) or false (F).

1 The patient was admitted with an injured foot. _____
2 The patient was admitted to the surgical ward. _____
3 The patient did not get the correct medication. _____
4 The patient died before he could be operated on. _____
5 The patient died of brain damage. _____
6 It was decided that the patient's death had been an accident. _____

2 Match the words (1–6) from the text with the correct definitions (a–f).

1 inquest
2 coroner
3 lawyer
4 counter
5 vascular
6 pulmonary

a of the blood vessels
b to act against something
c of the lung
d a person trained in the law who does legal work for other people
e a person who investigates the causes of death
f an inquiry to find out the facts

Inquest told of hospital error

A HOSPITAL error left a dying man on the wrong ward for two days as deep vein thrombosis (DVT) ravaged his body, an inquest heard. Stephen Melvin Newbold suffered massive brain damage when a blood clot formed in his veins. Now his family are considering legal action against York Hospital, saying that his death was 'untimely and unnecessary'.

Mr Newbold, a 52-year-old maintenance worker, went to York Hospital on November 3 complaining of a swollen right foot. He should have been sent to a surgical ward where he would have been treated with Fragmin, a drug which counters the effects of DVT. However, hospital staff wrongly admitted him to an orthopaedic ward, where he stayed for two days, before finally being transferred to the care of a consultant vascular surgeon. Twenty-four hours later, on November 6, doctors decided they would have to operate to remove his leg below the knee.

The operation went ahead on November 10, but two days later Mr Newbold suffered a cardiac arrest. A scan revealed he had had a pulmonary embolism, a condition related to DVT. Mr Newbold suffered brain damage and died in the hospital on November 16.

Giving evidence, the surgeon said he could not explain why Mr Newbold had been admitted to an orthopaedic ward where it was not policy to administer Fragmin. He did not know why his medical team had not given Mr Newbold the drug later.

York coroner Donald Coverdale said, 'From November 3 until the day of the operation, no Fragmin was given to Mr Newbold. If he had been admitted to a consultant vascular surgeon's care from day one, it is clear that Fragmin would have been prescribed. Fragmin reduces the risk of DVT, but does not eliminate it. It is impossible to say whether Mr Newbold would have suffered this DVT if he had received the Fragmin.' He recorded a verdict of death by misadventure.

Kim Daniells, Mr Newbold's family's lawyer, said, 'The family hope that the hospital will learn from the errors, and that no other families will have to suffer in the future.'

A spokeswoman for York Hospital's NHS Trust said, 'We would like to extend our sincere sympathies to the family of Stephen Newbold during this difficult time.'

4 Accidents in the home

1 Which of the categories in the text do these home accidents belong to?

1 Lucy Mann left a candle burning when she went to bed. ___________

2 Two-year-old Toby Smith fell into a neighbour's swimming pool. ___________

3 76-year-old Eric Baker slipped on a wet bathroom floor. ___________

4 One-year-old Ben Brown put a small toy in his mouth and it lodged in his throat. ___________

5 Jasvinder Singh cut his hand badly while opening a tin of peaches. ___________

6 Ten-year-old Jason Gold swallowed some of his father's medicine. ___________

7 82-year-old Iris Watts dropped a pan of boiling water on her foot. ___________

8 Nick Young suffered cuts, bruises, and a broken arm when he was putting up some shelves in his home. ___________

9 Lee Fenton was hit by a falling tree which he was cutting down. ___________

2 Join these word combinations used in the text.

1 safety	a resources
2 total	b leaflets
3 simple	c cost
4 limited	d services
5 advice	e guidelines
6 emergency	f campaigns

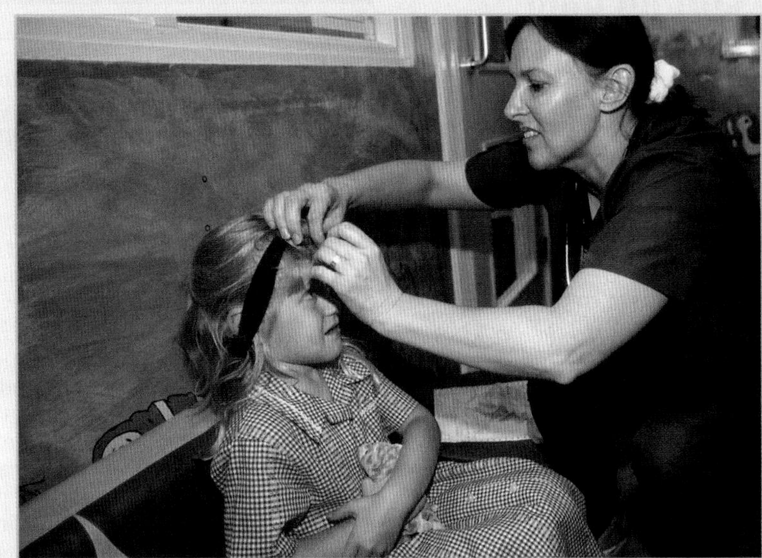

In the UK, about 2.8 million people every year seek treatment at an Accident and Emergency department after an accident in the home. More than 3,000 people die every year as a result of home accidents, and the total cost of home accident injuries has been estimated at £25 billion per year.

Research shows that most home accidents occur in the following categories:

- falls
- poisoning
- fires
- DIY accidents
- choking
- packaging accidents
- burns and scalds
- garden accidents
- drowning

Many of these accidents could be prevented by following simple guidelines. With this in mind, the government produces a range of safety campaigns and advice leaflets to warn people about dangers around the home. This would clearly reduce the load on Accident and Emergency departments and emergency services, such as police, fire and ambulance, allowing them to use their limited resources for other work.

5 Chronic pain

1 Read the text quickly and choose the best title.

a A cure for chronic pain
b Managing chronic pain
c New treatments for chronic pain

2 Read the text again. Choose the correct words to complete the sentences.

1 Chronic pain lasts for a *limited* / *long* period of time.
2 Chronic pain *sometimes* / *never* only exists in people's minds.
3 The causes of chronic pain are *simple* / *complicated*.
4 Chronic pain *can* / *cannot* be cured.
5 The programme helps patients use their *mind* / *mind and body* to manage their pain.
6 Patients *are* / *are not* helped to reduce their medication as part of the course.

3 Try to remember the verb used in these expressions. Then read the article again and check.

1 continue ______ for extended periods
2 m__________ a big difference
3 f__________ better about yourself
4 w__________ towards a meaningful, active, and satisfying life
5 w__________ closely with a team of physiotherapists
6 o__________ your fears
7 d__________ stretching and exercise sessions
8 ch__________ negative ways of thinking
9 a__________ depression
10 f__________ our programme

File Edit View Insert Format Tools Actions Help

What is chronic pain?

There are two kinds of pain, *acute* and *chronic*. Acute pain lasts for a limited time, and is usually the result of an injury, surgery, or medical illness. Chronic pain continues for extended periods of time, sometimes even after the original problem has healed. Treatments for acute and chronic pain are often quite different.

Is the pain all in my mind?

Many people ask this question when they can't understand why they have chronic pain, or because they feel that health professionals, family, and friends don't believe them. But pain is either present or absent – you can't imagine it. And we know that pain is caused by a mix of physical, psychological, social, and emotional factors.

Will my pain go away?

At present there is no known cure for chronic pain. Many patients say that their pain reduces during treatment on our programme, but only a few people find that it makes a big difference on its own. However, we aim to help you manage your day-to-day mood and outlook on life, and generally to feel better about yourself.

Should I give up all hope of a cure?

Advances in our understanding of pain are happening all the time, and who knows what the future may bring? However, it is more helpful to focus on working towards a meaningful, active, and satisfying life today, rather than on the possibility of a cure in the future.

What happens on the programme?

You will work closely with a team of physiotherapists, psychologists, nurses, doctors, and occupational therapists. We will teach you skills to help you address the challenge of living with chronic pain. We help you to understand your pain, and overcome your fears about it. We help you to reduce tablets that don't work. We do stretching and exercise sessions. And we help you to learn ways of relaxing and challenging negative ways of thinking, and so avoid depression.

Will this programme really help me to improve my life, even though my pain hasn't gone away?

Yes, it is possible. Many people who follow our programme, and similar programmes around the world, report that they have achieved a more balanced and fulfilling life. They achieve this despite their chronic pain.

6 Improving patient care

1 Before you read the text below, look at these words and phrases from the text and use them to predict what you think it is about. Use a dictionary to help you, if necessary.

misdiagnosis
diagnostic tool
information database
quality of care

2 Read the text. In which paragraph will you find information about the following?

1 how the diagnostic tool works _____
2 what happened to Isabel Maude at the local hospital _____
3 how the diagnostic tool can be used _____
4 who developed the idea for the diagnostic tool _____
5 who the system is for _____

3 Join these word combinations used in the text.

1	clinical	a	skills
2	diagnostic	b	recovery
3	secondary	c	failure
4	full	d	error
5	decision	e	characteristics
6	organ	f	infection

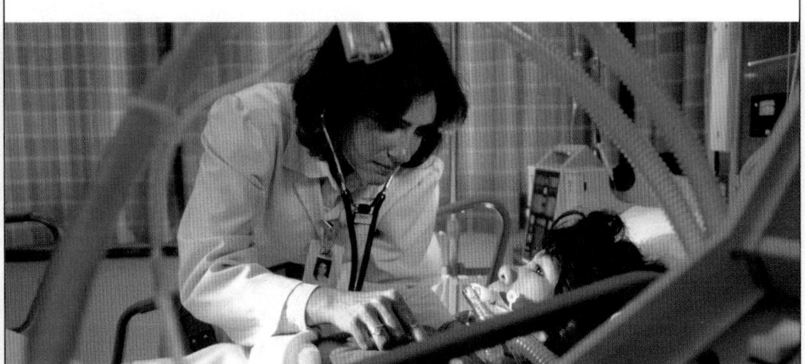

IMPROVING PATIENT CARE

A In July 1999, Jason and Charlotte Maude's three-year-old daughter, Isabel, developed chickenpox. The illness followed the normal patterns at first, but then her symptoms got worse. Doctors told her parents it was all normal, but Isabel had to be rushed to the Accident & Emergency department of their local hospital. Here her condition continued to deteriorate. She went into multiple organ failure as a result of a secondary infection.

B Isabel was taken to another hospital, where she spent two months suffering from toxic shock syndrome and necrotizing fasciitis (also known as 'the flesh-eating bug'). Fortunately, Isabel eventually made a full recovery. But her parents were devastated by the experience – their family doctor and her local A & E department had not diagnosed her symptoms correctly, and their daughter had almost died.

C During the time that their daughter was in hospital, the Maudes and paediatrician Dr Joseph Britto, who helped to treat Isabel, came up with the idea of a diagnostic tool to try to stop the kind of misdiagnosis that had caused them and their daughter so much suffering. The Maudes left their jobs to set up a medical charity to pursue their idea.

D The company's mission statement is 'Our mission is to help reduce diagnosis and decision error, and provide clinicians with relevant knowledge in their workflow to help them improve the quality of care.'

E The product the Maudes developed, called Isabel, uses software to search medical texts. It allows medical staff to key in symptoms, signs, results of tests and investigations, etc. The database then delivers a list of possible diagnoses. The user can click on each diagnosis to access information and images. The software is accessible via the Web, or integrated into an electronic medical records system.

F Initially, the system was designed for paediatric patients, but it now includes adults as well. It covers all the major specialties, including internal medicine, surgery, gynaecology and obstetrics, geriatrics, and oncology.

G Isabel is being used in the UK, USA, Ireland, and India. At one hospital in the USA, a paediatrician listed the main clinical characteristics of every medical admission to the paediatric intensive care unit for one month, and Isabel included the correct diagnosis in every case. Other hospitals who have used it say it is especially useful for cases which are difficult to diagnose. For experienced physicians, it can serve as a reminder. For less

7 Secrets of a long life

1 Read the article and decide if the sentences are true (T) or false (F).

1 Genetic factors explain the long life of Okinawans. ____

2 Elderly people in Okinawa usually eat large meals. ____

3 Elderly Okinawans are physically active. ____

4 Elderly Okinawans are usually cheerful and relaxed. ____

5 On Okinawa, elderly people are often involved in group activities. ____

6 Young Okinawans follow the same lifestyle as their grandparents. ____

2 Add these sentences to the end of the paragraphs (A–G) where they fit best.

1 All of these factors give Okinawans *ikigai*, or 'a reason for living', which makes their lives happier and more fulfilled. ____

2 The life expectancy of Brazilian Okinawans is 17 years lower than that on Okinawa itself. ____

3 Rates of osteoporosis, heart disease, strokes, cancer, and dementia are all low on Okinawa. ____

4 Okinawans under the age of 50 have Japan's highest rates of obesity, heart disease, and premature death. ____

Secrets of a long life

A A hundred years ago, not many people lived into their seventies. Today, it is fairly common to do so in developed countries. But on the Japanese island of Okinawa, people live longer than anywhere else in the world, with an average life expectancy of 81.2 years. Many people on Okinawa live to be over 100 years old – the highest ratio of centenarians per head of population in the world. And they don't just live longer, they live better.

B So what's the Okinawan secret? So far all the findings indicate that lifestyle, not genetic factors, is largely responsible.

C Okinawans eat a traditional diet of soya, fruit, and vegetables. They consume a lot of fish, such as tuna, mackerel, and salmon, which are rich in omega-3 fatty acids, and help reduce the risk of heart disease and breast cancer. They don't eat a lot of red meat, and their diet is low in fats. Many elderly Okinawans also live by the motto 'Eat until you are 80% full', and this helps them to control portion sizes.

D Elderly Okinawans enjoy walking, gardening, and T'ai Chi, and often work long after the usual age of retirement in Western countries. Interviews with elderly Okinawans reveal that they are optimistic, adaptable, and easy-going. They have strong religious beliefs, which give them comfort and support. They have a valued role in society and the family, and they are respected for their wisdom and experience of life.

E Most of them belong to *moai*, groups of old classmates, colleagues, friends, or neighbours that meet several times a week to drink tea and chat. These networks provide emotional and financial support throughout their lives.

F Unfortunately, younger Okinawans have abandoned these good habits. They have followed a more Western diet and lifestyle, and the results have been devastating.

G For Okinawans who move away from the island, the picture is similar. Around 100,000 Okinawans moved to Brazil and adopted the eating habits of their new home, including eating a lot of red meat. ■

8 Chocolate

1 Read the text quickly. Who is this information for?

a doctors
b nutritionists
c the general public

2 Read the text again and complete it using words from below.

unfortunately	after	tooth
decreases	slowly	full
hungry	mood	same
improves	before	risk
because	lower	high
quickly		

3 Match these words from the text with the correct definitions.

a pros and cons
b fatigue
c sensation
d addicted to
e contribute to
f clog up

1 to help cause something
2 feeling
3 tiredness
4 to block
5 good points and bad points
6 can't stop doing something, eating something, etc.

Is chocolate good for you? The pros and cons

Chocolate is made from the beans of the cacao tree, and has been popular for thousands of years. The Aztecs in South America used cocoa beans to make a chocolate drink which was refreshing and nourishing, but bitter to taste. In Europe, sweeteners were added, and modern chocolate contains cocoa butter, sugar, and cream or milk.

But is chocolate good for you? First, the good news:

Research at Harvard University suggests that people who eat chocolate three times a month will live almost a year longer than people who don't.

Chocolate contains flavenoids – substances that can reduce the __________[1] of coronary artery disease. Chocolate also contains small amounts of caffeine, which can be beneficial as it __________[2] your endurance and __________[3] feelings of fatigue.

Eating chocolate makes you feel good. Like other sweet food, chocolate stimulates the release of endorphins – natural body hormones that produce feelings of pleasure and help to lift your __________[4]. And because chocolate melts in the mouth at body temperature, it produces a wonderful, silky sensation that people love. According to psychologists, this is one of the main reasons why people can become addicted to chocolate.

But it's not all good news. __________[5], chocolate contains a lot of calories – just 100 g of milk chocolate contains 520 kcals, while dark chocolate contains 510 kcals. That's about the __________[6] number of calories as 2.5 kg of grapes or 300 g of grilled chicken.

The Harvard research also suggests that people who eat too much chocolate have a __________[7] life expectancy. Chocolate is __________[8] in saturated fats and sugar, so eating too much can contribute to obesity and related health problems. And the sugar in chocolate can cause __________[9] decay.

But if you really can't resist chocolate, eat dark chocolate – it's higher in cocoa than milk chocolate and helps to increase levels of HDL, a type of cholesterol that helps prevent fat clogging up arteries.

And here are some more tips:

- Eat good-quality, dark chocolate, not milk or white chocolate.
- Don't eat more than 100 g per day.
- Eat chocolate after a meal, when you are __________[10].
- Clean your teeth __________[11] eating chocolate.
- Eat it with fresh fruit.
- Eat it __________[12] so that you can experience the full flavour.

9 Leeches

1 Read the text. Match each topic below with a paragraph (A–G).

1 Problems with leech therapy ____

2 How leech therapy works ____

3 Patient reaction to leeches ____

4 History of leech therapy ____

5 Benefits of using leeches ____

2 Find words in the text with the following meanings.

1 to make something become bigger or wider ________

2 cut off ________

3 dangers ________

4 outer openings in the body ________

5 a state of being blocked or too full ________

6 having a feeling of extreme dislike ________

3 In your own words, explain

- the job that leeches do
- some benefits and dangers of using leeches.

A Imagine having a bloodsucking worm attached to your body – by a doctor! It may sound incredible, but it happens, and it's known as leech therapy.

B Leeches are a type of earthworm, and their use in medicine dates back 2,500 years. In Europe, the surgical removal of a patient's blood using leeches was practised widely until the 19th century. They were thought to cure many things, including headaches, obesity, eye disorders, and mental illness. For most of the 20th century the use of leeches went out of fashion, but since developments in microsurgery in the 1980s, they have been making a comeback.

C Leeches are often used today in plastic or reconstructive surgery, especially where a part of the body, such as a finger, hand, toe, or ear has become severed and has to be re-attached. This is how it works: sometimes a patient's veins are unable to take blood away from the body part and so the blood builds up, causing 'venous congestion'. When this happens, the re-attached part of the body turns blue and lifeless, and is at risk of being lost. Leeches attached to the body will suck the blood away, allowing the re-attached body part to survive until the veins begin to work normally.

D The leech bite doesn't hurt because leech saliva contains a natural anaesthetic. Leech saliva also contains substances which prevent the blood from clotting, and dilate the blood vessels to increase blood flow. When a leech is full of blood, it simply falls off.

E Leeches are inexpensive to buy, and easy to look after. And studies have shown that leech therapy can double the success rate of transplanted tissue flaps – for example, where a flap of skin is taken from one area of the body to cover a defect or injury in another area, as in facial reconstruction following cancer. This is a much higher success rate than that achieved through drugs or further surgery.

F As you might imagine, patients are often disgusted at the thought of having slimy worms attached to their wounds. But when the benefits are explained to them they usually accept the treatment – most would rather have leech therapy than lose a part of their body.

G However, there can be problems. Hazards associated with leech therapy include infection, excessive blood loss that may require blood transfusion, and allergic reactions. Sometimes the leeches slip off patients and re-attach themselves to other parts of the body that are not in need of treatment. Once they are full, leeches will look for a warm, dark place to digest their meal, and may burrow into wounds or enter the patient's mouth or other orifices. To prevent escapes, nurses must keep careful count of the leeches.

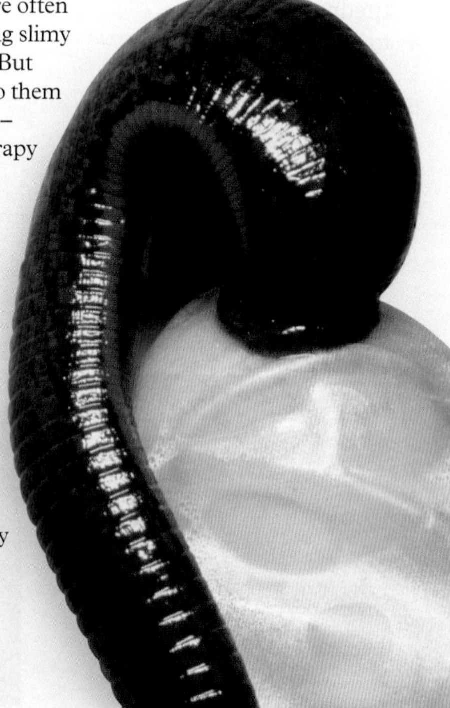

10 Death and dying customs

1 Read the text quickly and answer the questions below.

1 Who is this information for?
 a patients
 b healthcare professionals
 c religious leaders

2 What is the writer's intention?
 a to describe the process of dying and death
 b to help people from different religions deal with grief
 c to explain how different religions view dying and death

2 Read the text again. Decide whether each statement relates to Buddhism, Islam, or Judaism, and write *B*, *I*, or *J*. There may be more than one answer.

1 The dying person should be kept quiet and calm. ____
2 The dying person should not be left alone. ____
3 The body is washed by family members. ____
4 Any open wounds should be covered. ____
5 Burial should take place within 24 hours. ____
6 Cremation is not acceptable. ____
7 Burial or cremation are acceptable. ____

Death and dying customs

Death is a cultural as well as a biological event. It is important for you to be aware of the cultural and religious beliefs and customs of your dying patients and their families. These guidelines will help you to respond in an appropriate way in order to provide a culturally-aware service.

ISLAM

When a Muslim dies in hospital, the family may experience a great deal of anxiety if they feel that healthcare staff are unfamiliar with Muslim traditions. Firstly, it is important to put on some gloves so that you do not touch the body directly. The face of the person who has died should be turned towards Mecca. Straighten the arms and legs and close the mouth and eyes. After death, the body is washed by family members of the same sex and is wrapped in white linen cloth. According to Islamic tradition, a dead person should be buried as soon as possible, preferably within 24 hours. A Muslim is always buried, never cremated. Post-mortem examinations are discouraged, unless they are required by law.

BUDDHISM

According to Buddhist beliefs, in death the consciousness departs from one life and begins the journey into another new life. For Buddhists, death is a process in which the consciousness gradually separates from the body. This can take up to three days, which is when death occurs. It is very important to provide as much peace and quiet for the dying person as possible. The more composed and calm the mind is at death, the greater the opportunity for a better rebirth. Immediately following signs of physical death, Buddhists believe that it is best to keep the body in a peaceful state. Traditionally, the body is taken to the home, and for a period of three days or so prayers are said and the body is not touched. The deceased may be cremated or buried, depending on the wishes of the family. Generally speaking, post mortems are acceptable as the body is considered less important after death.

JUDAISM

By religious law, someone should stay with the dying person so that the soul does not feel alone. The body should also not be left alone after death. It is important to leave in place any catheters, drains, and tubes, as the fluid in them is considered to be part of the body, and must be buried with it. Cover them with gauze or bandages. Any wound dressings that have body fluids on them must also be left on the body. Any incisions or cuts must be covered. The body is prepared for burial as soon as possible after death, preferably within 24 hours. The body is prepared by members of the *chevra kaddisha*, or burial society, and the body is covered with a sheet. Post-mortem examinations are discouraged, unless they are required by law.

11 Typhoid Mary

1 Read the text and complete it using words from below.

co-operate	disease	cured
quarantine	forcibly	samples
confirmed	examples	freely
transmitted	discuss	sent
developed	infection	causes
provided	infected	helped
investigation	isolated	

2 Decide if these sentences are true (T) or false (F).

1 Mary Mallon was born in the United States. ____

2 Mary was often ill. ____

3 George Soper discovered that Mary was a typhoid carrier. ____

4 Mary wanted to help the authorities. ____

5 After 1910, Mary did not work with food again. ____

6 Mary was kept in hospital for a total of 26 years. ____

7 Mary died of typhoid. ____

Mary Mallon (1869–1938) was an Irish immigrant who was the first known healthy carrier of typhoid in the USA. She probably contracted a mild case of typhoid, although she may not have been aware of it, and was never ____________[1]. In this way, she became a carrier, and spread the disease.

Typhoid is an infection of the digestive system caused by a bacterium, *Salmonella typhi*. Among other symptoms, it ____________[2] weakness, high fever, a rash of red spots, chills, sweating, and in serious cases inflammation of the spleen and bones, delirium, and erosion of the intestinal wall leading to haemorrhage. It is ____________[3] through contaminated food or drinking water.

Mary was the cause of several outbreaks of typhoid in the New York City area between 1900 and 1907. She worked as a cook in a number of different households, and on each occasion, members of the family or other servants ____________[4] typhoid. 22 people became ill, and one died. At the time, typhoid was a serious problem, especially in cities, and killed around 10% of sufferers.

In the summer of 1906, New York banker Charles Henry Warren hired Mary to be a cook for his family at their rented summer house. When six of the eleven members of the household became ill with typhoid, the owners of the house employed George Soper, a sanitary engineer with experience in typhoid outbreaks, to look for the source.

After some months of careful ____________[5] into Mary's background and her previous jobs, George Soper was certain that she was the cause of the outbreak, and so he asked her for blood, urine, and stool ____________[6]. She did not believe him – in fact, she resisted violently and attacked him with a large fork. At that time, the idea that a person could spread a disease and still remain healthy was not widely known.

Mary resisted two other visits from health officials, shouting and swearing at them and running away. Mary was a strong-minded woman, but it must also have been very frightening for her to be confronted in this way. Eventually the New York City Health Department sent five police officers and an ambulance and ____________[7] took her to hospital.

The New York City health inspector carried out some tests and ____________[8] that Mary was a carrier. In 1910 she was transferred to an island near New York City, where she lived in isolation for three years. She was then released but told that she should not work with food again. However, in 1915 she took a job as a cook in a hospital and ____________[9] 25 doctors, nurses, and other hospital staff – two of them died. Mary was then seized again and kept in ____________[10] for 23 years, living alone in a one-room cottage.

In December 1932, Mary suffered a massive stroke, which left her paralysed. She died in 1938 of pneumonia.

Today 'Typhoid Mary' is a term used to describe a carrier of a dangerous ____________[11] who refuses to take precautions or ____________[12] with the authorities.

12 Myths and facts

A 'myth' is something that is not true. The information here examines myths about mental illness and the facts behind them.

1 Match the myths with the facts.

1 _____
2 _____
3 _____
4 _____
5 _____
6 _____
7 _____
8 _____

2 Identify three things in this information that have improved your understanding of mental illness.

Myths and facts about mental illness

1 Myth People with mental illness are violent and unpredictable.

2 Myth Mental illness is a figment of the imagination.

3 Myth Mental illness cannot affect me.

4 Myth Therapy and self-help are a waste of time.

5 Myth Mental illness only affects people in rich countries.

6 Myth There is no hope for people with mental illness.

7 Myth If I have a mental illness, it's a sign of weakness – it's my fault.

8 Myth Most people with mental illness live on the streets or are in mental hospitals.

a Fact People with mental illness may work with therapists, counsellors, psychologists, psychiatrists, nurses, and social workers. They also use self-help strategies and community support. All can play their part in the recovery process.

b Fact Despite the image portrayed in the media, statistics show that people with mental illness are no more violent than the general population. People with psychotic illnesses like schizophrenia are more likely to be frightened and confused than violent.

c Fact Mental illness isn't your fault, any more than heart disease or diabetes is your fault. Mental illness is a product of biological, psychological, and social factors. Research shows that schizophrenia, depression, and alcoholism can be linked to genetic and biological factors. Social influences, such as the loss of a loved one or a job, can also contribute to the development of mental illness.

d Fact Mental illness is surprisingly common, and can affect anyone. A 2004 survey by the World Health Organization of 60,000 adults in fourteen countries revealed that a significant number of the people interviewed had had an episode of mental illness in the last year. This varied across countries – for example, from 4.3% in China to 26.4% in the USA.

e Fact Mental and brain disorders are found among people in developed countries as well as in developing nations. In a study of 27 countries carried out by the World Health Organization, no country was found to be free of schizophrenia. Alcohol abuse is another common disorder around the world.

f Fact Most people with mental illness live in the community. Most people who need hospitalization are only there for brief periods to get treatment and then return home. You probably know someone with a mental illness and don't even realize it.

g Fact Mental illness is real. It causes suffering and disability, and can even shorten life. The symptoms are a sign of real illness which needs treatment and diagnosis.

h Fact There is a wide range of treatments, therapy, and community support for mental illness. Most people with mental illness get better. Many recover completely and lead active, productive lives. Science has shown that having hope is an important factor in an individual's recovery.

13 Anaesthesia

1 Choose the best headings (1–6) to match the sections of the text (A–D). There are two more headings than you need.

1 Some types of anaesthesia ____
2 Death on the operating table ____
3 A short history of anaesthesia ____
4 Anaesthetic nurses ____
5 What is 'anaesthesia'? ____
6 Anaesthesia today ____

2 Answer these questions about the text.

1 How do anaesthetic drugs work?
2 Why do you think patients were held or strapped down before anaesthetic drugs were available?
3 What difference did anaesthetic drugs make to the work of surgeons?
4 Which was safer to use – ether or chloroform?
5 Which was easier to use – ether or chloroform?
6 Do patients lose consciousness during regional anaesthesia?
7 Is death resulting from anaesthesia common?

3 Find words or phrases in the text with these meanings.

a having a strong effect ____
b loses the power to feel ____
c disappear gradually ____

FACTFILE

ANAESTHESIA

A 'Anaesthesia' means 'loss of sensation'. Drugs that cause anaesthesia work by blocking the signals that pass along your nerves to your brain. This stops you feeling pain. When the drugs wear off, you start to feel normal sensations again.

B The development of effective anaesthetics in the 19th century was an important factor in successful surgery. Before this time, few operations were possible, and surgeons were judged by their speed. Some doctors used alcohol or morphine to reduce the pain, but patients were usually held or strapped down. Many died on the operating table. Anaesthesia meant that surgeons could take more time and perform more complex procedures.

Ether was one of the earliest anaesthetics, but it had some drawbacks – for example, it could cause vomiting. It was quickly replaced by chloroform, which was more potent and easier to use than ether. However, it was not as safe to use as ether, and could cause sudden death. By the 1920s, intravenous induction agents were introduced. They enabled patients to fall asleep quickly and pleasantly. In the 1940s muscle relaxants became available.

C Anaesthesia can be given in different ways, and not all anaesthesia makes you unconscious.

- Local anaesthesia numbs a small part of your body. You stay conscious but free from pain.
- Regional anaesthesia can be used for operations on larger or deeper parts of the body. The most common regional anaesthetics (also known as regional 'blocks') are spinal and epidural anaesthetics. These can be used for operations on the lower body, such as Caesarean sections, bladder operations, or hip replacements. You stay conscious but free from pain.
- General anaesthesia is a state of controlled unconsciousness, and you feel nothing. It is essential for some operations such as abdominal surgery. As the anaesthetic drugs wear off, your consciousness starts to return.

D Modern monitoring systems and a greater understanding of the functions of the body mean that anaesthesia is now very safe. Fewer than 1 in 250,000 deaths during operations are directly related to anaesthesia.

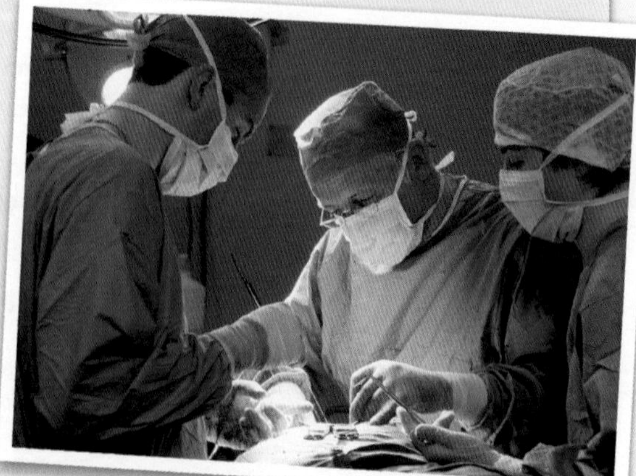

14 The return of Thalidomide

1 Read the article and decide if the sentences are true (T) or false (F).

1 One of the side effects of Thalidomide was nausea. ____
2 40% of mothers who took Thalidomide had normal children. ____
3 The tests carried out on Thalidomide were not strict enough. ____
4 Thalidomide can cure leprosy. ____
5 Thalidomide can damage the autoimmune system. ____
6 We still don't know exactly how Thalidomide works. ____

2 Add these sentences to the end of the paragraphs (A–E) where they fit best.

1 It has been so successful in many cases, that it is seen by some as a 'wonder drug'. ____
2 At least this drug, which caused such tragedy when introduced, can now offer hope to sufferers of conditions that are otherwise incurable. ____
3 Investigations began immediately into what had gone wrong. ____
4 However, Garry does suffer from side effects of the drug such as muscle pain, and numbness in the hands and feet. ____
5 Drugs must now undergo thorough testing on human subjects before being made available for general use. ____

A In 1961 an Australian doctor, William McBride, noticed a sudden increase in the number of babies being born with one or more limbs missing. He realized that all their mothers had taken the same drug during pregnancy, and he alerted the medical world. The drug, Thalidomide, had been used since the late 1950s to combat nausea during pregnancy. When its catastrophic effects were realized – 40% of affected children died in their first year – it was withdrawn from use.

B The drug had been believed safe, as it had been thoroughly tested on animals. Tests had shown that rats could be given massive doses without any ill-effects. Today's strict rules for drug-testing owe a great deal to Thalidomide.

C The drug remained out of use until 1964, when Dr Jacob Sheskin found some old boxes of it in his French clinic, and decided to try it as a sedative to relieve the suffering of a patient with leprosy, a disease that eats away at the flesh and bones. Within three days, lesions had healed and the leprosy disappeared. Since then, the drug has cautiously been trialled as a treatment for a wide range of conditions.

D The powerful anti-inflammatory properties of the drug make it effective at treating arthritis, AIDS, multiple sclerosis and over 100 other conditions, including many autoimmune disorders. It is also believed to restrict the growth of blood vessels in cancerous tumours. Garry Edlin, a patient whose rare form of cancer, mantle cell lymphoma, has been successfully treated by Thalidomide at Derriford Hospital in the UK, said, 'Within ten days the huge lumps had gone – it's like a miracle cure.'

E Although Thalidomide is known to be effective, we do not fully understand how it works. For this reason, and because of the memories of its devastating introduction, it will take some time before Thalidomide is widely accepted as a treatment.

15 The best medicine?

1 Find the answers to these questions in the text below.

1 In what two ways is laughter good for patients, according to Dr Tim Crick?
2 Where were the first laughter therapy sessions held?
3 Why might laughter help diabetics?
4 How does laughter help fight infection, according to some studies?
5 According to Dr Crick, why is laughter a powerful healer?

2 Match the highlighted words in the text with the meanings below.

1 hormones produced in the brain that reduce pain ___________
2 designed to help treat illness or to help you relax ___________
3 the effect that you are trying to achieve ___________
4 to increase something ___________
5 makes something begin to happen ___________
6 recovery after illness or injury ___________

It's not a noise that you usually hear coming from a hospital room. 'Ha ha haa! Hee hee!' You open the door to see twelve patients – all sick, several in wheelchairs – tickling each other with long balloons and laughing as hard as it's possible to laugh.

Joining in with the fun is Dr Tim Crick, and this is his weekly session of laughter therapy at Leeds City Hospital. The **aim** of these 30-minute sessions is not only to help patients forget that they are sick, according to Dr Crick: 'Laughter gives the lungs and the muscles a good workout, which is important in long-term patients. But more than this, I believe that laughter can actually speed up **recuperation** from sickness.'

Laughter therapy's recent history begins in the 1980s, when writer Norman Cousins described in *Anatomy of an Illness* how he used comedy films to successfully give himself some relief from a painful medical condition. This prompted academics to begin looking at the physiological effects of laughter. The spread of **therapeutic** 'laughter clubs' began in India in the 1990s with Dr Madan Kataria, who began taking patients for sessions in a public park.

So is there any science behind the claims that laughter speeds recovery? Certainly, it **triggers** a range of reactions in the body. Some studies have shown that the ability to use and respond to humour may raise the level of infection-fighting antibodies, and **boost** the level of immune cells. A recent study with diabetics showed that laughter helped control blood sugar levels. And research at the University of Maryland showed that laughing helped blood flow by keeping blood vessels relaxed.

For Dr Crick, it is in laughter's ability to relax us that its healing power lies. 'After a good laugh, our muscles relax, our mind stops focusing on pain or negative thoughts, and **endorphins** start to flow in our brains. It puts the body in a situation where it can begin to heal itself. When we are healthy we can achieve this state through physical exercise, social contact, and so on – things that are more difficult when you are in hospital. Laughter, in the same way as music, can bring relaxation into the wards.'

While many are doubtful about the scientific basis of laughter therapy, it would be impossible for even the most extreme sceptic to watch these twelve patients in Leeds laugh until tears run down their faces without thinking, 'This is doing them good.'

Reading bank key

1 Pet visits (p.52)

1 1T 2F 3T 4F 5F

2 Possible answers

The pet should be in good health / clean / stay with the family or patient at all times.

The hospital should check that patients in beds nearby are not afraid of or allergic to the animal. The doctor should approve every visit. The family must sign a consent form releasing the hospital from liability.

2 Mobile medical units (p.53)

1 Possible answers

The hospital has no electricity or running water. Hospital buildings / equipment are damaged. The hospital runs out of / cannot get supplies. The hospital staff are killed, injured, or cannot get to work. The number of patients increases.

2
1 wars, health services for rural areas
2 Possible answers
It can be used in different places. It is easy to pack / transport. The modules can be used in different combinations.
3 yes
4 two
5 Medical Officer module
6 no

3
1 sustained 2 durable
3 operational 4 autoclaves
5 disposables 6 triage

3 Hospital error (p.54)

1 1T 2F 3T 4F 5T 6F

2 1f 2e 3d 4b 5a 6c

4 Accidents in the home (p.55)

1
1 fires
2 drowning
3 falls
4 choking
5 packaging accidents
6 poisoning
7 burns and scalds
8 DIY accidents
9 garden accidents

2 1f 2c 3e 4a 5b 6d

5 Chronic pain (p.56)

1 b

2
1 long 2 never
3 complicated 4 cannot
5 mind and body 6 are

3
2 make 3 feel
4 work 5 work
6 overcome 7 do
8 challenge 9 avoid
10 follow

6 Improving patient care (p.57)

1 Students' own answers

2 1E 2A 3G 4C 5F

3 1e 2a 3f 4b 5d 6c

7 Secrets of a long life (p.58)

1 1F 2F 3T 4T 5T 6F

2 1D 2G 3A 4F

8 Chocolate (p.59)

1 c

2
1 risk 2 improves
3 decreases 4 mood
5 Unfortunately 6 same
7 lower 8 high
9 tooth 10 full
11 after 12 slowly

3 a5 b3 c2 d6 e1 f4

9 Leeches (p.60)

1 1G 2C 3F 4B 5E

2
1 dilate 2 severed
3 hazards 4 orifices
5 congestion 6 disgusted

3 Students' own answers

10 Death and dying customs (p.61)

1 1b 2c

2
1 Buddhism 2 Judaism
3 Islam 4 Judaism
5 Islam, Judaism 6 Islam
7 Buddhism

11 Typhoid Mary (p.62)

1
1 cured 2 causes
3 transmitted 4 developed
5 investigation 6 samples
7 forcibly 8 confirmed
9 infected 10 quarantine
11 disease 12 co-operate

2 1F 2F 3T 4F 5F 6F 7F

12 Myths and facts (p.63)

1 1b 2g 3d 4a 5e 6h 7c 8f

2 Students' own answers

13 Anaesthesia (p.64)

1 1C 2– 3B 4– 5A 6D

2
1 They block the signals passing from nerves to the brain.
2 Because operations were very painful before anaesthesia.
3 They could take more time and perform more complex procedures.
4 Ether
5 Chloroform
6 No
7 No, it is rare.

3 a potent b numbs c wear off

14 The return of Thalidomide (p.65)

1 1F 2F 3T 4T 5F 6T

2 1C 2E 3A 4D 5B

15 The best medicine? (p.66)

1
1 It exercises the lungs and muscles, and it speeds up recovery from illness.
2 India
3 It helps control blood sugar levels.
4 It may increase the number of antibodies and immune cells.
5 Because it relaxes us.

2
1 endorphines 2 therapeutic
3 aim 4 boost
5 trigger 6 recuperation

9 Blood

Scrub up

1 There are four main blood groups: A, B, AB, and O. Each type can be followed by + or –. Do you know your blood group?

2 Not all blood types can be mixed together. Read the information below, and work with a partner to solve the puzzle.

A–
A+
O+
AB+
B+
Who's who? Can you work out the names of the women in the picture?
Maddy's blood can't be given to the other women.
Holly could receive blood from Katie and Alex.
Only Katie could donate blood to Freya.
Four of the women could give blood to Maddy.
Alex can't be given blood by any of the others.
A– = ____ A+ = ____ O+ = ____
AB+ = ____ AB– = ____
This chart shows which blood types can mix.

RECEIVER	DONOR A–	A+	B–	B+	AB–	AB+	O–	O+
A–	✓						✓	
A+	✓	✓					✓	✓
B–			✓				✓	
B+			✓	✓			✓	✓
AB–	✓		✓		✓		✓	
AB+	✓	✓	✓	✓	✓	✓	✓	✓
O–							✓	
O+							✓	✓

Vocabulary

Testing blood

Complete the text using the words below. Use your dictionary to help you.

slide	drop	microscope	syringe
vein	test tube	pipette	

Use a __________ [1] to take some blood from a __________ [2] in the patient's arm. Put the blood into a __________ [3]. Then, use a __________ [4] to put a __________ [5] of the blood onto a __________ [6]. Examine it under a __________ [7]. What do you see?

Listening 1

Blood types

1 🎧 Listen to some student nurses learning about how different blood types mix together. Which two blood types are mixed together in each picture?

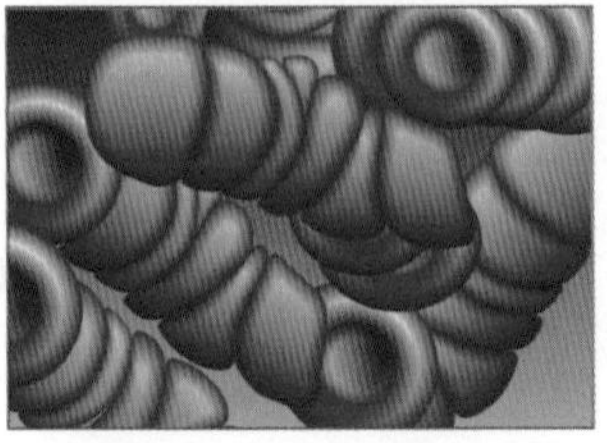

a= type _____ +type _____

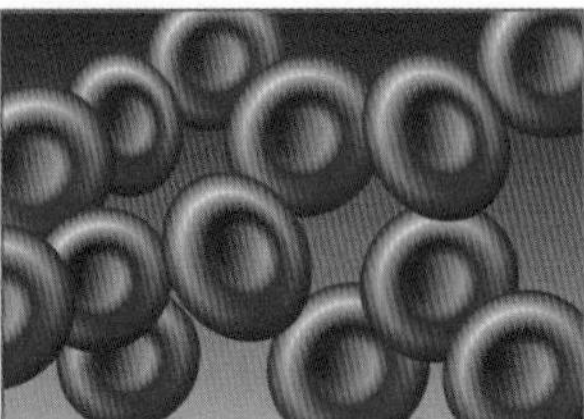

b= type _____ +type _____

2 Which blood type is most useful for emergencies?

In this unit

- talking about blood types
- describing blood samples
- doing a blood test and giving the results
- describing logical sequences using *if* and *when*
- the heart

Writing

Describing blood cells

1 Identify each type of blood cell in the picture below.

__*c*__ platelets
_____ white blood cells
_____ red blood cells

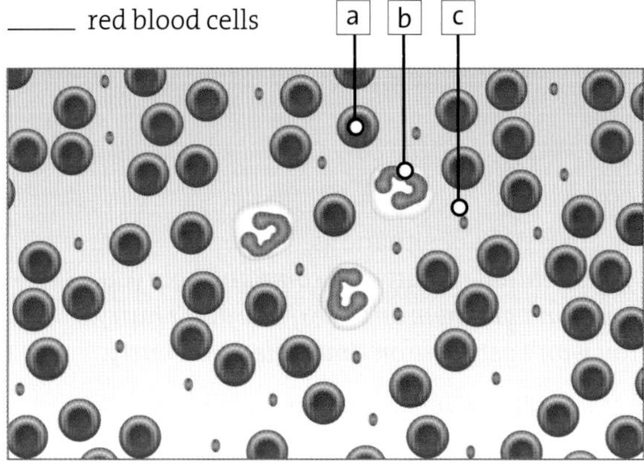

2 Find three more mistakes in this description.

There are many ~~rectangular~~ *circular* red blood cells moving freely in the plasma. The centres of the red blood cells are a light colour and the cells are all the same size. There are three white blood cells in the diagram. They are more regular in shape than the larger red blood cells. There are many platelets in this drop of blood. They are the small, dark, oval-shaped bodies.

3 This blood has cancer. Write a description of what you see in the diagram.

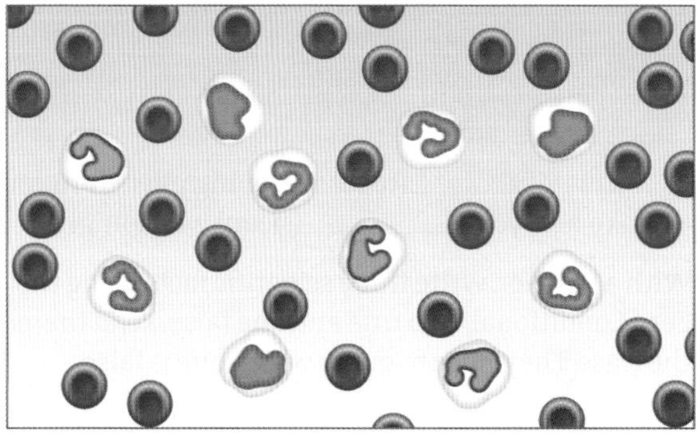

Speaking 1

You are going to read about our knowledge of blood. Work in pairs. Student A go to p.110. Student B go to p.113.

About 500 BC	Alcmaeon
About 200 BC	Chinese scientists
1492	doctors in Rome
1658	Jan Swammerdam
1818	James Blundell
1874	William Ostler
1901	Karl Landsteiner
1912	Roger Lee
1917	Oswald Robertson
1940	Karl Landsteiner
1948	Dr Carl Walter
1962	Max Perutz

The + or – sign after a person's blood group shows whether or not the blood has the **Rhesus factor** on the surface of their blood cells. This is an **antigen**, which causes people who do not have it to produce **antibodies** when their blood comes into contact with it. This causes their blood to become too thick.

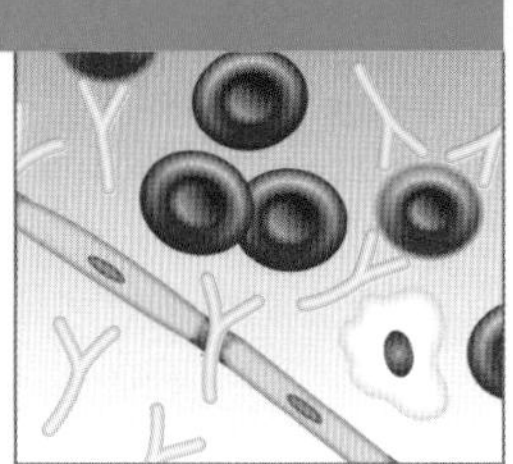

Listening 2

A blood test

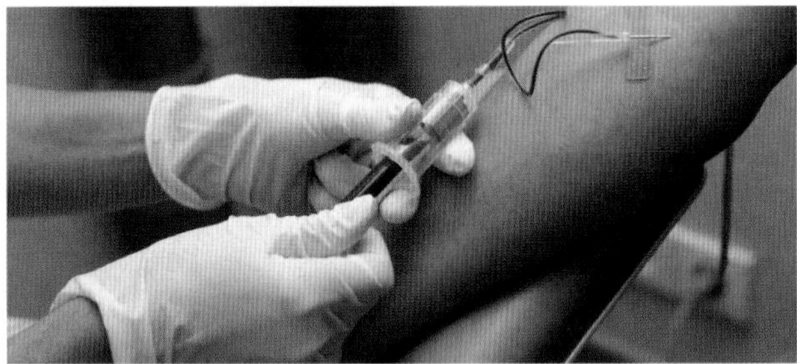

1 Complete this description of a Complete Blood Count (CBC) with the words below.

infection	platelets
haemoglobin	oxygen
clot	red blood cells
white blood cells	

A CBC measures the number of different cells that make up the blood. It looks at:

- __________[1] – these take __________[2] from the lungs to the body's tissues, and take carbon dioxide away at the same time. The CBC also measures the amount of __________[3] (a protein in the cells that carries the oxygen), and looks at the size and shape of the cells.
- __________[4] – these protect the body against __________[5].
- __________[6] – these make the blood __________[7].

2 Listen to the dialogue and answer the questions.

1. How does the patient feel?
2. How much blood is the nurse going to take?
3. What problem does the test result show?
4. How many million red blood cells per microlitre does it show?
5. How can the patient correct the problem?
6. How is the shape of the red cells?
7. How is the patient's white blood cell count?
8. How are her platelets?

Language spot

Zero and First Conditional

- We use the Zero Conditional to talk about what always happens in a particular situation. It is often used to talk about scientific facts.
  *If you **heat** water to 100°C, **it boils**.*
  ***When you get** pregnant, **you put on** weight.*
- The Present Simple tense is used in both parts of the sentence.
  *What **happens** to the blood when you **take** aspirin?*
- We use the First Conditional to talk about possible future actions or situations.
  *If **you remind** me later, **I'll come** and help you.*
  *You **won't get** there on time **if you don't hurry**.*
  *You **won't get** there on time **unless you hurry**.*
- We don't use *will / won't* after *if / when / unless*. We use the Present Simple.
  *If **you go** through the swing doors, you'll see the office on the left.*

Underline examples of the Zero and the First Conditional in the Listening script for *Listening 1* on p.129.

» Go to **Grammar reference** p.120

1 Complete these sentences using the Zero or the First Conditional.

1. If you explain the problem to Sister, she __________(tell) you what to do.
2. When you have an anaesthetic, it __________(stop) you feeling pain.
3. If I have time this evening, I __________(help) you with your homework.
4. You __________(have) a fever if your temperature __________(be) over 37.5°C.
5. If a person's brain __________(not get) oxygen, they __________(die).
6. If you __________(take) a sleeping pill before you go to bed, you __________(sleep) well tonight.

2 With a partner, write three scientific facts using the Zero Conditional, two true and one false. Read them to the class. They have to guess which one is false.

3 Finish these sentences with true information, then discuss them with a partner.

1 When I get home tonight, I'll ...
2 If the weather's good at the weekend, ...
3 I'll be very happy if ...
4 I'll be very disappointed if ...

Body bits

The heart

Look at the diagram and complete the descriptions with the words below.

pump
leaves
valve
enters
artery
flows
atrium
fills
aorta
opens
closing
beat

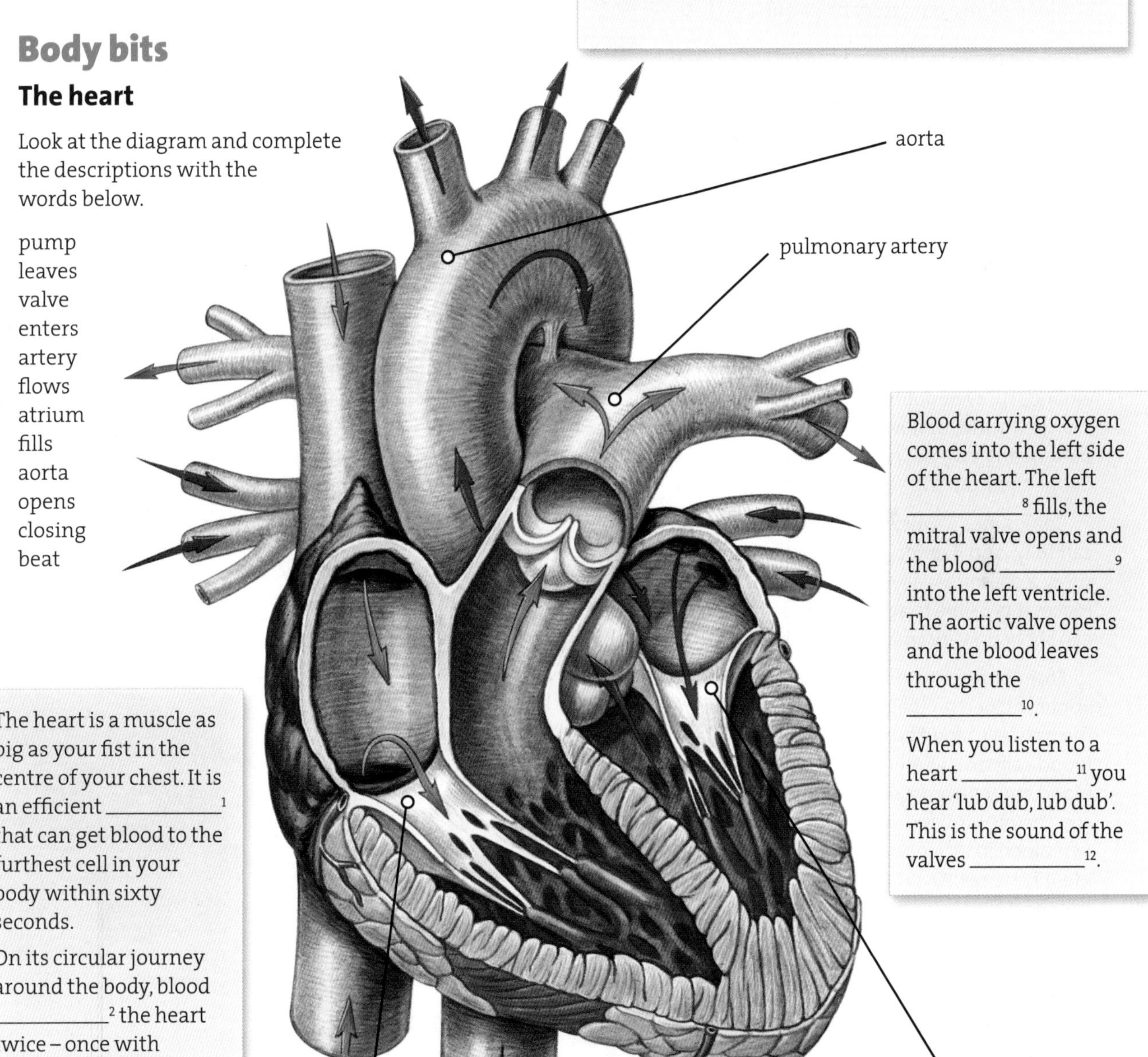

The heart is a muscle as big as your fist in the centre of your chest. It is an efficient ___________[1] that can get blood to the furthest cell in your body within sixty seconds.

On its circular journey around the body, blood ___________[2] the heart twice – once with oxygen and once without oxygen.

Blood without oxygen comes into the right side of the heart. It ___________[3] the right atrium. Then the tricuspid valve ___________[4] and the blood goes into the right ventricle. Then the pulmonary ___________[5] opens and the blood ___________[6] through the pulmonary ___________[7].

Blood carrying oxygen comes into the left side of the heart. The left ___________[8] fills, the mitral valve opens and the blood ___________[9] into the left ventricle. The aortic valve opens and the blood leaves through the ___________[10].

When you listen to a heart ___________[11] you hear 'lub dub, lub dub'. This is the sound of the valves ___________[12].

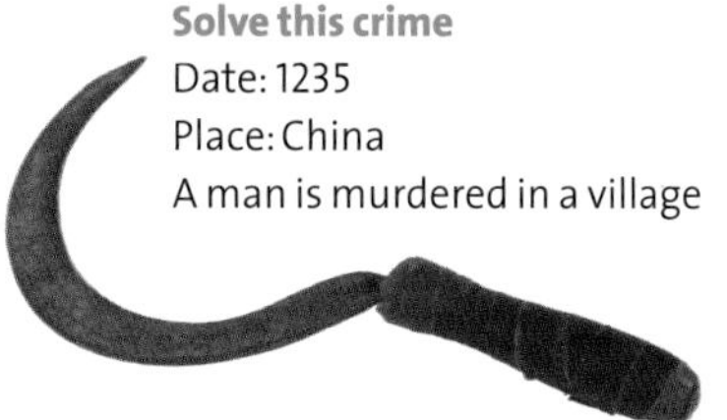

Solve this crime
Date: 1235
Place: China
A man is murdered in a village

The investigator knows the murderer used a sickle. But he can't find the murder weapon because all the sickles in the village are clean. He lays them all out in the sun and watches. Soon he knows which sickle was used in the murder. How?

Reading

1 Do you know of any murders where blood analysis has helped the police to catch the killer? Tell the class.

2 Read the article, and decide if these sentences are true (T) or false (F).

1 Blood from a cut artery drips out. ____
2 Blood pattern analysis looks at the shape of drops of blood. ____
3 Luminol tells you the blood type. ____
4 Male blood is different from female blood. ____
5 Graham Backhouse's neighbour shot himself. ____

3 Find words in the text with these meanings.

1 (used about a thick liquid) to move slowly o________
2 a knife, gun, or other thing used to hurt people w________
3 saliva, semen, and other liquids in the body b________ ________
4 people who the police believe committed a crime s________
5 hurt by a weapon w________
6 responsible for a crime g________

BLOOD PATTERN ANALYSIS

Even a tiny drop of blood at the scene of a violent crime can give important information to the police. Blood is there either because it has dripped out of a small wound, sprayed out from an artery, oozed out through a large wound, or flown off a weapon. Using blood pattern analysis, police can learn a lot about what happened from the shape of the blood drops.

Sometimes a murderer cleans the crime scene very carefully, and if detectives cannot see any blood they spray a chemical called Luminol across the scene. This makes it possible to see the blood in the dark. Luminol can show up very small drops of blood.

From blood at the scene of a crime, police can learn about the person the blood came from. They can tell the person's blood type and, because male and female blood cells are different, they can also work out if the blood comes from a man or woman. Also, 80% of us are 'secretors', which means our blood type is contained in other bodily fluids. This can also help identify suspects.

In 1984 a man, Graham Backhouse, was found injured near his home with deep cuts across his face and chest. A neighbour lay dead nearby. Backhouse said the neighbour attacked him, and so he shot the neighbour to defend himself. But the shape of the blood drops showed that Backhouse was standing still when he was wounded, and there was also no blood from Backhouse on his gun or near the victim. Police were sure Backhouse shot his victim and then wounded himself. He was found guilty of murder.

Project

Research one of these topics, and present what you find out to other students.

- forensic analysis of hair, DNA, and fingerprints
- a crime that was solved using forensic analysis

Speaking 2

1 Have you ever been in a car accident? Have you ever seen one? Describe what happened.

2 Read about the results of a car accident. Then close your book and check you have understood the same details as your partner.

Three people have been seriously injured in a road accident, and brought to hospital. In one car was twelve-year-old **Sally Cook** and her 70-year-old grandfather **William Cook**. Sally has lost a lot of blood, and needs a transfusion. Her grandfather is unconscious, and needs a bed on ICU and a ventilator (= a breathing machine) to keep him alive.

Fred Ellis is 21 years old, and was driving the second vehicle. Police say Fred caused the accident. He has severe injuries, and he will need a ventilator and a bed on ICU.

3 Discuss the following problems in small groups.

1 Sally's parents belong to a religious group which is against organ and blood donation. They do not want their daughter to have someone else's blood. Should the hospital respect their wishes, or should they give her a transfusion?

2 There is only one bed available on ICU. Who should have the bed, William Cook or Fred Ellis?

Checklist

Assess your progress in this unit. Tick (✔) the statements which are true.

- I can describe a blood sample under a microscope
- I can talk about blood tests and their results
- I can use *If* sentences to talk about general or future situations
- I can understand a description of how the heart works
- I can understand an article about forensic analysis of blood

Key words

Blood
artery
bodily fluids
cell
clot
drip
drop
forensic analysis
haemoglobin
platelets
vein

Equipment
microscope
pipette
slide
syringe
test tube

Look back through this unit. Find five more words or expressions that you think are useful.

10 Death and dying

Scrub up

Work in pairs. Discuss the questions.

- Which is more common in your culture, burial or cremation?
- What is a typical funeral like?

Vocabulary

Talking about dying

1 Match these words with a definition.

1	terminal	a	(of an accident or illness) that causes death
2	fatal	b	to become more and more weak or ill
3	go downhill	c	an examination of a body to find out how the person died
4	coma	d	the use of machines to keep a person alive
5	life-support	e	(of an illness) that cannot be cured, and causes death
6	pass away	f	a room in a hospital where dead bodies are taken and stored
7	mortuary	g	an unconscious state that a person cannot wake from
8	post-mortem	h	a polite word meaning 'to die'

2 Complete these sentences using the words in 1.

1 This boy has serious head injuries. He has been in a ___________ for a week.

2 The patient stopped breathing, and is now on a ___________ machine.

3 We need a porter to take the body to the ___________.

4 I'm afraid your father ___________ in his sleep last night.

5 There was a ___________ accident outside the hospital – both drivers were killed.

6 The ___________ showed that the elderly lady died of a stroke.

7 After a bad fall, Mr Deans ___________ very fast and died the following week.

8 This gentleman has ___________ cancer. With treatment, he may live another year.

3 Choose one of the words. Tell a true story which includes it.

In this unit
- talking about dying
- the body after death
- expressing possibility
- discussing euthanasia

Listening

Report of a death

1 A nurse visited Henry Jacobs in the days before he died. Listen to him reporting to his supervisor, and answer the questions.

1 When did the nurse first visit Mr Jacobs?
2 What happened at four on Monday?
3 When did Mr Jacobs die?

2 These are some of the things that can happen when a person is dying. Listen again and tick (✓) the things that the nurse mentions.

1 ☐ The patient's hands, arms, and feet become cool.
2 ☐ They become incontinent.
3 ☐ They hallucinate (see people or things that are not really there).
4 ☐ They want to sleep all the time.
5 ☐ They have difficulty breathing.
6 ☐ They become restless (unable to rest).
7 ☐ They lose consciousness.
8 ☐ They become confused about time, place, and who people are.
9 ☐ The colour of their skin changes.
10 ☐ Their breathing becomes irregular.
11 ☐ They don't want to eat or drink.

Body bits

The body after death

1 What happens to the different parts of the body when we die? Discuss it with a partner.

2 Look at the diagram and complete the labels with the words below.

beating	breathing	slightly	cools	stops
rigid	release	ceases	open	enlarge

1 Brain activity ___________.
2 The skin ___________.
3 The eyelids ___________ slightly and the pupils ___________.
4 The pulse ___________.
5 The jaw relaxes and opens ___________.

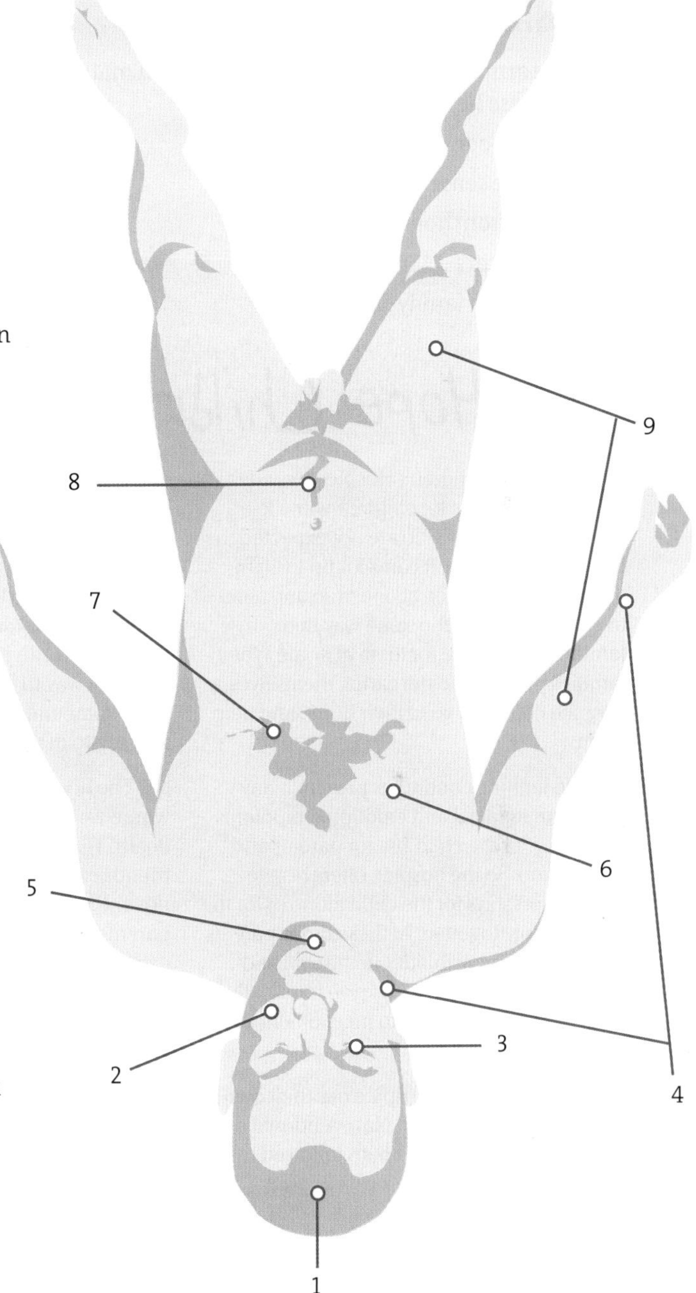

6 ___________ stops.
7 The heart stops ___________.
8 The bowel and bladder ___________ their contents.
9 The limbs become ___________.

hospice (n) a hospital for people who are dying

Reading

1 Read the article about a children's hospice, and match each of these headings to a paragraph.

1 Saying goodbye ______
2 Using the senses ______
3 A home from home ______
4 Personal care ______
5 Helping the family ______

2 Read the article again and answer the questions.

1 Do children have to stay at the hospice all the time?
2 How does the hospice help the children's families?
3 How many children does each carer look after?
4 What can children do in the multi-sensory room?
5 How is music used at the hospice?
6 How are the special quiet rooms used?

The Hope Children's Hospice

A The Hope Children's Hospice provides free specialist care for children with life-limiting conditions who are not expected to live into adulthood. It cares for up to eight terminally-ill children at one time, and aims to care for them in the same way their families would care for them at home. When families prefer to do the caring themselves, a hospice carer will go to their home and help them.

B Life-limiting conditions present many long-term medical and emotional problems – not only for the child, but for parents and siblings too. So the hospice offers respite care – short stays for the child alone or for the whole family together. At these times, parents hand over responsibilities to the staff and have a 'holiday'. Short stays give terminally-ill children an opportunity to meet others with similar conditions.

C Each child at the hospice has their own carer and their own care plan. A normal day might start with a jacuzzi bath followed by a massage from a complementary therapist. Some children go to school, while others play with hospice play specialists.

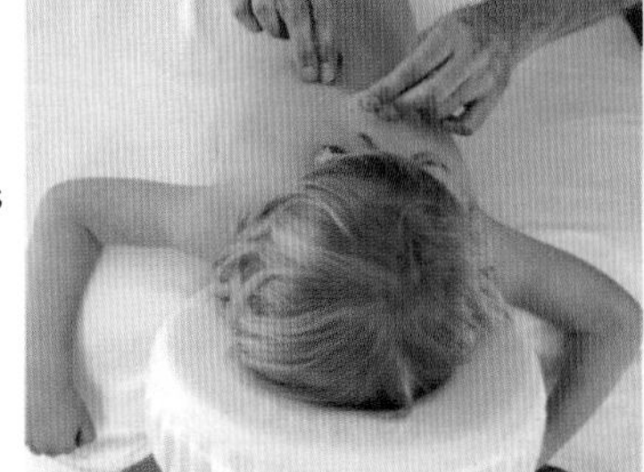

D The hospice has a multi-sensory room. This is a special room which stimulates the children's senses with lights, music, touch, and smell. It has touch-screen computers, video games, paddling pools, and space for wheelchair dancing. Children have music therapy and can record their own music, not only as a way to express their feelings, but to leave something for their family and friends to listen to in the years to come.

E The hospice has a number of quiet rooms where we care for children during and after death. These are places where families and friends can say goodbye. Our support does not end with death. We help not just grieving parents, but also siblings who are experiencing bereavement. We give everyone opportunities to discuss their fears about death and dying.

Patient care

Breaking bad news

1 Medical staff sometimes need to give sad news, for example that an illness is terminal, or that a relative has died. Here are some tips for breaking bad news. Discuss the reasons for each one with your partner.

- allow a lot of time
- find a private place
- express sympathy
- use simple and honest language

2 Add three more tips.

Language spot

Expressing possibility

- When you are not sure about something, you can use the modal verbs *may*, *might*, or *could*. The verbs all have a similar meaning.

They're going to try a new drug. It ***might work*** *and it* ***might not***.
He's been diagnosed with cancer. He ***may have*** *only weeks to live.*
Mrs Carr has developed a rash. She ***could be*** *allergic to Penicillin.*

- You can use these verbs to talk about possible future plans or schedules.

I'm tired, so I ***might not go out*** *tonight.*
I ***may be working*** *nights next Friday – I'll have to check.*

- Here are some other ways to express possibility.

He says his ear hurts. ***Perhaps*** *he has an infection.*
Mrs Ferreira is talking to herself. ***Maybe*** *she's having hallucinations.*
It's possible that *the growth is cancerous, so we'll need to do tests.*

» Go to **Grammar reference** p.120

1 Complete these sentences using an item from the top group, and a verb from the bottom group.

may	might	could
maybe	perhaps	It's possible that

left   's   has gone   be   go   have to

1 I can't find my phone. I __________ __________ buy another one.
2 I __________ __________ a little late for my shift – my bus isn't here yet.
3 I __________ __________ to the cinema tonight – I haven't decided yet.
4 Marie isn't here? __________ she __________ ill today.
5 The bed's empty. __________ Mrs Lewis __________ home.
6 You've lost your notebook? __________ you __________ it at reception.

2 Work with a partner. Discuss what these symptoms could indicate in a patient.

a fever	diarrhoea
a rash	sleeplessness
stomach ache	crying (in a baby)
extreme tiredness	painful fingers

EXAMPLE
A *A fever might indicate an infection.*
B *Or it could be flu.*
A *Or maybe the person has …*

3 Spend five minutes thinking about your plans for your free time in the next week. Note down your definite schedule, your possible schedule, and things you haven't decided yet.

EXAMPLES
I'm working tomorrow night.
I could be meeting my friend on Sunday morning – I'll check my diary.
I might go shopping, or I may stay in and study.

4 Work in pairs. Talk about your plans and schedule.

Speaking 1

1 When a patient dies in hospital, a nurse will prepare the body if relatives want to see it. Discuss with a partner what you need to do to the body. Think about the following.

- eyes
- mouth
- hair
- washing
- position
- jewellery
- lines (IV, catheters, etc.)
- the room

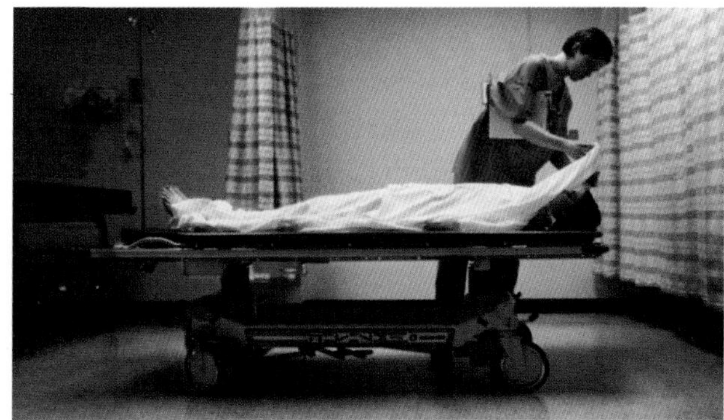

2 Student A go to p.78. Student B go to p.113.

In the UK, before a body can be buried or cremated, a doctor must issue a **death certificate** stating the cause of death. If there is doubt about how a person dies, the doctor reports the death to the **coroner**, an official who investigates causes of death.

euthanasia (n) the practice (illegal in most countries) of killing without pain a person who is suffering and cannot be cured

Student A

Read these guidelines for preparing a body, and draw simple pictures in your notebook to help you remember them. Then close this book and exchange information with Student B. Ask questions, for example *What do you do with the mouth? What about washing?* etc. Make notes as you listen to Student B.

- **eyes** Close the eyes if you can. It is not always possible.
- **mouth**
- **hair** Comb the hair. You may need to use a wet comb to make it tidy.
- **washing**
- **position** Sit the body up on a pillow. Place the patient's arms by their sides and outside the bed sheets, so that relatives can touch or hold them.
- **jewellery**
- **lines** If there is going to be an autopsy, leave all IVs and catheters in. If there is no autopsy, you can remove them. But remember that the site can bleed post-mortem, so cover these with gauze.
- **the room**

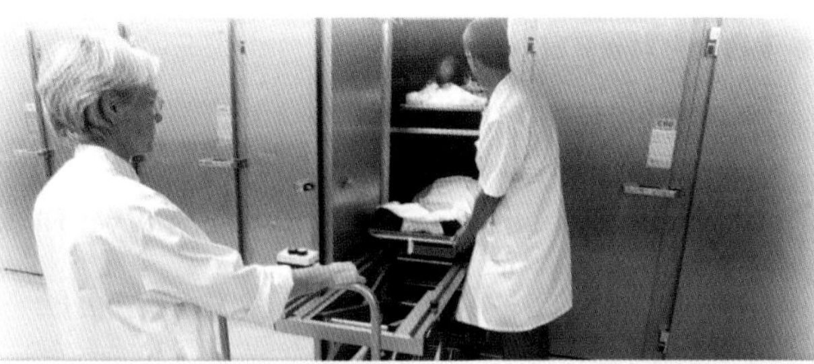

Death certificate

Name	Tariq Khamina
Age	72
Date of Death	16.10.07
Place of death	City Hospital
Date last seen by the doctor	16.08.07

Please tick one of the following:
– There ☐ will / ☑ will not be a post-mortem
– ☐ The death will be reported to a coroner

Cause of death

1a Primary cause of death	stroke 4 days before death
1b due to	heart disease (5 years)
1c due to	high blood pressure (20 years)

Other important conditions
Diabetes (10 years)
Dementia (6 months)

Writing

Death certificate

1 Work with a partner. Close your books and write down what information you would expect to find on a death certificate. Then open your books and look at the certificate to compare.

2 Complete this summary with the prepositions below.

for with by for in from for

Tariq Khamina suffered __________[1] diabetes __________[2] ten years, and was diagnosed __________[3] dementia six months ago. He started to receive treatment __________[4] heart disease five years ago, and has also been treated __________[5] high blood pressure. He suffered a stroke caused __________[6] heart disease and died __________[7] hospital.

3 Listen to two doctors talking about a patient who has died, Martin Webb. Make notes as you listen.

4 Write about Martin Webb's medical history and death. Use your notes and the text about Tariq Khamina to help you.

Speaking 2

Terminally ill with motor neurone disease, Diane Pretty lost her legal battle in the UK to allow her husband to help her commit suicide.

1 Work in small groups. Discuss the questions.

- Do you know of any cases of **euthanasia** that have been in the news?
- In your opinion, do we have the right to choose when we are going to die?
- Do we have the right to choose when another person is going to die?

2 Read the true story below.

> **A doctor, seeing his 87-year-old father suffering from terminal cancer, injected him with drugs, causing his death immediately. The judged decided that the doctor**

3 Discuss the questions.

- In your opinion, is the doctor guilty of murder?
- If you were the judge, would you send him to prison? If so, for how long?

4 Your teacher will tell you what the judge said.

Checklist

Assess your progress in this unit. Tick (✔) the statements which are true.

- I can talk about what happens before and after a person's death
- I can understand a text about what happens to the body after death
- I can understand an article about hospices
- I can express possibility in different ways
- I can understand a death certificate
- I can write a report about a patient's death

Key words

Nouns
body
bereavement
burial
carer
cremation
dementia
funeral
life-limiting condition
siblings
sympathy
therapy

Verbs
diagnose
lose consciousness

Adjectives
grieving
multi-sensory

Look back through this unit. Find five more words or expressions that you think are useful.

11 Hygiene

Scrub up

Test your knowledge of hygiene by doing this quiz.

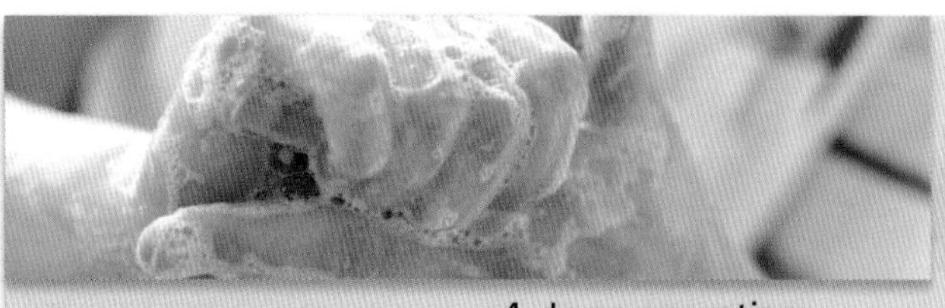

1 What is MRSA?
   a a virus
   b a bacterium
   c an antibiotic

2 How do you catch MRSA?
   a by eating from dirty plates
   b from poor hospital hygiene
   c by drinking bad water

3 Which of these things has nothing to do with bacteria?
   a wine making
   b yoghurt
   c the common cold
   d bad smells

4 In an operating theatre, which of these things breaks hygiene rules?
   a wearing your mask over your nose
   b wearing your hair loose
   c wearing make-up

5 Which of these things is most important in stopping the spread of MRSA?
   a hospital staff should wash their hands between patients
   b cleaners should disinfect door handles
   c visitors should wear masks

6 Where do staphylococcus bacteria live?
   a in noses
   b in soil
   c in toilets

7 When Florence Nightingale, founder of modern nursing, worked in a hospital during the Crimean war (1854-1856), the death rate dropped from 60% to 2.2%. Why?
   a She made nurses wash their hands
   b She gave her patients fruit and vegetables to eat
   c The ventilation was improved

8 How long should you wash your hands in hot water to be sure they are clean?
   a fifteen seconds
   b half a minute
   c one minute

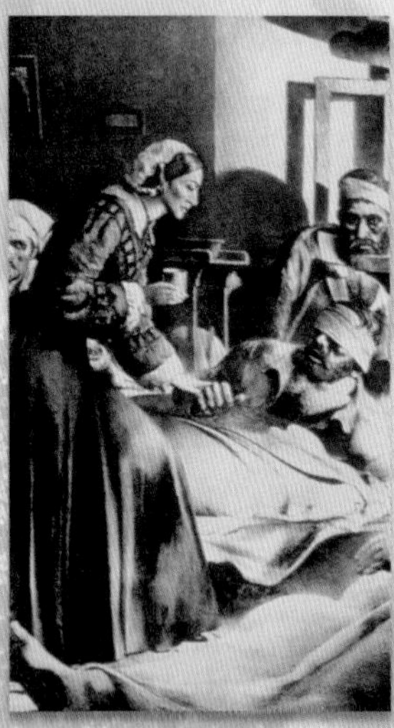

Vocabulary

Hygiene equipment

1 Match each of these items of hygiene equipment to a picture.

bin ____ clinical waste disposal bag ____

bucket ____ detergent ____

cloth ____ disposable gloves ____

mop ____ paper towels ____

sink ____ soap dispenser ____

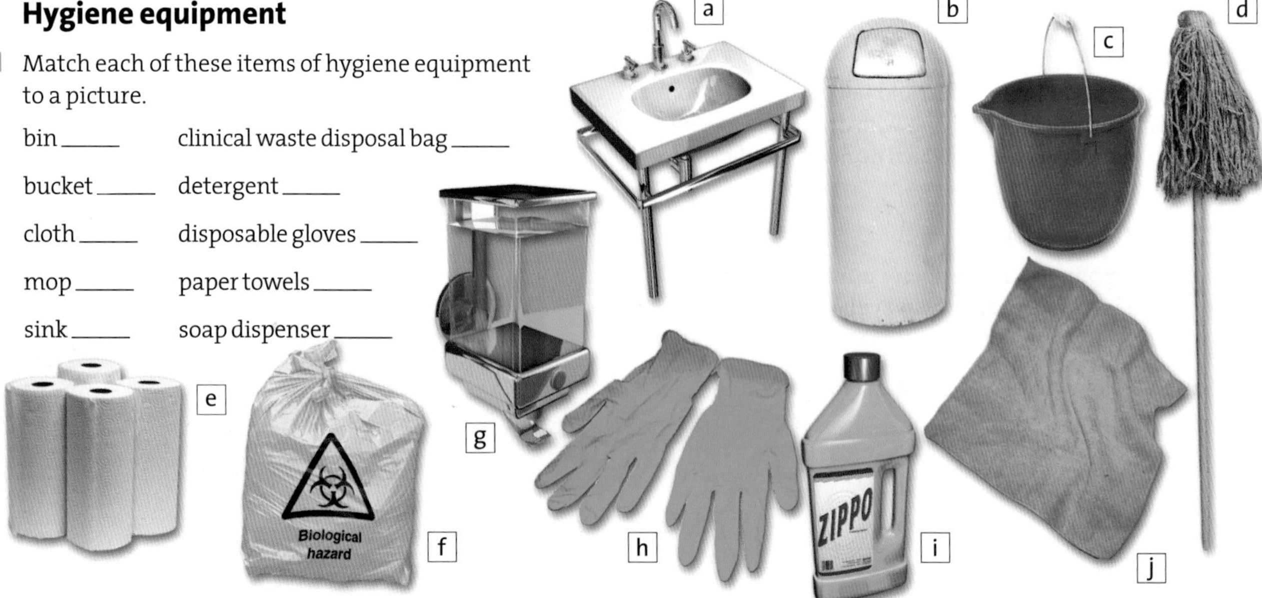

In this unit

- hospital hygiene quiz
- talking about the spread of infections
- understanding a hygiene inspection report
- talking about obligation
- MRSA
- completing a Pathology lab report

2 Complete the sentences with the words below.

contamination	disinfectant
antimicrobial agent	susceptible
pathogens	resistant
swab	spotless

1 An __________ will kill microorganisms.

2 Use a sterile __________ to get a sample from the back of the throat.

3 Our bodies have ways to kill __________ such as viruses and bacteria.

4 The old, the young, and the very ill are most __________ to hospital infection.

5 Staphylococcus is __________ to most antibiotics.

6 There is a risk of __________ from urine and blood.

7 Wash floors and door handles with __________.

8 A home doesn't have to be __________, but it does have to be clean.

Listening 1

A hygiene report

1 Listen to a hospital administrator talking to the ward matron about the hygiene report for her ward, and answer the questions.

1 Did the ward get a good or a bad score?

2 What reasons does the ward matron give for the ward's score?

2 Read through the sentences from the report. Then listen again and underline the correct version.

1 The door handles *are / are not* regularly cleaned.

2 Beds *are / are not* always cleaned between patients.

3 The toilets are cleaned *three times / twice / once* daily.

4 Floors are cleaned *four times / twice / once* daily.

5 The average time for cleaning up spillages of bodily fluids is *5 / 10 / 10–30 / more than 30* minutes.

6 Nurses' knowledge of MRSA is *good / fair / poor.*

7 Nurses *always / do not always* wear gloves.

It's my job

1 Before you read, discuss these questions with a partner.

- In the hospitals and clinics you know, how much time do nurses spend cleaning?
- What is the best way to make sure staff follow hygiene procedures?

2 Read about Harriet Banks and answer the questions.

1 What is the ward matron's rank?

2 What type of hygiene is Harriet Banks especially strict about?

3 Why does Harriet have real power in the hospital?

4 How does Harriet encourage nurses to follow hygiene procedures?

Harriet Banks

I wear a blue uniform because I am a Sister, and I am responsible for ward hygiene and the quality of patients' food.

My job is to do everything necessary to prevent and control infection. Because a lot of infection spreads by hand, I make sure that everyone follows the cleanliness procedures. For example, hands must be washed before and after patient contact, before and after taking off gloves, and after helping a patient use the toilet.

I am in charge of ward budgets, and controlling the money means I have real power. Sometimes I refuse to pay cleaning and catering companies if I'm not happy with standards.

But I don't like to be strict all the time. I like to encourage staff to think about infection and the spread of disease, and to lead by setting a good example.

A survey was done in 2004 to find **the cleanest country in the world**. Can you guess which country it was?

Hungarian **Ignaz Semmelweis** (1818-65), **the father of hand hygiene**, died from an infection that spread from a small cut on his finger.

• Language spot

Talking about obligation

1 Match these examples with the rules.

a *Sorry, I have to go. I'm on duty in ten minutes.*
b *You mustn't forget to put gloves on.*
c *We need to clean the floors more often.*
d *You don't have to wash Mrs Shah's face. She can do it herself.*
e *Two beds need changing.*
f *All visitors must wash their hands.*

must

• We use *must* in rules, and to say when things are necessary.

1 ________________

We must follow procedures more carefully.

NOTE: It can sound very strong to say *You must* ...
Use *must* + verb NOT ~~*must to* + verb~~

have to

• We use *have to* to talk about things that other people oblige us to do.

2 ________________

mustn't

• We use *mustn't* to say it is necessary that you do NOT do something.

3 ________________

don't have to

• We use *don't have to* to say something is not necessary.

4 ________________

need to

• We use *need to* to say it is necessary to do something

5 ________________

need + ing

• We use *need + ing* to say what jobs it is necessary to do

6 ________________

» Go to **Grammar reference** p.121

2 Complete the sentences with *need to, must, need(s), don't have to, mustn't, has to*. Use the verbs below.

use	cutting	cut	order
complete	~~mop~~	change	emptying

1 You'll *need to mop* the floor – there's been a spillage.
2 You ________________ gloves after contact with each patient.
3 The bins ________________ – they're all full.
4 You ________________ Mr Mills's nails – I've just done them.
5 You ________________ your mobile phone inside the building.
6 The Ward Matron ________________ a hygiene report every month.
7 My hair ________________ – I can't keep it all under my hat.
8 I ________________ some more paper towels – they've nearly all gone.

Speaking

Student A, working in pairs with another Student A, go to p.110. Student B, working in pairs with another Student B, go to p.114.

Writing

A notice

Work in pairs. Following the hygiene inspection, the Ward Sister has asked you to make a notice reminding nurses about good hygiene practice. Write a list of rules and instructions for the nurses.

HYGIENE REMINDER!

1 You must report all spillages immediately.

2 All visitors should ...

Between 1994 and 2004, deaths in the UK from MRSA infection rose 400%.

Signs and symptoms

MRSA

1 Work with a partner. Read about the symptoms of MRSA. Tick the symptoms that affect the skin.

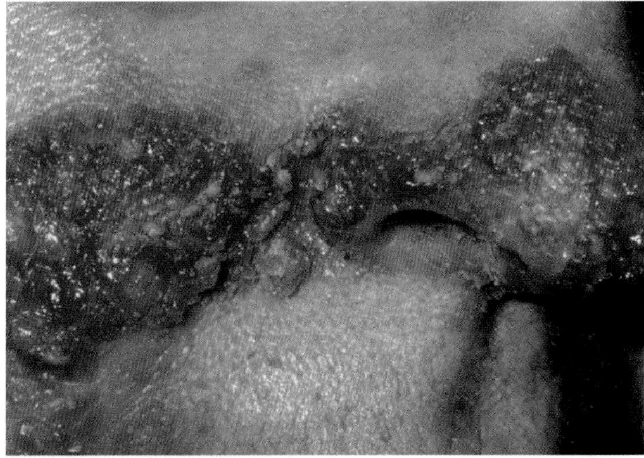

The newspapers call MRSA 'the flesh-eating superbug'. This is because symptoms are nasty, and include infection under the skin (usually on the arms or legs). Some people are carriers – they have MRSA but don't show any of the symptoms.

MRSA can cause:

abscesses ✓
boils ____
bone infections ____
fever ____
septicaemia ____
toxic shock syndrome ____
urinary tract infections ____
heart-valve infections ____
pneumonia ____
redness ____
septic wounds ____
swelling ____
tenderness ____
impetigo ____
headache ____

Research done at a New York hospital found that the **ties** that doctors wear are a major source of dangerous bacteria.

A species of tree in Brazil known as **Pau d'Arco** or the Inca tree of life (Tabebuia avellanedae) contains substances which kill Staphylococcus aureus. This tree could be our next weapon against MRSA.

Listening 2

Test results

1 A nurse on Ward 5 gets a phone call from the Pathology lab. Listen and complete this report.

Patient's Name ________________

Identified bacterium ________________

Place of infection
(show on diagram)

Tests done
urine ☐ *blood* ☐ *throat* ☐ *nose* ☐ *skin* ☐

White blood cell count __________

Test for Escherichia coli
negative ☐ *positive* ☐

Test for Staphyloccocus aureus
negative ☐ *positive* ☐

Resistance to antimicrobial agents

	Resistant	*Susceptible*	*Non-resistant*
Penicillin	☐	☐	☐
Cefazolin	☐	☐	☐
Methicillin	☐	☐	☐
Erythromycin	☐	☐	☐
Clindamycin	☐	☐	☐
Tetracycline	☐	☐	☐
Mupirocin	☐	☐	☐
Vancomycin	☐	☐	☐
Oxacyllin	☐	☐	☐

2 Now complete this summary of the report by choosing the correct word in italics.

When medical staff *suspicion / suspect* that Mrs Browning has MRSA, they send blood samples and swabs to the Pathology lab for tests. The test results show that she has *infected / an infection / infect* from the bacterium Staphylococcus aureus. This bacterium has *resistant / resistance / resists* to some antibiotics, it is *susceptible / susceptibility* to one antibiotic, and there are two antibiotics it cannot *resistant / resistance / resist* .

Mrs Browning will be isolated in a separate room and, to avoid any *contamination / contaminate* by pathogens, the ward will be thoroughly *disinfected / disinfectant* .

Reading

1 Read the questions to Nurse Anthea and her answers, and decide if these sentences are true (T) or false (F).

1 Dirt can be good for you. _____
2 Children who live with pets are more susceptible to allergies. _____
3 Antibiotics kill all bacteria. _____
4 Vancomycin will always be 100% effective. _____
5 VRSA is a stronger bacterium than MRSA. _____
6 We are losing our protection from bacteria. _____

2 Find words in the text with these meanings.

1 moving around on your hands and knees __________
2 regular contact with something __________
3 particles of solid waste from the body __________
4 completely without dirt __________
5 to not be killed by something __________
6 something that you use to fight with __________
7 not at all effective __________

Ask the Nurse –

Nurse Anthea answers your questions.

This week's topic is **bacteria**.

Q *I'm worried about my baby. She is crawling around on the floor and putting all sorts of things into her mouth.*

Don't worry. Children who live in spotlessly clean houses do not have much exposure to bacteria, so their immune systems don't get the practice of fighting bacteria. Research shows that children living in houses that are not spotlessly clean, who have contact with animals and faecal matter, get fewer illnesses than children living in spotless homes. And there's evidence that children who live with pets get fewer allergies.

Q *I've heard that we shouldn't use too many antibiotics. Why is this?*

Antibiotics kill the weak bacteria but allow the strong ones to survive and get stronger. This means that there are more and more bacteria around that are resistant to antibiotics.

Q *Is there a cure for MRSA?*

There's an antibiotic called Vancomycin. This is our last weapon against MRSA, but in time it will be useless too. One type of Staphylococcus aureus is now resistant to Vancomycin – so it is VRSA – Vancomycin resistant. There is a possibility of a bacterium which will be resistant to *all* antibiotics.

We have been winning the war against bacteria for about fifty years, but soon bacteria will make a comeback and we will be where we were in the nineteenth century – with no protection from bacteria.

Checklist

Assess your progress in this unit. Tick (✔) the statements which are true.

I can talk about good hospital hygiene practices

I can understand a hygiene inspection report

I can talk about obligation

I understand the symptoms and causes of MRSA

I can understand a Pathology lab report

Key words

Nouns
antimicrobial agent
bacteria
bin
catering
contamination
disinfectant
immune system
infection
pathogen
procedure
spillage
virus

Adjectives
resistant
spotless
susceptible

Look back through this unit. Find five more words or expressions that you think are useful.

12 Mental health nursing

Scrub up

1 Which of these people do you think may have a mental illness? Discuss each one with your partner.

2 With your partner, try to explain what 'mentally ill' means. Finish this sentence in your own words.

A person is mentally ill if he / she ...

Stephen Gough has walked naked across Britain. 'Nakedness is natural,' he says every time he is arrested.

By the time Salma Perrin goes to bed, she will have washed her hands over a hundred times. She says, 'I know they're clean, but I can't stop myself.'

David Leary is seventeen. He sleeps all day, and at night he sits in his room playing his guitar. He says, 'Life sucks!'

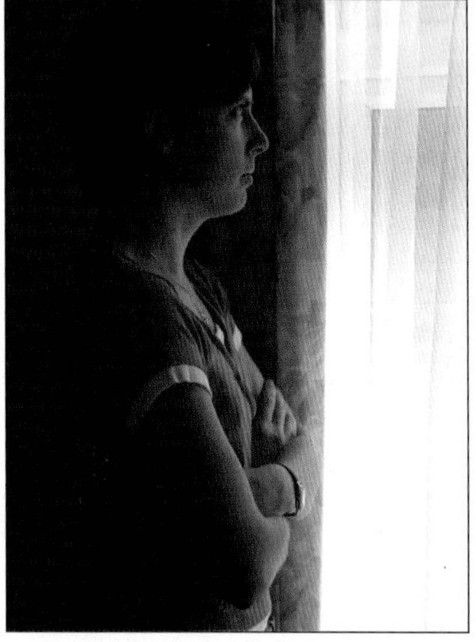

Barbara Scott believes she is in danger, and never leaves her house. She talks to the people on the television and says, 'They're my real friends.'

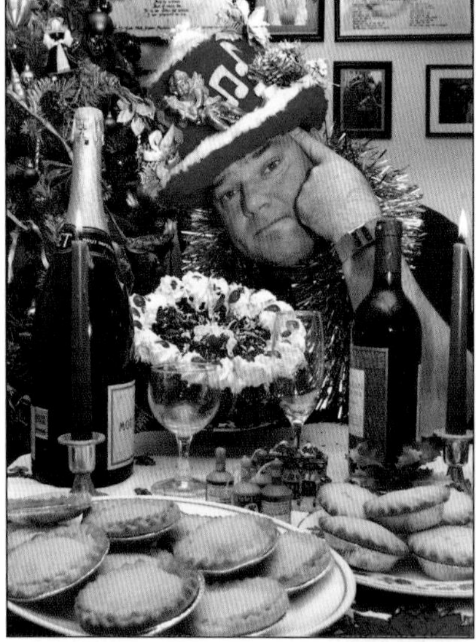

Andy Park has celebrated Christmas every day for the last twelve years. He lives alone and says, 'Every day I give presents to myself'.

Every time Diego Ferri gets into a car, he becomes a monster. 'Other drivers are mad,' he says.

In this unit

- describing the symptoms of mental illness
- Present Perfect v Past Simple
- a case conference
- schizophrenia
- writing a job application
- Tourette syndrome

Vocabulary

Mental illness

1 Match each word with its definition.

1 posture	a the false belief that somebody is trying to harm you, or that you are somebody very important
2 unemotional	b not sure where you are
3 hallucinations	c not wanting to talk to people
4 manic	d not logical; not making sense
5 paranoia	e behaving in an abnormally excited way
6 disoriented	f not showing your feelings
7 uncommunicative	g a way of standing or sitting
8 delusions	h feelings of extreme, uncontrollable sadness
9 irrational	i strange and false ideas that somebody believes are true
10 depression	j occasions when you imagine you see things that are not really there

Pronunciation

Stress patterns

1 Match these stress patterns to the ten words from *Vocabulary* above.

a ••●•	5	e ••●••	______
b •●•	______	f •●••	______
c ••●•••	______	g •●•••	______
d •••●•	______	h ●•	______

2 Listen and check.

Language spot

Present Perfect v Past Simple

We use the Present Perfect

- to talk about past actions in an unfinished period of time, for example 'in my whole life', or 'today'.
*I'**ve** never **done** this before.*
***Have** you **seen** Ana this morning?*

- when a past action has a result in the present.
*He'**s had** his medication and is feeling sleepy.*

- when we give news of recent, finished events.
*The psychiatrist **has** just **spoken** to the patient's family.*

- when we say how much we have completed, how many times we have done something, etc.
*I **have told** him six times to take his medication.*

- with *yet*, to talk about whether or not tasks have been completed.
*I've taken Mr Pool's temperature, but I **haven't checked** his blood pressure **yet**.*

- with *for* and *since* to talk about when a present situation started.
*I'**ve worked** at this hospital for six months.*

We use the Past Simple, not the Present Perfect

- when we talk about a finished time in the past, especially with time expressions such as *ago*, *last week*, *in 2006*.
*I **graduated** from college two years ago.*

» Go to **Grammar reference** p.122

1 Complete each sentence using one of the verbs below. Use the Present Perfect where possible. In other sentences, use the Past Simple.

attend	go	see	study
be	have	start	write
finish	reply		

1 We ______ the assessment. You'll get the report tomorrow.
2 The doctor ______ the patient three times today.
3 I ______ working here a year ago.
4 Mrs Linton is no longer in hospital. She ______ home.
5 I ______ three letters to the consultant, but he ______ yet.
6 I ______ until 11 o'clock last night.
7 The patient ______ the clinic since January.
8 The patient ______ in hospital for a week now.
9 ______ you ever ______ a general anaesthetic?

The novelist André Malraux suffered from **Tourette syndrome**, which showed in a nervous facial tic and muscular and vocal activity. He was well-known for his energetic style of public speaking.

The novelist Virginia Woolf suffered from **bipolar disorder**. She had her first mental breakdown when she was thirteen, and made several suicide attempts. She killed herself when she was 59 by walking into a river.

2 Paula is a nursing assistant. She is finishing her shift, and Jack is starting his. Jack is checking the list of things to do. Listen to the conversation, and write a tick (✓) or a cross (✗) next to each job on the list to show if Paula has done it yet.

change patients' dressings
Mrs Eriksson – blood pressure
Mr Sissoko – temperature
clean up spillage
Mrs Wong – urine specimen

3 Write five sentences in your notebook about what Paula has done and hasn't done yet.

4 Write the past participle of these verbs.

be	*been*	give	______
watch	______	work	______
forget	______	talk	______
take	______	try	______

5 Write questions using *Have you ever* ... and the verbs above to find out about your partner's experience as a student nurse.

EXAMPLES

Have you ever been late for class?

Have you ever watched an operation?

6 Work in pairs and ask your questions. Each time you receive the answer *yes* to your first question, use questions in the Past Simple to get more information.

EXAMPLE

A *Have you ever been late for class?*
B *No, I haven't.*
A *Have you ever watched an operation?*
B *Yes, I have. It was last week.*
A *What was it?*
B *It was an appendectomy.*
A *Really! How long did ...*

Listening

A case conference

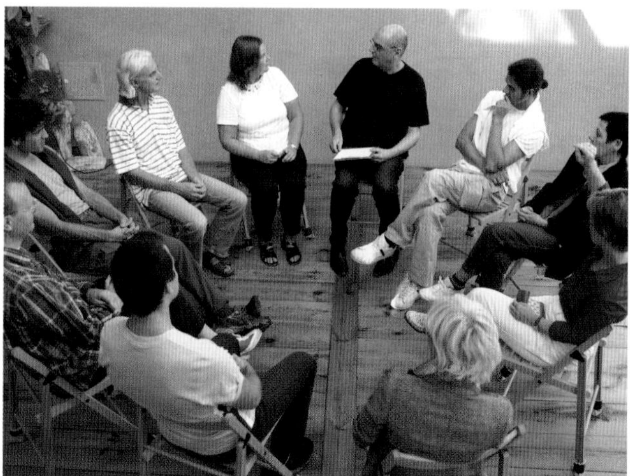

Listen to the psychiatric case conference discussing a patient, Delroy Moseki. Tick (✓) the symptoms of schizophrenia that they say Delroy has.

a ☐ strange posture
b ☐ confused and disoriented
c ☐ cries a lot
d ☐ unclear speech
e ☐ uncommunicative
f ☐ makes irrational statements
g ☐ unable to sleep
h ☐ manic
i ☐ hears voices in the head
j ☐ unable to retain information

Speaking

Work in pairs. You are going to read about Delroy Moseki's life. Student A go to p.110. Student B go to p.114.

Project

Many talented painters, writers, actors, etc. suffer from mental illnesses. Find out about two famous people and write about how mental illness affected their life.

Mental illness is far more common than cancer, diabetes, heart disease, or arthritis. **One person in three** suffers some sort of mental illness at some time in their lives.

Reading

1 Read this article about schizophrenia and decide if these sentences are true (T) or false (F).

1 There are 1.5 million sufferers of schizophrenia. ____
2 A psychotic episode is a symptom of schizophrenia. ____
3 People with schizophrenia are usually not violent and dangerous. ____
4 Suicide is not connected with schizophrenia. ____
5 We understand what causes schizophrenia. ____

2 Join these word combinations without looking at the text, then look at the text to check your answers. Choose some of the combinations to learn.

1	changes	a	relatively normal life
2	facial	b	completely
3	the onset of	c	side effects
4	think	d	suicide
5	commit	e	expressions
6	reduce the	f	treatment
7	have bad	g	the illness
8	lead a	h	in behaviour
9	recover	i	logically
10	long-term	j	symptoms

Schizophrenia – the facts

Every year 1.5 million people worldwide are diagnosed with schizophrenia. It is a mental illness which has periods called 'psychotic episodes'. During a psychotic episode, a sufferer shows disturbing changes in behaviour. They may seem very cold and unemotional, using few facial expressions, and say strange things in a slow, flat voice. They may lose all interest in life and spend days doing nothing at all, not even washing or eating. These distressing symptoms are shocking for family members who, of course, remember what the sufferer was like before the onset of the illness.

During a psychotic episode there may be hallucinations. Hearing voices that other people do not hear is the most common type of hallucination. The voices give orders and carry on conversations. Sometimes the voices swear and make threats.

Someone with schizophrenia may have delusions, believing for example that they are a famous, historically important person, or that people on television send them special messages.

People with schizophrenia may not think logically. They are isolated because conversation with them is very difficult, so they have no one to communicate with.

It is relatively common for schizophrenia sufferers to commit suicide – 10 per cent of people with schizophrenia (especially younger adult males) kill themselves. Violence and threats against others, on the other hand, are not symptoms of the illness.

There is medication that can reduce the symptoms, but it often has bad side effects, and some sufferers discontinue treatment because of this. Although many sufferers can continue to lead a relatively normal life, it has been estimated that no more than one in five individuals recovers completely, and most will require long-term treatment.

We do not yet know the cause of schizophrenia. Researchers have looked at links with genes, with brain development, with infections before birth, and with traumatic life events.

It's my job

1 Work in pairs. Discuss the questions.

- Have you done any work placements?
- How did you feel when you started?
- What difficult situations did you have to deal with?

2 Read about Juliet Francisco and answer the questions.

1. How did she feel when she started her placement?
2. What two activities does she talk about from her placement?
3. What went wrong each time?

Juliet Francisco

I've just finished my training and am now a qualified mental health nurse. The course was in two parts, half general nursing and half mental health nursing. I've studied a lot of theory, but the real learning has come from my placements in psychiatric wards.

My first placement was on a ward for elderly people. The patients were all very quiet, but I was still terrified when I started. I thought some of the things the patients said and did were really strange.

One day I took a relaxation group. But no one told me that doing relaxation can start a psychotic episode. We were all lying down on the floor – all nicely relaxed. Suddenly a woman in the group started screaming. I was so shocked that I almost screamed too.

Another time, I took a patient out for a walk round the town. Suddenly he ran off down the street. What should I do? Run after him? No, I took a chance. I just stood and watched him. He stopped and looked back. I smiled and gave a friendly wave, then turned around and walked slowly back towards the hospital. A minute later he joined me. He was laughing. I was quite proud of myself that day!

Writing

Email job application

Read this advertisement for a job, then put the expressions in the correct places in Juliet's email.

skills and qualifications	to meet with you
I believe	relevant work experience
I am attaching	to apply for

City Hospital
Psychiatric Unit

Job title: mental health nurse
CITY HOSPITAL PSYCHIATRIC UNIT
Good salary and conditions. Would suit newly qualified nurse
Apply to Chief Nursing Officer
John Till: j.till@cityhospital.nhs.uk

File Edit View Insert Format Tools Actions Help
Send Options...

From... Juliet Francisco
To... j.till@cityhospital.nhs.uk
Subject: post of mental health nurse

Dear Mr Till

I am writing ____________[1] the job advertised on the City Hospital website. I am 22 years old, and I have just qualified as a mental health nurse. I also have ____________[2]. I have done placements on a geriatric ward, and in a prison unit. Last summer I worked as a volunteer on a camp for children with learning difficulties.

____________[3] that I have the necessary ____________[4] for working on your unit.

I would welcome an opportunity ____________[5]. My phone number is 01632 960081.

____________[6] a copy of my CV.

Yours sincerely

Juliet Francisco

Signs and symptoms

Tourette syndrome

1 Read about the condition and answer the questions.

1 When does Tourette syndrome first appear?
2 What makes the symptoms worse?
3 What four categories of tic are there?

Tourette syndrome is a nervous disorder which first appears in childhood. A person with Tourette syndrome has frequent, repetitive motor and vocal tics (repeated movements or sounds that you cannot control).

Vocal tics may consist of repeating somebody else's words, or sudden outbursts of swear words.

Tourette tics are often worse when a sufferer is tired or under stress. Sufferers can hold back their tics for hours, though this leads to a strong outburst of tics later.

Motor and vocal tics are classified as either 'simple' or 'complex'. Simple tics are sudden, short movements, and complex tics are movements or speech that use more than one set of muscles.

2 This is a list of some tics. Work with a partner. Using your dictionaries to help you, write *M* (for motor) or *V* (for vocal) next to each one.

M	clapping	____	making faces
____	kicking	____	scratching
____	muttering	____	smelling things
____	spitting	____	belching
____	hiccuping	____	stuttering
____	swearing	____	shivering
____	blinking	____	shouting
____	chewing clothes	____	sniffing
____	licking things	____	throwing things
____	offensive gestures	____	sticking the tongue out

3 Write down the verbs that are new to you.

Checklist

Assess your progress in this unit. Tick (✔) the statements which are true.

I can talk about the symptoms of mental illness

I can understand an article about schizophrenia

I can use the Present Perfect

I can write a job application

Key words

Verbs
concentrate
swear

Adjectives
distressing
long-term
psychiatric
psychotic
qualified
traumatic

Nouns
bipolar disorder
onset
placement
side effects
suicide
threat
tic

Look back through this unit. Find five more words or expressions that you think are useful.

13 Monitoring the patient

Scrub up

1 Look at the pictures below. Describe what the nurse is doing in each one.

2 Work with a partner. Match each reading 1–4 with a vital sign a–d.

1 120 bpm	a temperature ____
2 38.5°C	b blood pressure ____
3 150/90	c heart rate ____
4 18 bpm	d respiration ____

3 Listen and check.

4 Can you answer these questions?

1 What two things does bpm mean?
2 What do 150 and 90 refer to?
3 Are these readings normal? What is the normal range for each?

5 Take your partner's pulse. What should their maximum heart rate be when they exercise?

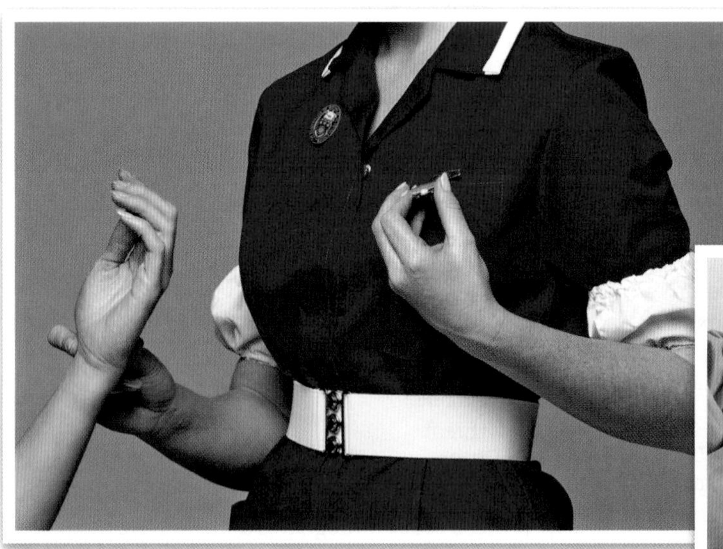

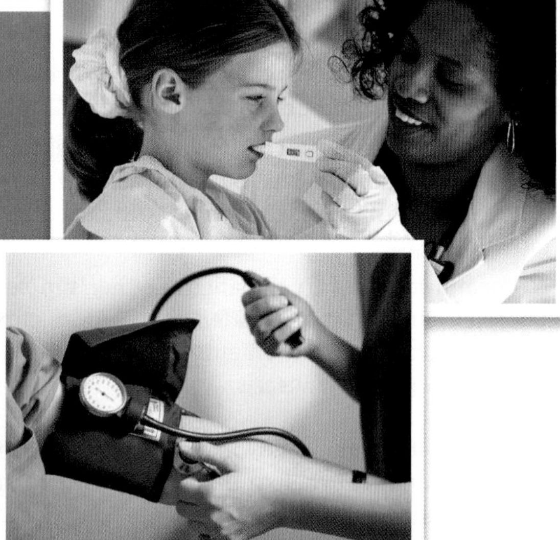

Pronunciation

Taking readings

1 Which words or expressions from *Scrub up* do these phonetics represent?

1 /ˈhɑːt reɪt/ __________
2 /ˈtemprətʃə/ __________
3 /pʌls/ __________
4 /reˈspɪrətri reɪt/ __________
5 /ˈblʌd ˌpreʃə/ __________
6 /ˌvaɪtl ˈsaɪn/ __________

2 Listen and check.

Patient care

Taking vital signs

1 Put these words in order to make sentences in your notebook. Which vital sign is the nurse taking in each case?

1 tongue pop your under just this.
2 roll your can up you sleeve?
3 cold a feel bit your may on chest this.
4 and out in just normally breathe.
5 relax me for your arm.
6 shirt you undo please your , me for could?

2 Listen and check.

In this unit

- saying measurements
- describing changes in measurements
- recording vital signs
- hypothermia
- using the Passive to describe procedures
- general anaesthetic

Vocabulary

Describing readings

Complete the sentences with the words below, and match each one to a graph.

's up	rising	fell
stable	up and down	went up
varies	back to	

1 *b* His temperature was ________ all night, but now it's ________ at 37.5.

2 ____ Her heart rate ________ to 20 bpm, but now it's ________ again.

3 ____ His blood pressure ________ from 120/80 to 160/100.

4 ____ Her pulse rate was extremely low, but now it ________ to 70.

5 ____ His respiratory rate ________ between 10 and 25 bpm.

6 ____ He was running a fever, but his temperature's ________ normal now.

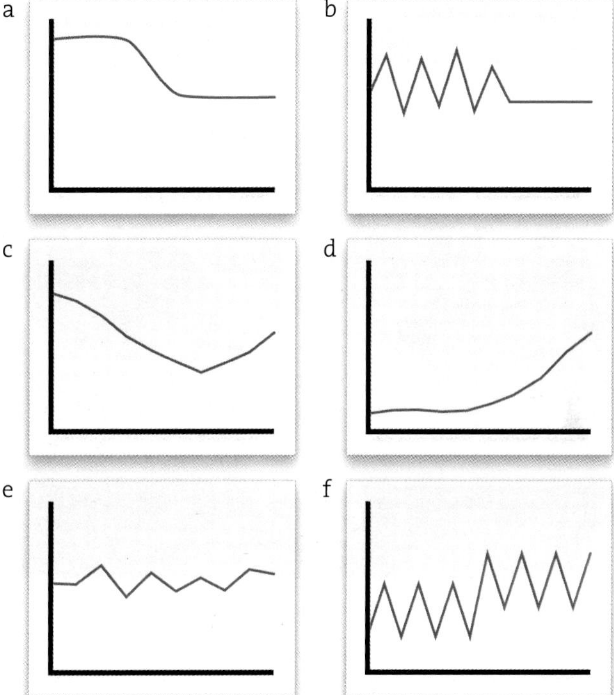

Listening 1

A coma patient

1 The patient, Grant Forrester, is suffering from a Traumatic Brain Injury (TBI) and is in an Intensive Care Unit (ICU). It is 11 p.m. and the nurse is reporting the patient's progress to the doctor on call. Listen and decide if these sentences are true (T) or false (F).

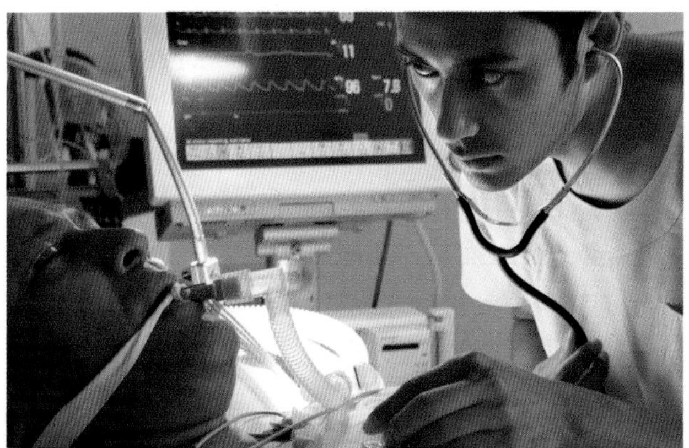

1 The patient is awake. ____

2 The patient is getting worse. ____

3 An ICP of twenty is OK. ____

4 The doctor is going to go to the hospital. ____

2 Listen again and complete this table.

Time	BP	ICP
2000		
2100		
2200		
2300	*170/120*	

Signs and symptoms

Hypothermia

1 Before reading, discuss with a partner what you know about hypothermia.

2 Make a list of the symptoms of hypothermia by joining the two halves of these phrases.

Moderate hypothermia (35–34°C)

lack of	speech
violent	behaviour
slurred	co-ordination
irrational	shivering

Severe hypothermia (33–30°C)

shivering	skin
inability to	walk
rigid	breathing
shallow	pulse rate
pale	muscles
falling	stops

Speaking 1

A man has been rescued from the sea, and has hypothermia. In pairs, you are going to exchange information about his vital signs. Student A go to p.111. Student B go to p.114.

• Language spot

The Passive

• Passive verb forms are very common in medical English. We use Passive verbs to say what is done to people and things.
The patient's progress ***is monitored*** *every hour.*
Mr West ***was treated*** *for multiple injuries.*

• Often, you can choose whether to use an Active form or a Passive form. Compare these sentences.
(Active) *Paramedics* ***treated*** *the man for hypothermia.*
(Passive) *The man* ***was treated*** *for hypothermia.*

• The Passive form focuses on the action, not on the person or thing that does the action. If you want to say who does the action, use *by*.
The man ***was treated*** *for hypothermia* ***by*** *paramedics.*

» Go to **Grammar reference** p.123

1 Underline the correct form of the verbs in italics.

Mrs Ramone *admitted / was admitted*[1] to hospital for an operation. She *didn't give / wasn't given*[2] food for eight hours. She *brought / was brought*[3] to theatre at sixteen hundred hours.

She *was prepared / prepared*[4] for theatre. The nurse *was shaved / shaved*[5] the area which was going to *cut / be cut*[6], and Mrs Ramone *put on / was put on*[7] a theatre gown. Her dentures *removed / were removed*[8], and her wedding ring taped to her wrist.

2 Ken Miah was woken up one night by severe abdominal pains. Read the notes, and write sentences in your notebook to describe his experience using the Passive. You can say who did each action if you want to.

EXAMPLE
admit / hospital
He was admitted to hospital.

1 give / general anaesthetic
2 perform / appendectomy
3 insert / stitches / wound
4 prescribe / painkillers
5 discharge from hospital

A preparation that is commonly used in general anaesthetics comes from the drug **curare**. It is the paralysing poison South American Indians use on the tips of their arrows.

Reading

1 Discuss these questions with a partner.

- Have you ever had a general anaesthetic? Describe what happened.
- Were you / Would you be nervous of having one?

2 Read the article and answer the questions.

1 How many types of drugs make up a general anaesthetic?
2 What are they?
3 What tells an anaesthetist if a patient is waking up?
4 Why do patients under general anaesthetic need a ventilator?
5 What two organs are *not* paralysed by general anaesthetic?

3 Work in pairs. Without looking back at the text, try to remember the missing verbs. Then look back and check.

1 The anaesthetist's job is to p__________ this from happening ...
2 The patient is g__________ a general anaesthetic in three parts.
3 ... an electroencephalogram (EEG), which will w__________ if you are waking up.
4 The second drug p__________ the muscles ...
5 An alarm will s__________ if it drops too low.
6 Despite the effects of the paralysing drug, the brain also still f__________.

GENERAL ANAESTHETIC

The thing about general anaesthetic that frightens everyone is the idea of waking up in the middle of an operation. The anaesthetist's job is to prevent this from happening by monitoring the patient every step of the way.

The patient is given a general anaesthetic in three parts. The first part is a drug that puts you to sleep. It works very fast. You are told to count backwards from 100, and you are usually asleep before you reach 95. From that point onwards, your brain waves are monitored by an electroencephalogram (EEG), which will warn if you are waking up.

The second drug paralyses the muscles, so you need a ventilator to breathe. The percentage of oxygen in the air is controlled by the ventilator. An alarm will sound if it drops too low.

The heart still works under general anaesthetic, and your heart rate is recorded by an electrocardiogram (ECG). The anaesthetist also monitors the percentage of haemoglobin in the blood and level of carbon dioxide. Body temperature is constantly measured because hypothermia can occur under general anaesthetic.

Despite the effects of the paralysing drug, the brain also still functions. So if you wake at the wrong time, you may be able to hear surgeons and nurses talking, and understand what is going on. You will be unable to call out, open your eyes, or move, because your muscles will be paralysed. However, you will feel no pain because of the third part of the anaesthetic – a painkiller, such as morphine.

The drugs of a general anaesthetic are powerful and can cause hallucinations, which may explain the 'near death' experiences described by people who are given general anaesthetic. Many of them say the same thing – they rose out of their body and went down a corridor towards a bright light, and sometimes they have reported hearing a voice telling them to return.

The scientist **Sir Humphrey Davy** (1778–1829) discovered the anaesthetic properties of **nitrous oxide**. When he breathed in the gas, he began laughing uncontrollably before losing consciousness. He named it 'laughing gas'.

One of the first women to give birth painlessly using chloroform named her new baby **Anaesthesia**.

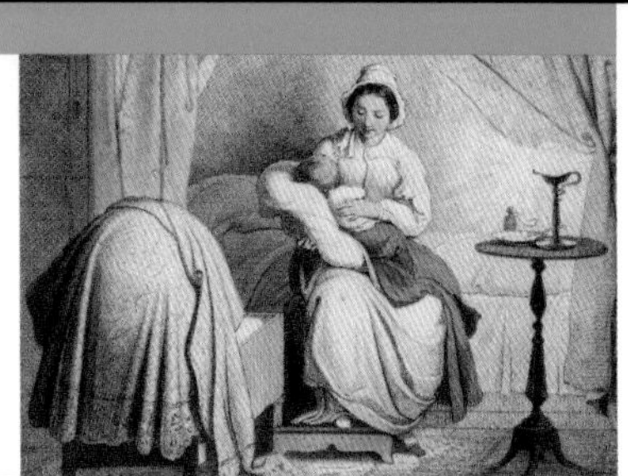

Speaking 2

1 Work with a partner. Decide what the logical order for the pictures is.

1 _____ 2 _____ 3 _____ 4 _____

5 _____ 6 _____ 7 _____ 8 _____

2 Work in pairs. Use the notes in the *Speaking activities* section to describe half of the anaesthetic procedure. Use the Passive where possible. Make notes while listening to your partner. Student A go to p.111. Student B go to p.114.

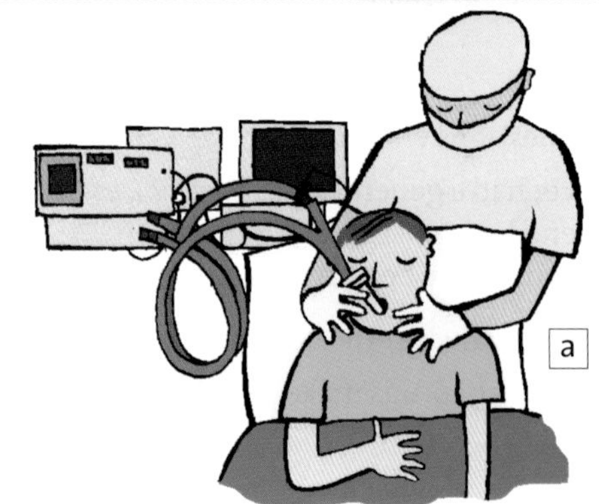

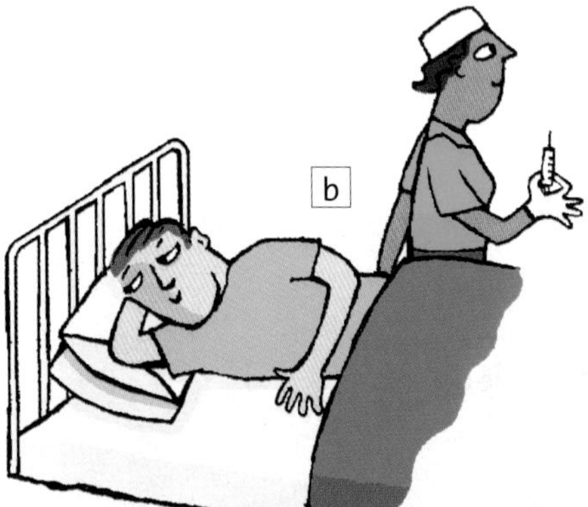

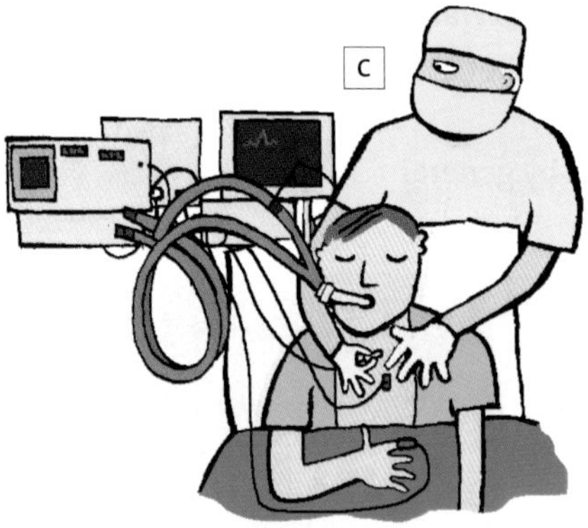

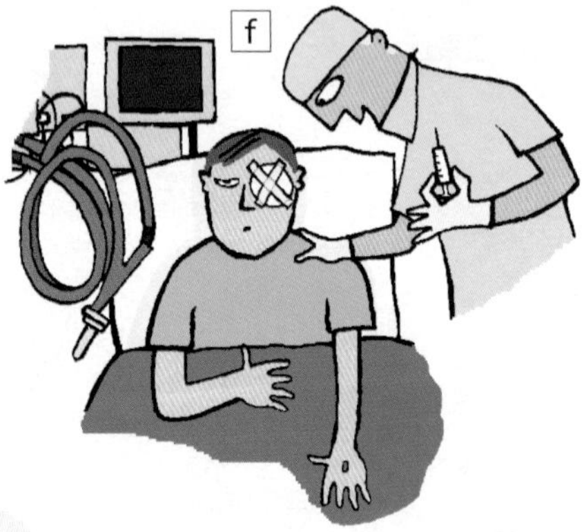

Writing

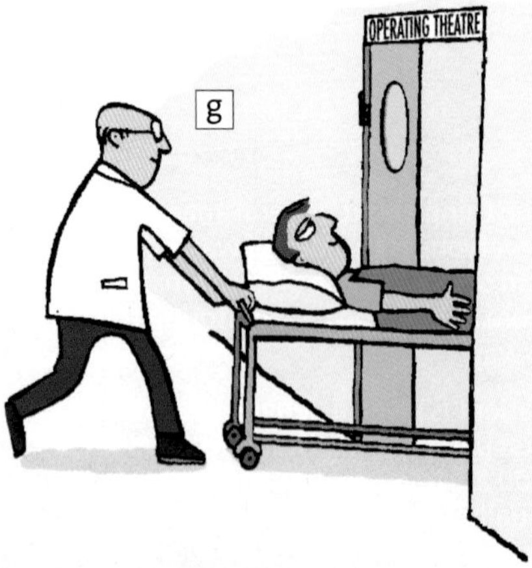

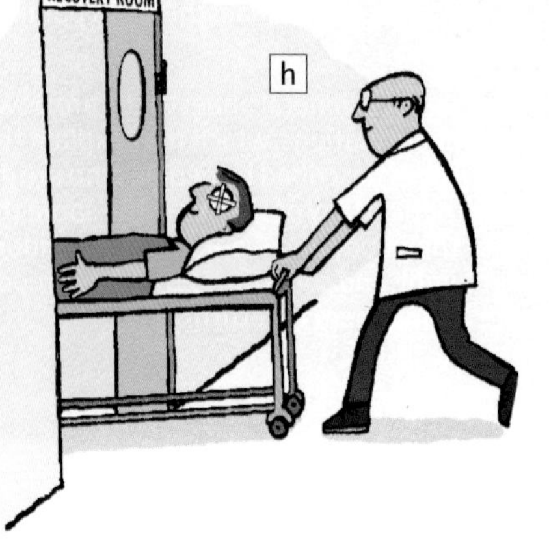

Describing a procedure

Use your notes from *Speaking 2* to write a description of what happens when a patient has a general anaesthetic. Add details of your own.

EXAMPLE

First, the patient is asked questions to assess their health and history. Then, he is given a pre-med and ...

Checklist

Assess your progress in this unit. Tick (✔) the statements which are true.

- I can express the results of the main methods of monitoring
- I can understand and record a patient's vital signs
- I can use the Passive
- I can understand a text about general anaesthetics

Key words

Monitoring
bpm
brain waves
ECG
heart rate
oximeter
scan
ultrasound
vital signs

Nouns
abnormality
co-ordination
pre-med
shivering
transducer
ventilator

Verb
paralyse

Look back through this unit. Find five more words or expressions that you think are useful.

Listening 2

A scan

1 Look at the picture. Talk with your partner about what's happening.

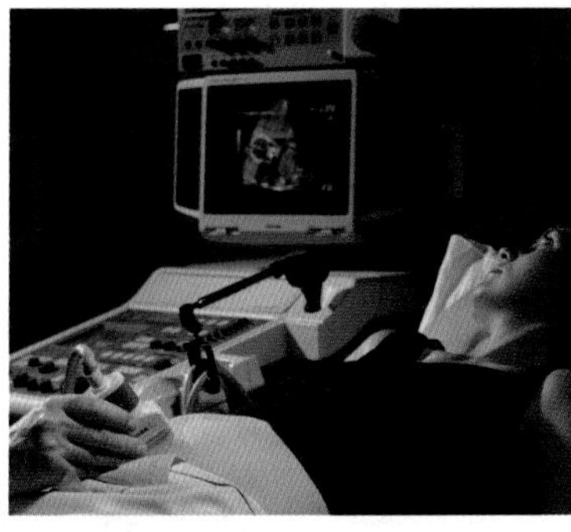

2 Listen to the dialogue between Mrs Murphy and the nurse, and decide if these sentences are true (T) or false (F).

1 Mrs Murphy drank nothing before the scan. ______
2 Before the scan, Mrs Murphy was worried about the baby. ______
3 Mrs Murphy's pregnancy has just started. ______
4 Mrs Murphy's scan shows abnormalities. ______
5 She doesn't want to know the sex of the baby. ______
6 The heartbeat is very weak. ______

3 Complete the sentences with the verbs below. Then listen again and check.

looks	putting	makes	shows up
lie back	passing	work	stopped

1 ...just __________ on this examination table.
2 I'm __________ some gel onto your abdomen.
3 That helps the ultrasound __________ well.
4 Your notes say the baby has __________ moving.
5 ...and it __________ a picture here on the monitor.
6 It __________ any abnormalities.
7 I'm __________ the transducer over your abdomen now.
8 The baby's alive and __________ good.

4 Discuss these questions with your partner.

- Do you know any traditional ways of testing if the baby is a boy or a girl?
- Are there any advantages in knowing if a baby is going to be born a girl or a boy?
- Would you want to know?

14 Medication

Scrub up

1 Work in pairs. Match these pictures with the medical problems.

1 an infection
2 a cut
3 an insect bite
4 constipation
5 obesity
6 vitamin deficiency
7 an infectious disease
8 an allergy

2 Tell your partner about a time when you had one of these conditions. What treatment did you have? Did it work?

Vocabulary

Types and forms of medication

1 Complete each sentence with a type of medicine.

A painkiller	An antihistamine
A sedative	A stimulant
An anti-inflammatory	An antidepressant
An inoculation	A laxative
An antibiotic	A supplement

1 __________ kills bacteria and other germs.
2 __________ protects you against infectious diseases.
3 __________ relieves pain.
4 __________ reduces swelling.
5 __________ encourages bowel movements.
6 __________ provides a substance that the body lacks.
7 __________ treats allergies.
8 __________ increases activity in the body.
9 __________ reduces feelings of extreme sadness.
10 __________ makes you relaxed and sleepy.

2 Work in pairs. Look at the list of words in 1. Circle the syllable that you think is stressed in each word.

EXAMPLE
painkiller

3 Discuss with a partner which type of medicine you could use to treat the people in *Scrub up*.

In this unit

- types of medication
- methods of giving medication
- understanding instructions for giving medication
- *be going to* v Present Continuous for future
- writing up an experiment

4 Match the pictures with these names.

1 syringe	_____	6 suppository	_____
2 inhaler	_____	7 adhesive patch	_____
3 ointment	_____	8 tablespoon	_____
4 capsules	_____	9 dropper	_____
5 IV drip	_____		

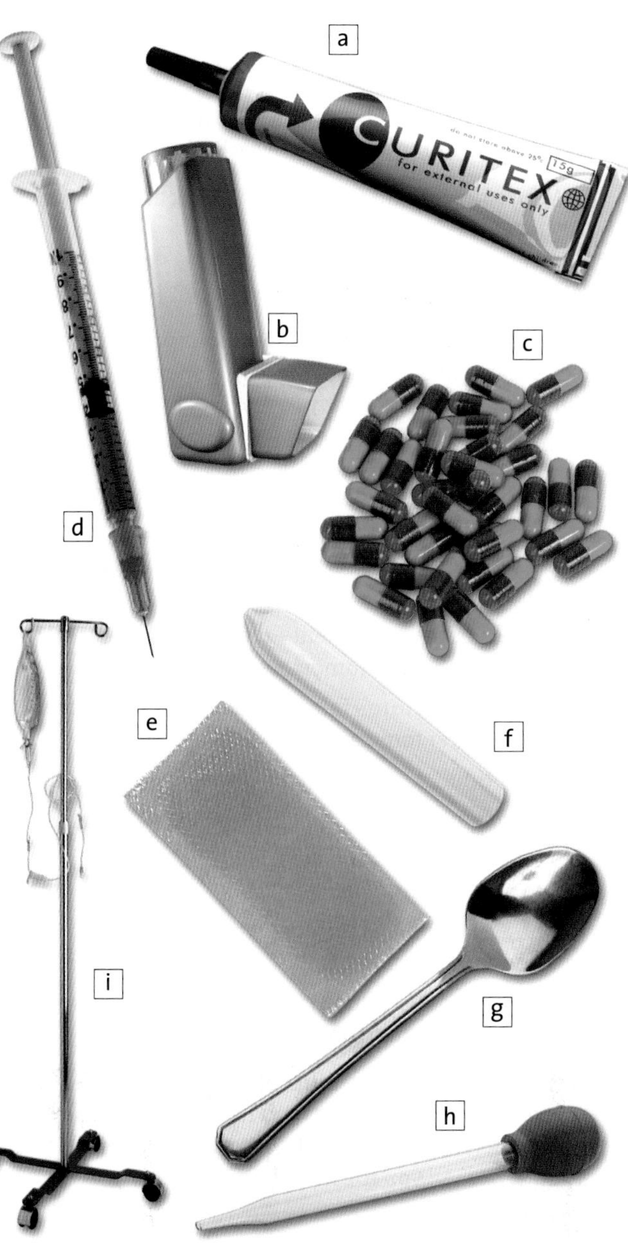

Listening

Patient medication

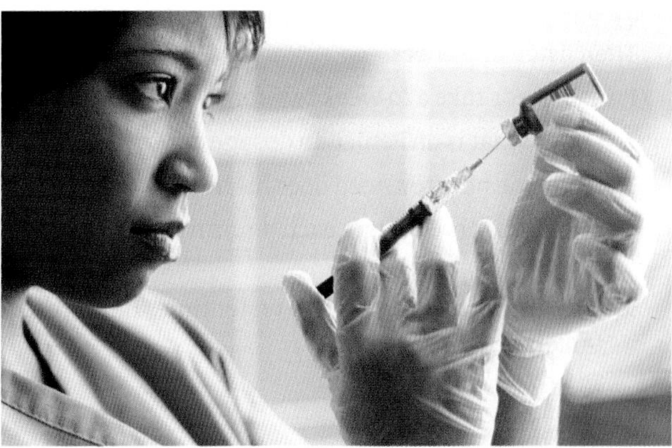

1 Listen to the nurse give information about patients' medication. Match each patient with the problem they have and with a medication type.

patient	problem	medication
Mr Gupta	allergy	antibiotic
Mr Gill	constipation	painkiller
Mr Sawyer	skin infection	laxative
Mr Thomas	respiratory tract infection	antibiotic
Mr Cheong	abdominal pain	antihistamine

2 Listen again and write down the dosage for each patient.

1. Mr Gupta — ________ mg of Morphine every ____ hours
2. Mr Gill — a ________ mg infusion of Clindamycin over a ________ hour period
3. Mr Sawyer — one ________ mg tablespoon of Metamucil, ________ times a day
4. Mr Thomas — ________ mg of Cephalexin every ________ hours
5. Mr Cheong — an injection of ________ mg of Dimotane every ________ hours

Patient care

Dosages

Put the words in the right order to make sentences. Then listen and check.

1 day needs take a to week two for twice she tablets a.
2 Oliver what is on Penicillin dosage of Mr?
3 medicine he often need does his how?
4 four drop Mrs 0.5 every each hours ml one eye give in Muben.
5 with mealtimes on day two water times he's a three tablets at.

Speaking

Work in pairs. You are going to exchange details about patients' medication. Student A look at this page. Student B go to p.115.

Student A

Ask Student B questions to complete this information about patients' medication.

Mrs Dupont	½ teaspoon		3 / day at mealtimes
Mrs Francis		painkiller	
Miss Wang	500 mg		1 / day x 2 days
Miss Ekobu		antihistamines	
Mr Strauss			1 / day on an empty stomach
Mr Rossi	75 mg capsule	Tamiflu	
Mr Metcalf		laxative	
Mr Takahashi	injection 30 mg		1 / 3 hours

• Language spot

be going to v Present Continuous for future

We can use *be going to*

- to make a prediction about the future, based on signs we can see now.
*The scan is very clear – you'**re going to have** twins!*

- to talk about your next action.
*I'**m** just **going to take** your temperature.*

- to talk about something you have decided to do.
*I'**m going to apply** for a job in New York.*

- We use the Present Continuous to talk about things we have scheduled in the future.
*I'**m seeing** my boyfriend tonight.*
*What shifts **are** you **working** next week?*

- We often use the Present Continuous with expressions like *next week*, *in May*, *tomorrow*, etc.
*I'**m taking** a week's holiday in April.*

» Go to **Grammar reference** p.123

1 Complete these sentences using *be going to* or the Present Continuous and the verb in brackets.

1 I <u>*'m going to ask*</u> (ask) you a few questions and fill in this form.
2 Here's your appointment – you ________ (see) the doctor at 11.45 tomorrow.
3 Your temperature's falling – you ________ (feel) much better tomorrow.
4 What time ________ (start) work tonight?
5 The consultant ________ (talk) to you later today.
6 I ________ (visit) some friends next weekend, so I'm out of town.
7 I ________ (ask) the doctor if you can have stronger painkillers.
8 ________ (you, have) your operation tomorrow morning or tomorrow afternoon?

2 Work in pairs. Ask each other about your future schedule, and about things you have decided to do in the future. Ask about tonight, next weekend, next summer, when you finish studying, etc.

EXAMPLE

A *What are you doing tomorrow night?*
B *I'm working until seven, then I'm going home to relax.*

A **pandemic** can start when these three conditions are met:

- a new disease appears
- the agent infects humans, causing serious illness
- the agent spreads easily among humans

3 Write sentences making predictions about people in your class. Give a reason for each one.

EXAMPLE

Grace is going to fall asleep this afternoon – she looks *very* *tired!*

Reading

1 Can you name any deadly infectious diseases that have spread around the world?

2 Read the sentences and decide if they are true (T) or false (F).

1 A pandemic is a type of virus. ____
2 Viruses reproduce outside your body. ____
3 More people died from Spanish flu than were killed in the First World War. ____
4 H1N1 is the name of a pandemic. ____
5 H5N1 is an antiviral drug. ____
6 Tamiflu is made by Roche. ____
7 Tamiflu stops H5N1 spreading. ____

3 What is the latest news on bird flu?

Pandemics and TAMIFLU

When someone who has flu sneezes nearby, you take tiny droplets of their saliva into your lungs. The droplets contain viruses that are looking for a new home. They get into your lungs and then into your blood, and can quickly take over your whole body, using it as a factory in which they can reproduce.

At any time, a deadly bacterium or a virus can become very successful and spread across the world, killing millions of human beings. When this happens it is called a 'pandemic'.

There was a pandemic in 1918. An influenza virus called H1N1, or 'Spanish flu', killed between 50 and 100 million people. More people died from H1N1 than were killed in the First World War .

A letter from a doctor in a military camp in 1918 describes the situation:

'... It is only a few hours until death comes. It is horrible. We have been averaging about 100 deaths per day. We have lost many nurses and doctors. Special trains carry away the dead. For several days there were no coffins and the bodies piled up.'

Since 1918, the H1N1 virus has mutated. Now there is a mutation called H5N1. When this mutation first appeared in China in 1996, there was a desperate search for a medicine to deal with it. The pharmaceutical company Roche came up with a drug called Tamiflu.

Tamiflu does not kill H5N1, but stops it making copies of itself. If given early enough, vaccinations of Tamiflu could perhaps save many lives. However, the virus will continue to mutate, and might become resistant to Tamiflu. The next mutation may already be with us by the time you're reading this!

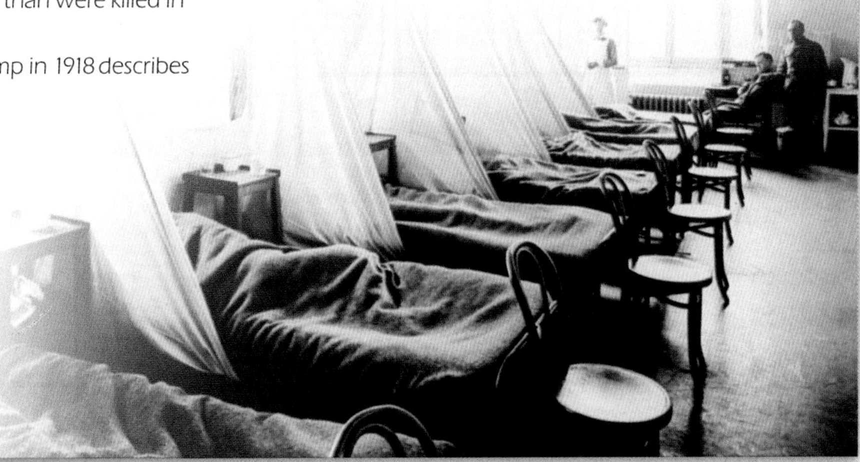

Writing

Writing up an experiment

1 In an experiment, a stimulant called Isoprenaline is given to a rat to see what happens to heart rate and blood pressure. Look at the data, and use the words and expressions below to complete the report.

dose	intravenous infusion
the effect of	returned
anaesthetized	administered
dropped	recorded

Experiment report

Aim To test __________[1] Isoprenaline on an __________[2] rat.

Method I __________[3] a small __________[4] of Isoprenaline by __________[5] to a rat and __________[6] the rat's heart rate and blood pressure .

Results The rat's heart rate went up to 500 and then __________[7] slowly to normal after three minutes.

The rat's blood pressure __________[8] after one minute. After two minutes the rat's blood pressure returned to 130.

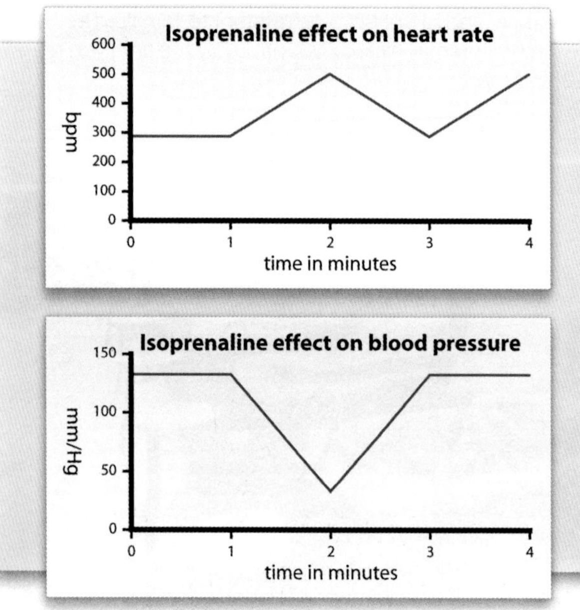

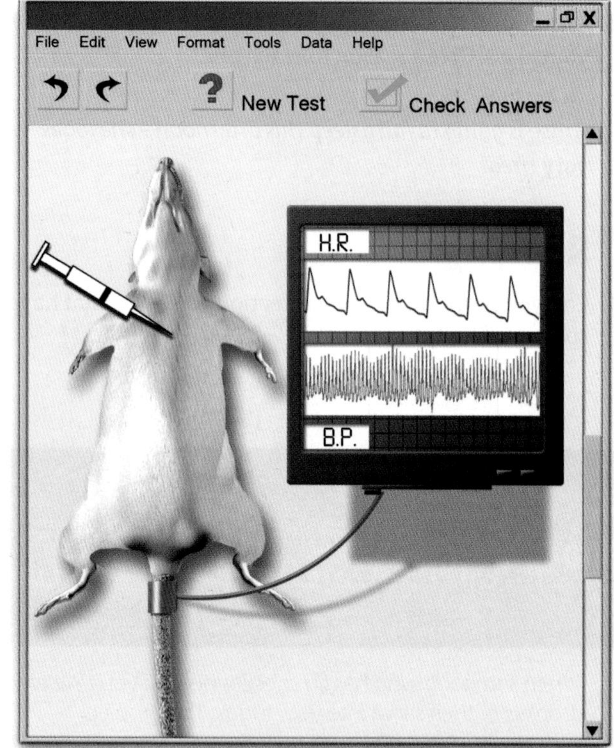

2 These two charts show what happened when an anaesthetic (Cocaine) was given to the rat. Look at the data carefully, then write up the report using the report in 1 to help you.

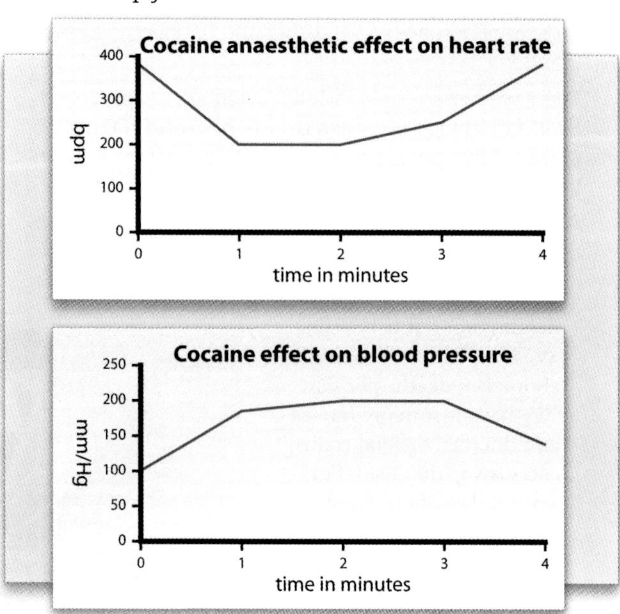

Project

1 Do you know who the man giving the injection is? Do you recognize the disease? Read the story.

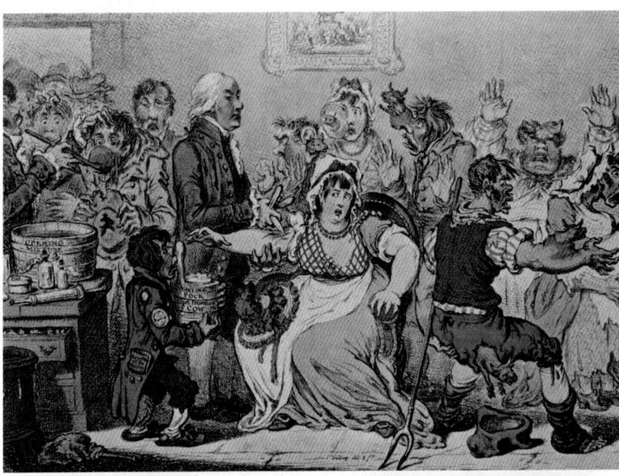

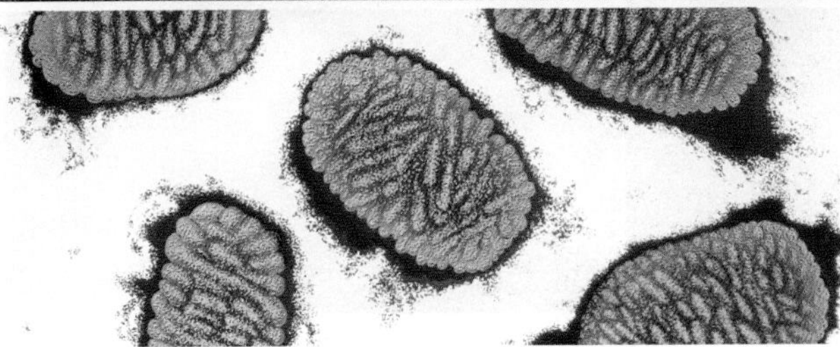

The British scientist Edward Jenner (1749–1823) found a cure for smallpox when he noted that milkmaids did not catch the disease because they already had a mild form of smallpox from milking cows. This made them immune – their bodies could resist the disease. Jenner invented vaccination – the injecting of a mild form of a disease into patients to make them immune. His discovery came at a time when smallpox was killing millions.

2 Research one of these drugs which has also changed history and prepare a mini-presentation for the class. Talk about its history, what it's used for, how it's taken, and any possible side effects.

- Penicillin
- Aspirin
- the pill (oral contraceptives)

Checklist

Assess your progress in this unit. Tick (✔) the statements which are true.

I can understand instructions for giving medication

I can use *be going to* and the Present Continuous to talk about the future

I can understand an article about pandemics

I can write up an experiment

Key words

Adjectives
antiviral
immune

Verbs
mutate
prescribe
spread

Nouns
bowel movement
constipation
deficiency
dose
droplet
germ
infusion
saliva
stimulant
suppository

Look back through this unit. Find five more words or expressions that you think are useful.

15 Alternative treatments

Scrub up

Work in pairs. Discuss the questions.

- What treatment is being performed in each picture?
- What do you know about it?
- Have you tried it? / Would you try it?

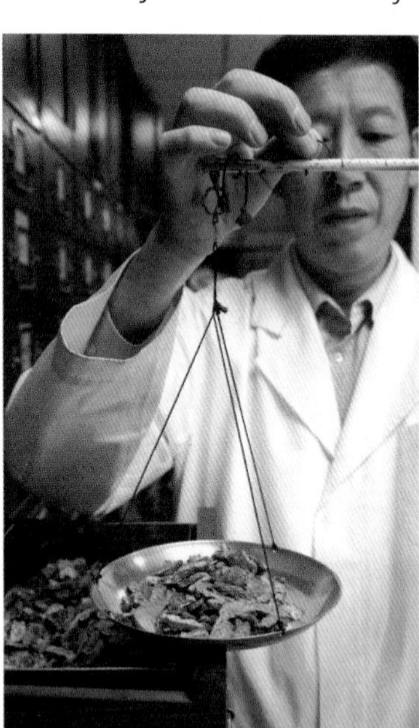

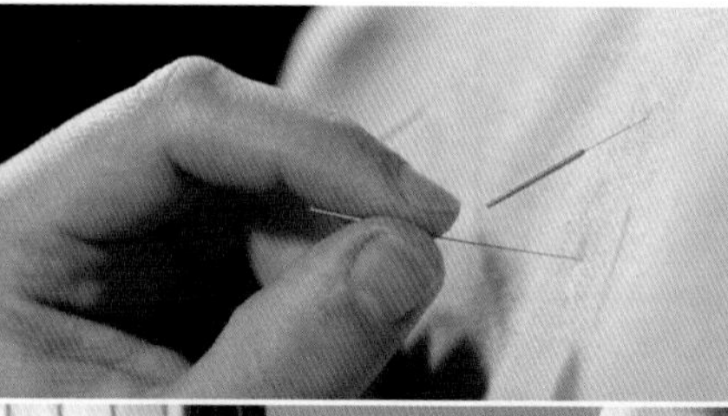

Vocabulary

Types of therapy

1 Complete the descriptions with the words below, and match each description to a therapy.

energy	herbs	channels	pressure points
stimulate	heal	therapist	functioning

a traditional Chinese medicine
b acupuncture
c music therapy
d cupping
e reflexology
f faith healing
g reiki
h hydrotherapy

1 Putting heated cups on the skin to suck bad __________ from the body __*d*__
2 The use of hot and cold water and underwater exercise to __________ the immune system _____
3 Massaging hands and feet to unblock energy __________ _____
4 Inserting needles into __________ on the body to control the energy called *qi* (/tʃiː/) _____
5 Using sound to help patients control pain and improve physical and mental __________ _____
6 Using prayer to ask a god or spirit to __________ the patient _____
7 Using Chinese knowledge of __________ to balance *yin* and *yang* _____
8 Laying of the __________'s hands on the patient to bring energy into the body _____

2 Discuss these questions with your partner.

- What alternative therapies do you believe in?
- Which are you most sceptical about?

In this unit

- describing alternative treatments
- natural medicines
- *Qigong*
- giving reasons
- healers
- arguing for and against something

Reading

1 Discuss these questions in pairs.

- Do you know any examples of animals using natural medicines to keep themselves healthy?
- What medicinal plants or other natural medicines do you know?

2 Guess which natural medicine (1–5) animals use to treat which condition (a–f). Then read the article and find out if you guessed correctly.

1	aromatic plants	a	labour
2	clay	b	skin conditions
3	grass	c	stomach problems
4	leaves	d	wounds
5	roots	e	tiredness
		f	worms

3 Work with a partner. Try to remember the verbs used in the article. Then read the article again to check.

1 Grass m__________ cats sick and cl__________ their stomach of worms.

2 Chimpanzees eat certain leaves to c__________ stomach aches and r__________ tiredness.

3 Bears ch__________ Ligusticum roots and a__________ the juice to wounds.

4 Elephants eat certain leaves before they g__________ b__________ to h__________ them with labour.

5 Many animals eat clay to b__________ d__________ poisons in their stomach.

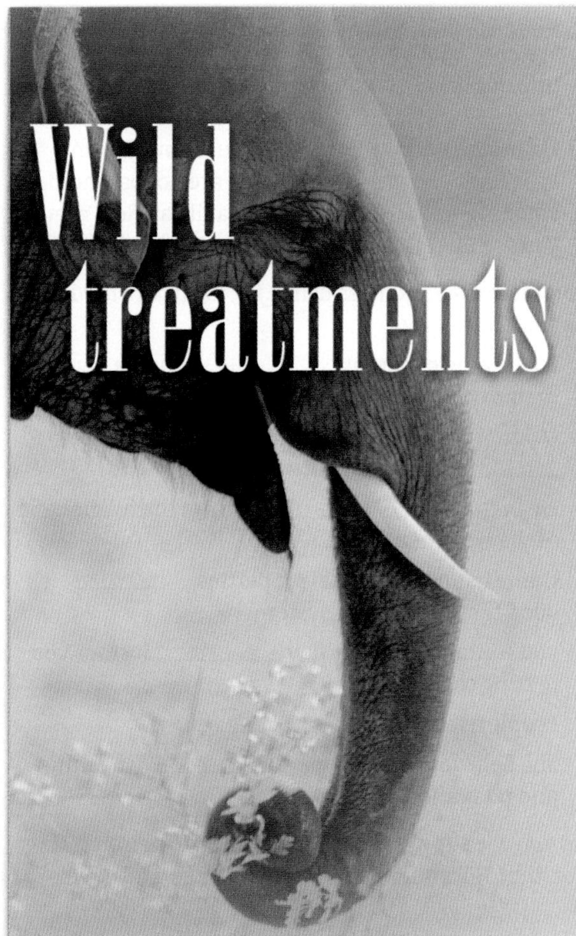

Wild treatments

A lot of knowledge which we call 'alternative medicine' has come from watching animals, because not every pharmacist is a human being – animals treat themselves with medicines too. You may have seen a dog or a cat eat grass, for example. They do this because it makes them sick, and clears their stomachs of worms.

In Tanzania, leaves from a tree which local WaTongwe people call 'the bitter leaf tree', are eaten by chimpanzees. Both the WaTongwe and the chimpanzees know that the leaves can cure stomach aches and relieve tiredness.

Bears know about the medicinal properties of the root of a plant called Ligusticum. They chew its root, and apply the juice to wounds as an antiseptic. Ligusticum is used by Navajo Indians too. A folk story says they were told about the plant by bears.

When African elephants are going to give birth, they will walk many kilometres to eat the leaves from a certain tree that will help labour. The leaves are used by Kenyan women for the same thing.

Clay is eaten by many animals, from cows to rhinoceroses, because it breaks down poisons in the stomach. It is also the main ingredient of kaolin, which is used in treatments for stomach illnesses in humans.

When some birds build their nests, they choose aromatic plants that will keep their babies healthy. The plants chosen by the birds are also used by herbalists for skin problems such as ulcers, sores, and eczema.

Because bacteria are becoming resistant to antibiotics, it is becoming more and more important to find alternatives, and zoopharmacognosy – a word from Greek meaning 'animals' knowledge of medicine' – may give us important new information about very old ways of dealing with illness.

If a patient believes that a drug will cure them, it often will, even if it is just a tablet with no active ingredient. This is known as the **placebo effect**.

Listening

Qigong

1 Listen to this radio programme about an alternative treatment called *qigong* (/tʃiːˈɡʊŋ/), and decide if these statements are true (T) or false (F).

1 *Qi* causes illness. ____
2 *Qi* is a treatment. ____
3 A 'holistic' treatment deals with the patient's mind, not the body. ____
4 *Qigong* corrects the body's energy balance. ____
5 External *qigong* healers pass their hands over the patient's body. ____
6 Professor Silver is sceptical about *qigong*. ____
7 Professor Silver believes in the placebo effect. ____
8 Professor Silver thinks that belief is the most important part of treatment. ____

2 What is your opinion of *qigong* healing? Put an *x* somewhere on this line to show your opinion.

x————————————————————x

I strongly believe in it — I am extremely sceptical about it

• Language spot

Giving reasons

We can give reasons for things in a number of ways.

• *for* + noun
*People take herbal medicines **for** good health.*
*I see a reflexologist **for** my back pain.*

• *for* + -*ing*
*Birds use these plants **for** build**ing** nests.*

• *to* + infinitive
*Chimpanzees eat these leaves **to** treat stomach aches.*
*I visited a healer **to** get relief from the pain.*

• *... so that ...*
*Elephants eat leaves **so that** their labour will be easier.*

• *... because ...*
*Animals put ants on their skin **because** they produce formic acid.*

• *... so ...*
*The juice is antiseptic, **so** bears put it on their wounds.*

• *That's why ...*
*I use only herbal medicines – **that's why** I am so healthy.*

» Go to **Grammar reference** p.124

1 Match the beginnings and the endings of the sentences.

1	Homeopathy works on animals,	a	that's why I feel so good now.
2	Acupuncture unblocks *qi*	b	for swellings.
3	We need a lot of information	c	so it cannot be a placebo.
4	They use massage	d	to make a diagnosis.
5	Use an ice pack	e	for relaxing the body and mind.
6	I gave up smoking –	f	because your yin and yang are not balanced.
7	You are ill	g	so that it can flow around the body.

2 Complete the sentences using *for, to, so that, because, so,* and *That's why*.

1 I have music therapy ________ improve my memory.
2 My mother doesn't believe in modern medicine, ________ she will not see a GP.
3 Lie in the water ________ you get the full benefit of the treatment.
4 Garlic has antibacterial properties. ________ it's good for the immune system.
5 I take vitamin C every day ________ it stops you getting colds.
6 People use this herb ________ burns.
7 She believes in homeopathy ________ healing and relaxation.

3 Do you use supplements, therapy, etc. to help you stay healthy? Tell your partner what you use, and why.

Project

Do some research on the Internet about a plant that is used as a medicine. Find out information such as

- what it looks like
- where it grows
- what it is used for
- how it is prepared for use.

Speaking 1

1 Student A – read about Pak Haji Haron on this page. Student B – read about Alma Gluck on p.115. Then cover the information and ask your partner the questions that follow the text.

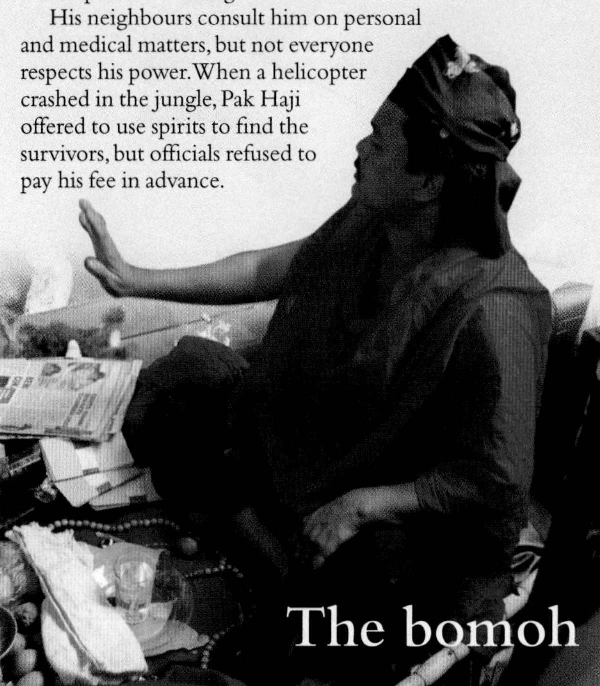

Pak Haji Haron is a bomoh – a Malaysian witch doctor. He learned his craft from his father who, in turn, learnt it from his father.

Pak Haji believes that a person gets ill because an enemy uses the magic of another bomoh. His speciality is making a 'sekatan' – a protection from other bomohs' bad magic.

Pak Haji uses a mixture of superstition and religion in his work. He uses the Koran, ghosts, and bones to raise spirits which perform healing.

His neighbours consult him on personal and medical matters, but not everyone respects his power. When a helicopter crashed in the jungle, Pak Haji offered to use spirits to find the survivors, but officials refused to pay his fee in advance.

The bomoh

Student A's questions:

- How did Alma learn to be a healer?
- How do Christian Scientists believe illness is cured?
- How does Alma give consultations?
- Does this form of healing really work?

2 With your partner, read the two texts again and translate the following key terms into your own language. If necessary, use a dictionary.

1 superstition ________
2 to consult ________
3 a fee ________
4 a course ________
5 give a consultation ________
6 to charge ________

Writing

Advice to a friend via email

1 This is part of an email which you have received from a friend who is ill with a dangerous tumour. What is she thinking of doing?

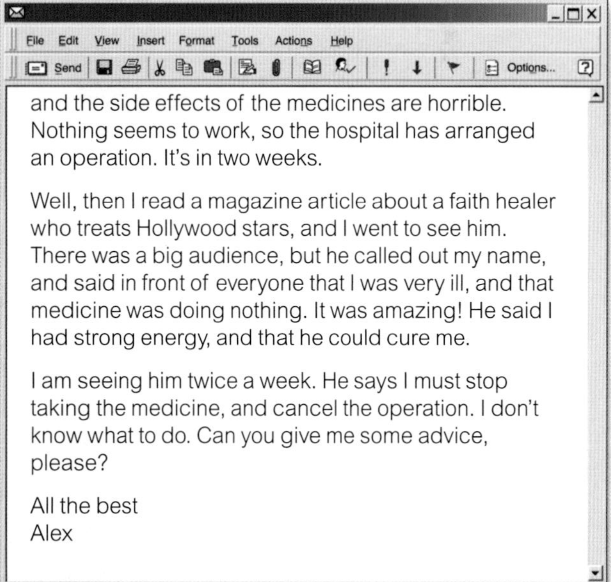

and the side effects of the medicines are horrible. Nothing seems to work, so the hospital has arranged an operation. It's in two weeks.

Well, then I read a magazine article about a faith healer who treats Hollywood stars, and I went to see him. There was a big audience, but he called out my name, and said in front of everyone that I was very ill, and that medicine was doing nothing. It was amazing! He said I had strong energy, and that he could cure me.

I am seeing him twice a week. He says I must stop taking the medicine, and cancel the operation. I don't know what to do. Can you give me some advice, please?

All the best
Alex

2 Write an email in reply. Ask questions about the faith healer. You can either encourage your friend to see the healer, or argue against the healer and try to persuade her to have the operation.

Body bits

Mind and body therapies

Read the descriptions of alternative treatments and complete them using the words below.

scalp	scent	habits	mental
beneficial	herbs	wrinkles	hair
contact	operation	pressure	fingers
concentrate	properties	adjustments	pressure
practitioner	posture		

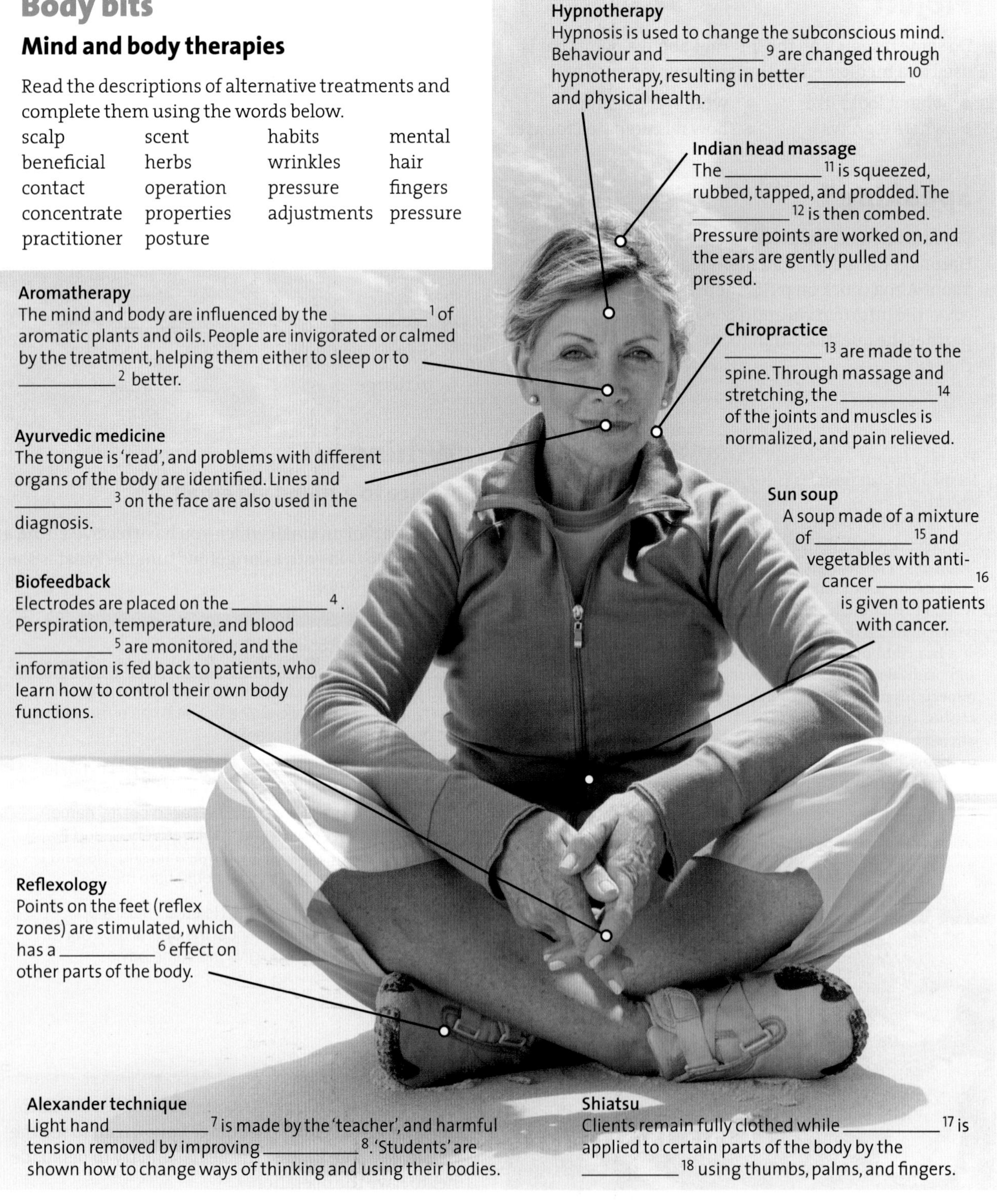

Aromatherapy
The mind and body are influenced by the ___________ [1] of aromatic plants and oils. People are invigorated or calmed by the treatment, helping them either to sleep or to ___________ [2] better.

Ayurvedic medicine
The tongue is 'read', and problems with different organs of the body are identified. Lines and ___________ [3] on the face are also used in the diagnosis.

Biofeedback
Electrodes are placed on the ___________ [4]. Perspiration, temperature, and blood ___________ [5] are monitored, and the information is fed back to patients, who learn how to control their own body functions.

Reflexology
Points on the feet (reflex zones) are stimulated, which has a ___________ [6] effect on other parts of the body.

Alexander technique
Light hand ___________ [7] is made by the 'teacher', and harmful tension removed by improving ___________ [8]. 'Students' are shown how to change ways of thinking and using their bodies.

Hypnotherapy
Hypnosis is used to change the subconscious mind. Behaviour and ___________ [9] are changed through hypnotherapy, resulting in better ___________ [10] and physical health.

Indian head massage
The ___________ [11] is squeezed, rubbed, tapped, and prodded. The ___________ [12] is then combed. Pressure points are worked on, and the ears are gently pulled and pressed.

Chiropractice
___________ [13] are made to the spine. Through massage and stretching, the ___________ [14] of the joints and muscles is normalized, and pain relieved.

Sun soup
A soup made of a mixture of ___________ [15] and vegetables with anti-cancer ___________ [16] is given to patients with cancer.

Shiatsu
Clients remain fully clothed while ___________ [17] is applied to certain parts of the body by the ___________ [18] using thumbs, palms, and fingers.

Speaking 2

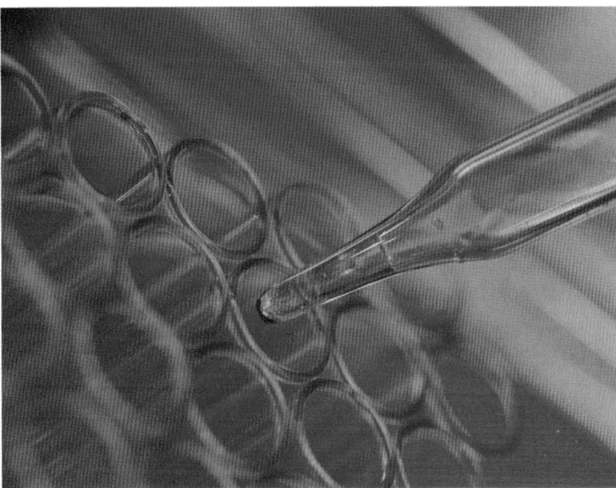

1 You are going to debate whether conventional medicine or homeopathy is better for a particular patient. First, prepare your ideas in groups. Copy the table below and note down your ideas.

- **Group A** You are in favour of conventional medicine, and against homeopathy.
- **Group B** You are in favour of homeopathy, and against conventional medicine.

	Group A		Group B	
	in favour of conventional medicine	against homeopathy	in favour of homeopathy	against conventional medicine
Are the practitioners qualified?				
How does it work?				
Are treatments tested?				

2 A patient has a number of problems. Her symptoms include diarrhoea, pains in the joints, and loss of hair. Should she see a doctor or a homeopath?

Each student from group A now talks with a partner from group B. Discuss the patient, and try to persuade the other person about your point of view.

Checklist

Assess your progress in this unit. Tick (✔) the statements which are true.

I can describe alternative treatments

I can give reasons in different ways

I can understand an article about zoopharmocognosy

I can express an opinion for or against something

Key words

Adjectives
holistic
medicinal
sceptical

Nouns
consultation
conventional medicine
eczema
fee
healer
herbalist
practitioner
root
sore
superstition
supplement
worms

Look back through this unit. Find five more words or expressions that you think are useful.

Speaking activities

Student A

Unit 8 p.49

1 Ask and answer questions until you both have all the information, for example *What's Heidi Klum's height in feet?*

	height	height	weight	weight
Heidi Klum	1.77 m		54 kg	
Robert Wadlow	2.72 m		223 kg	
Walter Hudson		6'1"		1402 lb

Unit 9 p.69

1 Read the information below, and draw very simple pictures to help you remember it in the grid on p.69. Do not write words.

2 Ask your partner questions to complete the grid, for example *What happened in about 200 BC? What did Chinese scientists do?* Write notes as you listen.

About 500 BC	The Greek scientist Alcmaeon saw that arteries and veins were different.
1658	In Holland, Jan Swammerdam used one of the first microscopes, and saw that there are different types of cells in the blood.
1874	William Ostler identified platelets.
1912	Roger Lee demonstrated that it is safe to give group O blood to patients of any blood group, and that blood from all groups can be given to AB patients.
1917	An American army doctor, Oswald Robertson, set up the first blood bank.
1948	Dr Carl Walter designed plastic bags for collecting and storing blood.

Unit 11 p.82

1 You are nurses on the ward pictured on p.83. There is going to be a hygiene inspection. Look around the ward, and find as many problems as you can. Decide what action to take about each problem.

EXAMPLE

The bin needs emptying. I'll find a cleaner.

2 Now each work with a Student B, the Hygiene Inspector. They will tell you what problems they have found. Tell them what action you have taken, or what action you're going to take, for example:

B *You need to empty the bin.*

A *Yes, I told a cleaner, and he emptied it. I'm going to check them every morning in future.*

Unit 12 p.88

Here is Delroy Moseki talking about his life, a few years after the case conference you listened to. Ask your partner questions to get the missing information, for example *How long has Delroy been ill?*

I've been ill since ______________. That's when I started to get the voice in my head.

I've seen doctors, psychologists, psychiatrists, and psychotherapists, and I've been in hospital seven times.

The first time I went into hospital, I was ______________ years old. They just put me on medication. Now I've stopped ______________ because it made me feel like I was dead.

I left the hospital. Then I got into serious trouble with the police and they sent me to ______________. I've spent three years in prison in my life. It wasn't a nice experience, but I learned to ______________ there. Since then I've read about my illness and I started to understand it.

When I got out of prison I met a group of travellers. I travelled all over Britain with them. That changed my life.

I've been off medication now for ______________ years. Am I winning the fight? Well, my life has been hard, but now I have friends I can talk to. I'm not isolated any more, and I've just got ______________.

Unit 13 Speaking 1 p.94

Describe the patient's temperature and heart rate for Student B to record. Then listen to the information about the patient's respiration and blood pressure and record the information in the graphs.

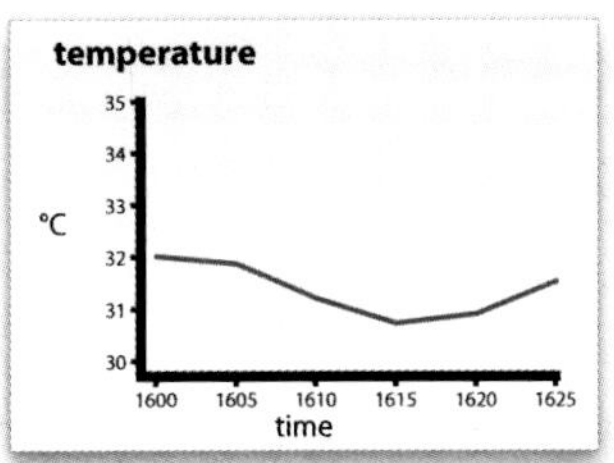

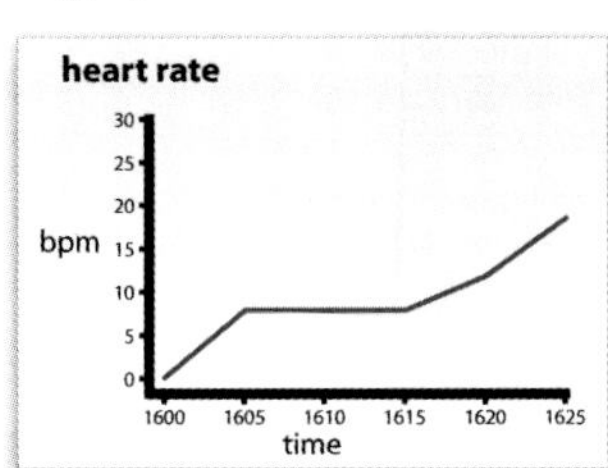

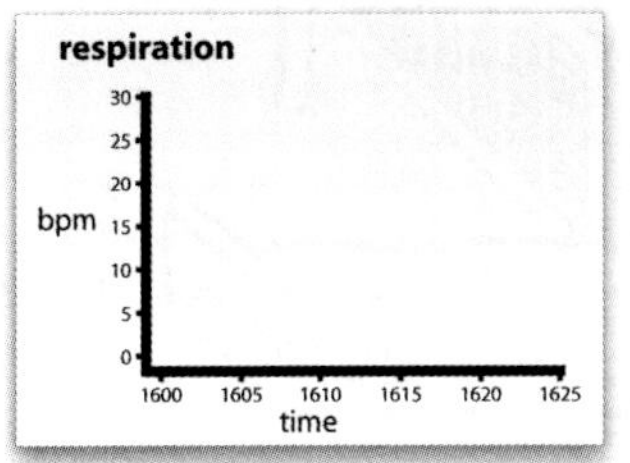

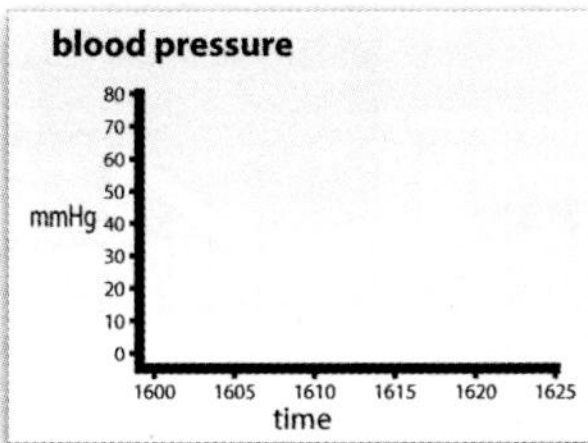

Unit 13 Speaking 2 p.96

Describe each stage in the anaesthetic process by making full sentences using the words given. Use the Passive form. You begin with picture 1, then Student B describes picture 2, and so on.

EXAMPLE

The patient is given a pre-med to make him sleepy and relaxed.

1

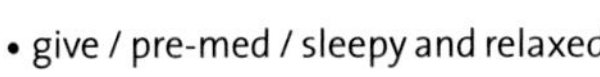

- give / pre-med / sleepy and relaxed
- administer / injection or by mouth

3

- insert cannula / hand
- administer / general anaesthetic / lose consciousness
- record / type and amount / drugs

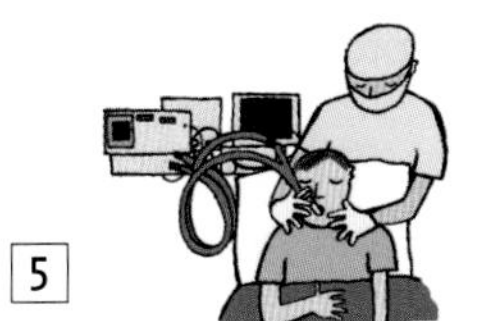

5

- insert / tube / airway
- connect / tube / ventilator / help / breathe
- deliver / anaesthetic gas / lungs / keep / unconscious

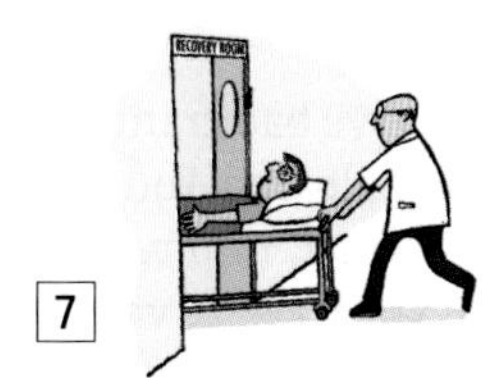

7

- disconnect / equipment / transfer / recovery room

Unit 6 Diagnosis table

	gastroenteritis	E.coli infection
aches	yes	yes
nausea	yes	yes
vomiting	maybe	no
blood in vomit	maybe	no
fever	yes	no
blood in stools	no	yes
cramps	yes	yes
diarrhoea	yes	yes
bloating	yes	yes

Student B

Unit 5 p.32

1 You are in pain after a fall the other day. Imagine the pain you might feel, and be ready to answer the nurse's questions in a lot of detail. Think about the following details:

- where?
- when?
- how bad?
- type of pain?
- same place or moving?
- getting better / worse?
- what helps / makes it worse?

2 Answer the nurse's questions.

	1	2	3	4
burning	☐	☐	☐	☐
stabbing	☐	☐	☐	☐
throbbing	☐	☐	☐	☐
shooting	☐	☐	☐	☐
constant	☐	☐	☐	☐
frequent	☐	☐	☐	☐
occasional	☐	☐	☐	☐
mild	☐	☐	☐	☐
moderate	☐	☐	☐	☐
severe	☐	☐	☐	☐
getting better	☐	☐	☐	☐
getting worse	☐	☐	☐	☐
staying the same	☐	☐	☐	☐

3 Change roles. Now you are the nurse. Ask Student A about the pain they are experiencing, and fill in the chart.

Unit 2 p.14

Describe your picture, and listen to Student A describe their picture.
Without looking at each other's pictures, find ten differences between them.

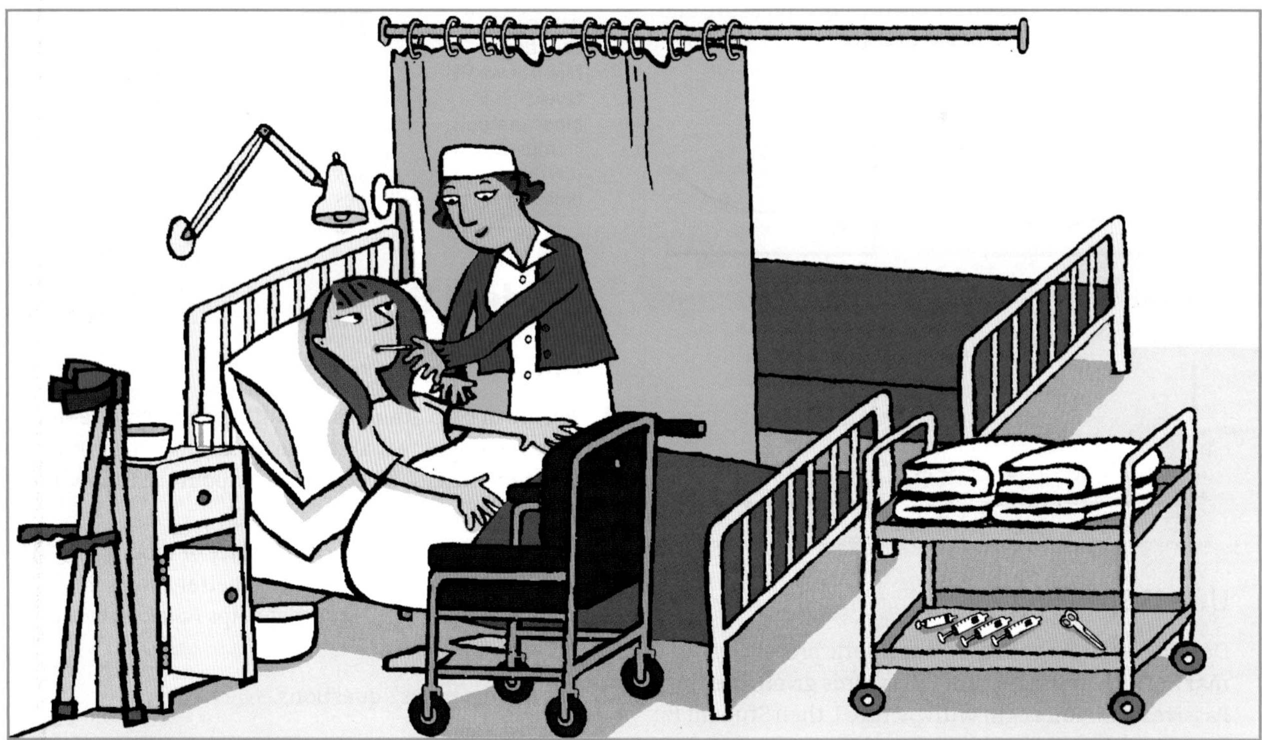

Unit 4 p.23

1 You are a nurse working on a telephone helpline. Listen to your caller explain the emergency, then use these notes to tell the caller what to do and to answer any questions.

EXAMPLE

Wash the wound with soap and water. Don't practise ...

- wound – wash ✓ (soap and water)
  - ice ✗
  - bandage ✓ (not too tight)
- immobilize the leg ✓ (lower than the heart)
- stand up, move ✗
- food, drink ✗
- hospital! ✓✓

2 A man you work with has spilt pesticide on his face, eyes, and mouth. Phone the emergency helpline for instructions. Explain the situation to the helpline nurse, then listen and use these notes to find out what to do. Note down the instructions that you are given.

- difficulty breathing – walk around?
- drink?
- mouth? eyes? skin?

Unit 6 p.37

1 You have a very bad stomach and decide to call a helpline nurse. Memorize these symptoms, then close your book.

You have bad cramps in your stomach, and you feel really bloated. You have bad diarrhoea, and there is blood in it. Your whole body aches. You feel a little sick, but you haven't vomited. Your temperature is normal.

2 Call the helpline and tell the nurse about your problem.

3 1 You are the helpline nurse. Ask the caller questions to find out exactly what the problem is. Use the notes below to help you, and make notes as you listen to the answer.

- What happened?
- pain? where?
- swelling?
- tender?
- bruising?
- skin painful?
- redness?
- deformed?
- hold weight?
- move it?

2 When you have all the answers you need, look at the diagnosis table on p.115. What do you think Student A's problem is?

Unit 8 p.49

1 Ask and answer questions until you both have all the information e.g. *What's Heidi Klum's height in metres?*

	height	height	weight	weight
Heidi Klum		5'9½"		119 lb
Robert Wadlow		8'11"		492 lb
Walter Hudson	1.84 m		636 kg	

Unit 9 p.69

1 Read the information below, and draw very simple pictures to help you remember it in the grid on p.69. Do not write words.

2 Ask and answer questions to complete the grid, for example *What happened in about* 500 *BC? What did Alcmaeon do?* Write notes as you listen.

about 200 BC Chinese scientists learned about the circulation of blood.

1492 Doctors in Rome performed the first blood transfusion. They gave blood from three boys to the Pope. The boys and the Pope all died.

1818 British doctor James Blundell made the first successful human blood transfusion.

1901 Austrian Karl Landsteiner discovered three main human blood groups – A, B, and O.

1940 Karl Landsteiner discovered the Rhesus factor.

1962 Max Perutz was awarded the Nobel prize for his discovery of haemoglobin.

Unit 10 p.77

Read these guidelines for preparing a body, and draw simple pictures in your notebook to help you remember them. Then close this book and exchange information with Student A. Ask questions, for example *What do you do with the eyes? What about the hair?* etc. Make notes as you listen to Student A.

- **eyes**
- **mouth** Put dentures in if worn. These will be difficult to put in later. Try to close the mouth if possible. Putting petroleum jelly on the lips may help.
- **hair**
- **washing** Wash the whole body. Make sure that the face and hands are perfectly clean before the family sees the body.
- **position**
- **jewellery** Put this in a bag marked with the patient's name to give to the family.
- **lines**
- **the room** Put chairs in the room for relatives to sit on. Put one or two boxes of tissues in the room. Clear away dirty linen, rubbish, and medical equipment that is no longer needed. Put on gentle music if appropriate.

Unit 11 p.82

1 You are hygiene inspectors, inspecting the ward pictured on p.83. Look around the ward, and find as many problems as you can. Discuss what action needs to be taken to correct each problem.

EXAMPLE
The bin's full. They need to empty bins regularly.

2 Now each work with a Student A, a nurse on the ward. Tell them what problems you have found, and find out what action they intend to take.

Unit 12 p.88

Here is Delroy Moseki talking about his life, a few years after the case conference you listened to. Ask your partner questions to get the missing information, for example *How many times has Delroy been in hospital?*

I've been ill since I was at school. That's when I started to get the voice in my head.

I've seen doctors, psychologists, psychiatrists, and psychotherapists, and I've been in hospital ______________ times.

The first time I went into hospital, I was 25 years old. They just put me on medication. Now I've stopped taking the medication because ______________ .

I left the hospital. Then I got into serious trouble with the police and they sent me to prison. I've spent ______________ in prison in my life. It wasn't a nice experience, but I learned to read there. Since then I've ______________ and I started to understand it.

When I got out of prison I met ______________. I travelled ______________ with them. That changed my life.

I've been off medication now for three years. Am I winning the fight? Well, my life has been ______________, but now I have friends I can talk to. I'm not isolated any more, and I've just got my own flat.

Unit 13 Speaking 1 p.94

Listen to the information about the patient's temperature and heart rate and record the information in the graphs. Then describe the patient's respiration and blood pressure for Student A to record.

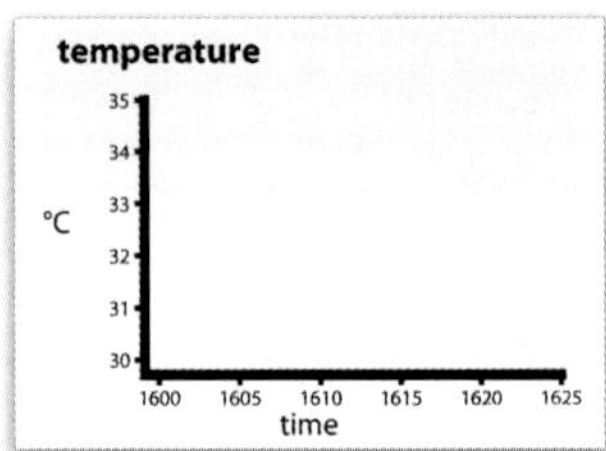

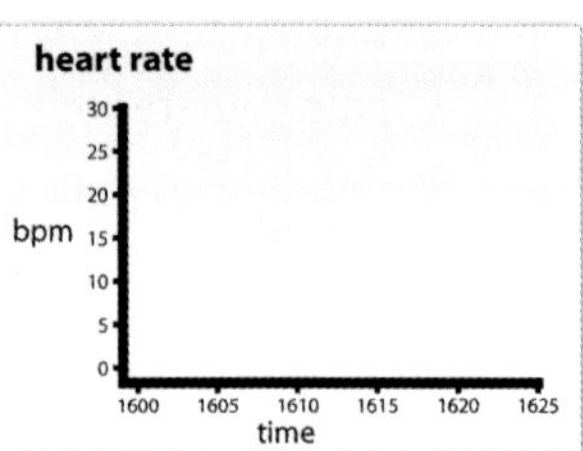

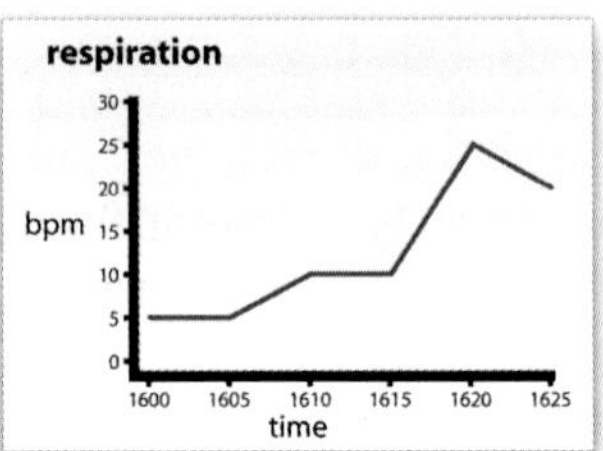

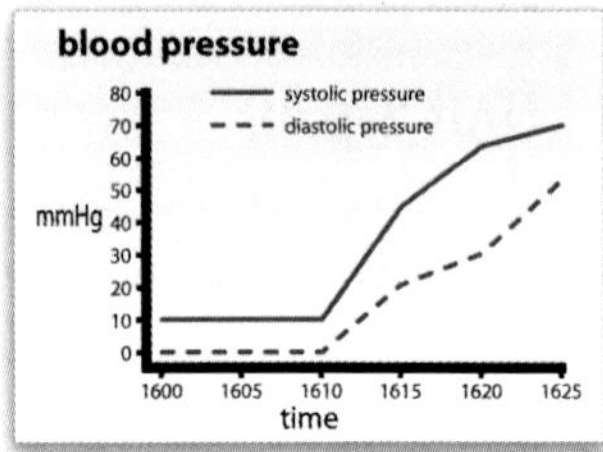

Unit 13 Speaking 2 p.96

Describe each stage in the anaesthetic process by making full sentences using the words given. Use the Passive form. Student A begins with picture 1, then you describe picture 2, and so on.

EXAMPLE
The patient is wheeled to the operating theatre.

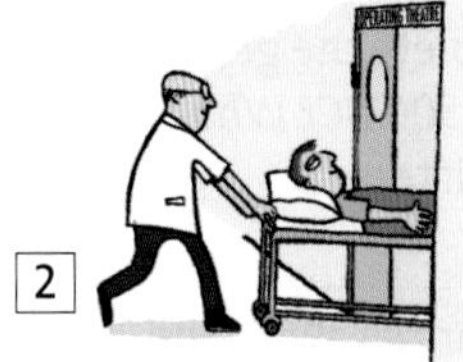

2

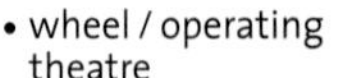

- wheel / operating theatre

4

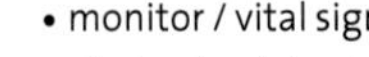

- monitor / vital signs
- electrodes / chest / measure / heart rate
- cuff / arm / measure / blood pressure
- oximeter / measure / blood oxygen level

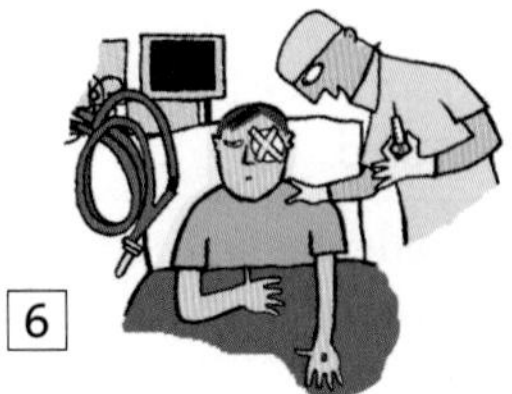

6

- patient / drugs / help / wake up

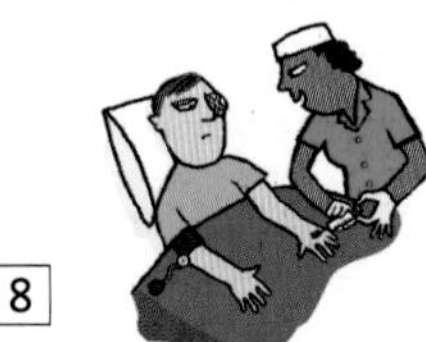

8

- care for / specialist staff
- monitor / level of consciousness
- give / medication / pain

Unit 14 p.100

Ask Student A questions to complete this information about patients' medication, for example *What dosage should I give Mrs Dupont / does Mrs Dupont need? What medication is Mrs Francis on?*

Mrs Dupont		antibiotic	
Mrs Francis	infusion		4 mg / minute
Miss Wang		iron supplement	
Miss Ekobu	2 capsules		one / 4 hours (with water)
Mr Strauss	1 capsule	vitamin supplement	
Mr Rossi			2 / day x 5 days
Mr Metcalf	1 teaspoon		when needed
Mr Takahashi		painkiller	

Unit 6 Diagnosis table

	bad strain	fracture	infection
swelling	yes	yes	yes
tenderness	yes	yes	yes
bruising	yes	yes	no
skin hurt	no	no	yes
redness	yes	no	yes
deformity	no	yes	no
movement → pain	yes	yes	no
hold weight	no	no	yes

Unit 15 p.107

The Christian Scientist faith healer

Alma Gluck belongs to an American religious group called The Christian Science Church. She took a two week course to learn to be a healer.

According to the Christian Scientists, illness is not made by God but by the Devil, so healing happens by being closer to God through prayer.

Alma believes that illness can be cured by prayer and strength of mind. She gives consultations by letter and email, and argues sick thoughts out of the mind.

Alma charges a small amount of money for a consultation on medical or personal matters, and her successes are published in the *Christian Science Journal*. It must be said that, in a test, a group of patients were prayed for and another group were not prayed for. Prayer made no difference.

Student B's questions:

- How did Pak Haji Haron learn to be a healer?
- What does Pak Haji believe causes illness?
- How does Pak Haji cure illness?
- Does everyone believe in Pak Haji's power?

Grammar reference

1 Present Simple v Present Continuous

Present Simple

Positive

I/You/We/They	**work**	in a team.
He/She/It	**works**	in a team.

= subject + infinitive

Negative

I/You/We/They	**don't**	**make** beds in my job.
He/She/It	**doesn't**	**make** beds in my job.

= subject + ***do not (don't) / does not (doesn't)*** + infinitive

Questions		Short answers
Do I/you/we/they	**want** a job?	Yes, I/you/we/ they **do**. he/she **does**.
Does he/she	**want** a job?	No, I/you/we/ they **don't**. he/she **doesn't**.

= ***Do / Does*** + subject + infinitive

We use the Present Simple to describe routines and duties, and to talk about things that are true at any time.

A ward orderly ***helps*** *around the wards.*
A surgeon ***doesn't drive*** *an ambulance.*
Do *anaesthetists* ***deliver*** *babies?*

Present Continuous

Positive

I	**am working**.
You/We/They	**are working**.
He/She/It	**is working**.

= subject + ***am / are / is*** + ***-ing*** form

Negative

I	**am not ('m not)**	**studying**.
You/We/They	**are not (aren't)**	**studying**.
He/She/It	**is not (isn't)**	**studying**.

= Subject + ***'m not / aren't / isn't*** + ***-ing*** form

Questions			Short answers
Am	I	**working** hard?	Yes, I **am**.
Are	you/we/ they	**working** hard?	you/we/ they **are**.
Is	he/she/it	**working** hard?	Yes, he/she it **is**. No, I'**m not**. you/we/they **aren't**. he/she/it **isn't**.

= ***Am / Are / Is*** + subject + ***-ing*** form

We use the Present Continuous to talk about things that are happening now, or around now. We often use a time expression such as *at the moment* or *this week*.

*At the moment, I'****m doing*** *a part-time course.*
Which department ***are*** *you* ***working*** *in this week?*

Note that there are some verbs which are not used in the Present Continuous. These are *have* (= possess), and thinking and feeling verbs such as *dislike, hate, know, like, love, remember,* and *want*.
I ***want*** *a new job.* NOT ~~*I'm wanting*~~ …

2 Prepositions of place and movement

Prepositions of place

We use the following prepositions to describe where something or someone is: *in, on, on top of, at the top / bottom of, inside/outside, near, next to, in front of, behind, opposite, under, over, at, on the left / right (of)*

The stairs are ***near*** *the reception.*
You'll find the restaurant ***on*** *the ground floor.*

Prepositions of movement

We use the following prepositions to describe movement: *along, up, down, into, out of, away, from, to, through, across, along, past, back to, around, left / right*

With prepositions of movement, we use verbs such as *bring, carry, come, get, go, push, run, take,* and *walk*.

You walk ***through*** *Orthopaedics to get to the exit.*
The porter brought the wheelchair ***up to*** *the ward.*

Go ***up to*** *the third floor. Ward 6 is* ***opposite*** *the lift.*
movement place

3 Past Simple v Past Continuous

Past Simple

Positive

I/You/We/They/He/She **slipped** on some ice.

= subject + Past Simple

Negative

I/You/We/They/He/She **didn't break** any bones.

= subject + ***did*** + ***not (didn't)*** + infinitive

Questions	**Short answers**
Did I/you/we/they/ he/she **fall**?	Yes, I/you/we/they/ he/she **did**.
	No, I/you/we/they/ she **didn't**.

= ***Did*** + subject + infinitive

Note that the *he/she/it* form does not change at all in the positive and negative or in questions.

Spelling rules for Past Simple

Infinitive		**Past Simple**
most verbs	infinitive + ***-ed***	*wait* → *waited*
verbs ending in ***-e***	infinitive + ***-d***	*arrive* → *arrived*
verbs ending in consonant + ***-y***	***-y*** → ***-i*** + ***-ed***	*try* → *tried*
verbs ending in vowel + consonant	double the consonant + ***-ed***	*stop* → *stopped*
except if final consonant is ***-w***, ***-x***, or ***-y***		*delay* → *delayed*

Many verbs have an irregular Past Simple form, which has to be learned separately. These include:

be – was	*break – broke*	*have – had*
fall – fell	*go – went*	*take – took*

We use the Past Simple to talk about an action that happened at a particular point in the past. We often use past time expressions such as *yesterday*, *last week*, and *in* + month / season / year.

*The doctor **examined** my leg **yesterday**.*

Past Continuous

Positive

I/He/She **was waiting** for the doctor.

You/We/They **were waiting** for the doctor.

= subject + ***was / were*** + ***-ing*** form

Negative

I/He/She **was not (wasn't) working** here then.

You/We/They **were not (weren't) working** here then.

= subject + ***was / were*** + ***not*** + ***-ing*** form

Questions

Was he **listening** to him?

Were you **listening** to him?

= ***Was / Were*** + subject + ***-ing*** form

We use the Past Continuous to talk about an action that was happening in the background when another event happened. It is often used in a sentence with *when* + Past Simple.

*He **was getting off** the bus **when** he **slipped**.*

We can change the order of the sentence.

*He **slipped when** he **was getting off** the bus.*

***When** he **was getting off** the bus, he slipped.*

4 Instructions

Instructions

There are several ways of telling someone what to do.

The Imperative is the most direct type of command.

Positive

Check the patient's temperature.

= infinitive

Negative

Do not / Don't move him.

= ***Do*** + ***not (Don't)*** + infinitive

We can use the imperative form *make sure* to emphasize the importance of an instruction.

***Make sure** you dispose of gloves safely.*
***Make sure** the dosage doesn't exceed 200 ml.*

Asking for instructions

We can use the Present Simple, *have to*, *shall*, and *should* to ask for instructions.

How **do** I **set** the charge on the defibrillator?

Where exactly **do** I **have to apply** the pads?

Shall I **tie** the bandage tightly?

Should I **remove** the burnt clothing?

= (question word +) ***do / shall / should*** + *I* + infinitive

5 Making comparisons

Comparative adjectives

We use comparative adjectives to make a comparison between two things or situations.

Adjective type		Example	Comparative
one syllable	+ *-er*	*mild*	*milder*
one syllable ending in *-e*	+ *-r*	*safe*	*safer*
two syllables ending in *-y*	*-y* → *-ier*	*easy*	*easier*
two or more syllables	+ ***more***	*painful*	***more*** painful
irregular		*good* *bad*	***better*** ***worse***

The pain is ***milder*** *now.*
Treatments today are ***more effective****.*

When we compare two things or situations directly, we use the comparative + *than*.

The fracture is ***more serious than*** *we realized.*

The opposite of *more* is *less*.

The treatment was ***less successful*** *than we had hoped.*

To make a comparison stronger, we use *much* before the comparative.

I'm feeling ***much better*** *today.*
My leg is ***much less painful*** *than it was yesterday.*

Superlative adjectives

We use superlative adjectives to make a comparison between more than two things.

Adjective type		Example	Superlative
one syllable	+ ***the -est***	*mild*	***the mildest***
one syllable ending in *-e*	+ ***the -st***	*safe*	***the safest***
two syllables ending in *-y*	+ ***the -y*** → ***-iest***	*easy*	***the easiest***
two or more syllables	+ ***the most***	*painful*	***the most painful***
irregular		*good* *bad*	***the best*** ***the worst***

This is ***the safest*** *treatment available.*
He had ***the most serious*** *type of fracture.*

The opposite of *the most* is *the least*.

This drug has ***the least severe*** *side effects.*

We can use *more*, *less*, and *most* + noun to talk about relative amounts.

More women *choose to give birth by Caesarean section nowadays. (more* = a higher number than before*)*

You will feel ***less pain*** *if you use gas and air. (less = a reduced amount)*

Most people *aren't very good at dealing with pain. (most* = the majority*)*

6 Question forms

There are several ways of asking a question. These are generally divided into those that require only a *yes / no* answer, and *wh-* questions, which ask for specific information.

yes / no questions

These begin with an auxiliary verb, such as *do / did*, *am / is / are*, *have / has*, *can*, *could*, *will*, *must*, etc.

Present Simple

Do you **have** a sore throat?

= ***Do / Does*** + subject + infinitive

Past Simple

Did she **see** the doctor yesterday?

= ***Did*** + subject + infinitive

Present Perfect

Have you **been** sick?

= ***Have / Has*** + subject + past participle

The verb *be* and modal verbs such as *can / could / must / should / will* are not formed with *do / does / did*.

Present Simple

Is the hospital near here?

= Present Simple of ***be*** + subject

Present Continuous

Is the pain **getting** worse?

= Present Simple of ***be*** + subject + *-ing* form

Modals

Could you **give** me your name?

= Modal verb + subject + infinitive

wh- questions

We begin a question with a question word when we want specific information. Question words include *what, who, when, where, why, which,* and *how*. We can use *how* in other combinations, such as *how much, how many, how long, how far, how safe*, etc. The question words *what, which, how much, how many* can be followed by a noun.

What does my x-ray show?

How much pain can you feel?

In the two sentences above, the question word is the object of the main verb. Note that *what, who, which, how much, how many* can also be the subject of a question. In this case, the word order is the same as in a positive sentence.

Who told you that?

= question word (+ subject) + verb

Question tags

A question tag is a short question that we add at the end of a statement. We use question tags when we want someone to confirm information. The verb used in a question tag depends on which verb is used in the statement.

In a positive question, the question tag is usually negative.

You'll tell me if you're uncomfortable, ***won't you?***

In a negative question, the question tag is usually positive.

My face is less swollen today, ***isn't it?***

Questions without a verb

In conversation, we can make a question without using a verb if we think the meaning is clear enough.

Sure? (= Are you sure?)
Any questions? (= Do you have any questions?)

7 *will*

Positive

The new hospital **will open** in 2012.

= subject + ***will ('ll)*** + infinitive

Negative

Your aunt **will not / won't be able to** walk.

= subject + ***will*** + ***not (won't)*** + infinitive

Questions

Which care home **will** I **go** into?

Will you **come** with me?

= (question word +) ***will*** + subject + infinitive

Short answers

Yes, I/you/he/she/it/we/they **will**.

No, I/you/he/she/it/we/they **won't**.

The short form *'ll* is found most commonly after a pronoun.

I'll ***get*** *you some water.*

We use *will* in a variety of contexts, for example
to talk about things that we know are definitely going to happen in the future

Your mother's memory ***will get*** *worse as she gets older.*

to make predictions and to express expectations about the future

Prediction	*I think most people* ***will live*** *to 100.*
	I don't think I'll ***enjoy*** *being old.*
NOT	*~~I think I won't enjoy~~ being old.*
Expectation	*I hope I'll* ***be*** *able to enjoy my old age.*

to express a decision that we have made suddenly

You look tired. I'll ***get*** *you a coffee.*

to make promises and requests

Don't worry – I ***won't be*** *away too long.*
Will *you* ***come*** *to the restaurant with me?*

Note that we can offer to do something by using the form *Shall I* + infinitive.

***Shall I call** the doctor for you?*

Remember that we can use *will / won't* in First Conditional sentences.

*If my cold gets worse, **I'll** go to the doctor.*
*We **won't** have the meeting if nobody is here.*

8 *should / shouldn't*

Giving advice

We use *should* and *should not (shouldn't)* to give advice and to offer an opinion.

Positive

A diabetic **should eat** a balanced diet.

= subject + ***should*** + infinitive

Negative

An obese person **shouldn't eat** sugary food.

= subject + ***should*** + ***not (shouldn't)*** + infinitive

Questions	**Short answers**
Should I **eat** a lot of bread?	Yes, you **should**.
	No, you **shouldn't**.

What **should** I **do** to improve my diet?

= ***Should*** + subject + infinitive
= question word + ***should*** + subject

We do not use the auxiliary *do / does* to form the negative and questions.

NOT ~~*Do I should*~~ *eat a lot of bread?*

Should is much weaker than *must*.

*You **must** take some exercise.* (= or your health will suffer)

*You **should** take some exercise.* (= it is a good idea)

We can offer advice by using other expressions.

***It would be a good idea to** see a nutritionist.*
***If I were you, I'd** take a multivitamin tablet.*
***I'd** take a multivitamin tablet **if I were you**.*

9 Zero and First Conditional

Zero Conditional

We use the Zero Conditional to talk about facts that are generally true, especially in a scientific context.

If you **expose** a wound to air, it **heals** more quickly.

= *If* + Present Simple	+ Present Simple
if **clause**	**main clause**

We can use *when* instead of *if*.

***When** you expose a wound to air, it heals more quickly.*

First Conditional

We use the First Conditional to talk about possible future situations.

If you **don't eat** less,	you'll get fat.
= ***If*** + Present Simple	+ ***will ('ll)*** + infinitive
if **clause**	**main clause**

We can also use *when* + Present Simple instead of *if*. In First Conditional sentences, *when* is slightly stronger than *if*, and means *only when* or *once*.

*Patient care will improve **when** there are enough nurses.*
***When** there are enough nurses, patient care will improve.*

We use *unless* + Present Simple to mean *if not*.

***Unless** we act quickly, he will die.*
*He'll die **unless** we act quickly.*

Remember that in Conditional sentences *if*, *when*, and *unless* are not followed by *will*.

10 Expressing possibility

may, might, could

We use *may*, *might*, and *could* when we are not certain about future situations, such as plans and schedules.

Positive

The hospital **may / might / could** close next year.

= subject + ***may / might / could*** + infinitive

Negative

The patient **may not / might not** want to eat.

= subject + ***may / might*** + ***not*** + infinitive

Questions

What symptoms **might / could** he have?

Might / could she lose consciousness?

= (question word +) ***might / could*** + subject + infinitive

Other ways of expressing possibility

We can express possibility in other ways.

Perhaps, maybe, it's possible that are used at the beginning of a sentence or clause.

Perhaps and *maybe* have the same meaning, while *it's possible that* is slightly more formal.

*His breathing has slowed down. **Perhaps / Maybe** I should call the nurse.*

*If she's asleep whenever you visit, **it's possible that** she's not sleeping at night.*

11 Talking about obligation

We use *must / mustn't* and *have to / don't have to* to talk about obligation.

must

Positive

We **must** stop the spread of MRSA.

= subject + ***must*** + infinitive

Negative

Theatre staff **must not (mustn't)** wear make-up.

= subject + ***must*** + ***not*** + infinitive

Must is not followed by *to*.

*You **must** use sterile instruments.* NOT *You ~~must to use~~ ...*

We do not form the negative with the auxiliary *do / does*.

*Visitors **mustn't** smoke in the hospital.*
NOT *Visitors ~~don't must~~ ...*

The question form of *must* is not frequently used. It is more common to use the question form of *have to*.

We use *must / mustn't* when giving rules or telling someone what to do or what not to do.

*Nurses **must** use an antimicrobial agent.*
*You **mustn't** leave spillages unreported.*

have to

Positive

Visitors **have to** leave the ward by 20.00.

= subject + ***have / has to*** + infinitive

Negative

Nurses **don't have to** wear gloves all the time.

= subject + ***don't / doesn't have to*** + infinitive

Questions	Short answers
Do I **have to** wash my hands?	Yes, you **do**.
Does he **have to** have surgery?	No, he **doesn't**.

= ***Do / Does*** + subject + ***have to*** + infinitive

We use *have / has to* + infinitive in positive sentences and questions to talk about things that we are obliged to do because of the circumstances, or because someone tells us to.

We use *don't have to / doesn't have to* + infinitive to talk about actions that are not necessary.

*Nurses **don't have to** clean the floor. That is the job of the cleaners.*

need to

Positive

You **need to** follow procedures.

= subject + ***need to*** + infinitive

Negative

Mrs Hassan **doesn't need to** be in a separate room.

= subject + ***don't / doesn't need to*** + infinitive

Questions	Short answers
Does this patient **need to** be moved to another ward?	Yes, she **does**.
Do I **need to** wear a mask?	No, you **don't**.

= ***Do / Does*** + subject + ***need to*** + infinitive

Need is formed in the same way as a regular verb, with *-s* added to the *he/she/it* forms in the positive, and the auxiliary *do* used in negative sentences and questions.

We use *need(s) to* + infinitive to say that an action is necessary. We use *don't / doesn't need to* in a similar way to *don't / doesn't have to*.

need + *-ing*

We use *need* + *-ing* to say what tasks it is necessary to do.

*The floor **needs cleaning**.*

= subject + ***need / needs*** + verb + ***-ing***

*The beds **don't need changing**.*

12 Present Perfect v Past Simple

Present Perfect

Positive

There **have been** many changes in this hospital over the past year.

= subject + ***have / has*** + past participle

Negative

Mrs Shaw **hasn't taken** her medication.

= subject + ***have / has*** + ***not (haven't / hasn't)*** + past participle

Questions	Short answers
Have you **had** any visitors?	Yes, we **have**. he/she/it **has**.
	No, we **haven't**. he/she/it **hasn't**.

= ***Have / Has*** + subject + past participle

We use the Present Perfect to talk about an action that happened during a period of time from the past to the present. It is not important exactly when it occurred. We often use time expressions such as *this year / month / week, today,* or *before*.

*Dr Bright **hasn't carried out** this type of surgery **before**.*
*Have you seen Sister Jones **today**?*

It is also used to give news of a recent, finished event.

*Mrs Linton **has had** a baby girl.* (= This happened recently but we do not know when. It is the event that is more important.)

It also describes a past action that has a result in the present.

*He **has had** the operation, and is in the recovery room.*

ever and *never*

Ever is used in questions to mean 'at some time in a person's life'.

Never is used in negative statements to mean 'not at any time in a person's life'.

*Have you **ever** had an operation?*
*She has **never** worked in this hospital.*

for, *since*, and *yet*

We can use both the Past Simple and the Present Perfect with *for* and the Present Perfect with *since* to answer the question *How long?*

for + period of time, to say how long a period of time lasted.

for eight months, for two hours

since + point in time to say when a period of time started.

since 2 o'clock, since 1993, since yesterday

Present Perfect: *I've worked here **for** a few months.*

Past Simple: *I was on the Children's Ward **for** six weeks.*

Present Perfect: *I've worked here **since** I was eighteen.*

We use *yet* in negative Present Perfect sentences and questions to talk about things that we expect to happen.

*They haven't arrived at work **yet**.*
*Has she talked to the consultant **yet**?*

Yet always appears at the end of the sentence.

Past Simple

Positive

I **failed** the exam twice.

= subject + Past Simple

Negative

We **didn't understand** what the psychiatrist said.

= subject + ***did*** + ***not (didn't)*** + infinitive

Questions	Short answers
Did you **have** a local anaesthetic?	Yes, I/he/she/it/we/ they **did**.
	No, I/he/she/it/we/ they **didn't**.

= ***Did*** + subject + infinitive

Note that the *he/she/it* form does not change at all in the positive and negative or in questions.

We use the Past Simple to talk about an action or event that happened at a particular point in the past.

My second placement **was** *in Casualty.*

With the Past Simple we can use expressions such as *in* + year / month / season, *last, before, after,* and *ago.* Note that *ago* comes at the end of the time phrase.

She first **saw** *a psychiatrist two years* **ago**.

We can use both the Past Simple and Present Perfect to talk about an action that happened today. However, when used with a Present Perfect verb, *today* means that the action may continue or be repeated, but the Past Simple suggests that the action is finished, or that the day is nearly over.

Present Perfect	*I've* **seen** *the doctor twice today.* (= it is possible I may see him / her again)
Past Simple	*I* **saw** *the doctor twice today.* (= it is unlikely that I will see him / her again today)

13 The Passive

The Passive is used when it is not important or relevant to mention who performs / performed an action (the 'agent'). It is often used when we describe medical and other procedures.

Present Passive

Positive

Temperature and heart rate **are monitored**.

=subject + ***am / is / are*** + past participle

Negative

The heart **is not paralysed** by the anaesthetic.

=subject + ***am / is / are*** + ***not*** + past participle

Questions	**Short answers**
Are dentures **removed** before an operation?	Yes, they **are**. No, they **aren't**.

=***Am / Is / Are*** + subject + past participle

We use the Present Passive to talk about procedures in general.

Past Passive

Positive

The patient **was prepared** for theatre.

= subject + ***was / were*** + past participle

Negative

She **wasn't diagnosed** until this morning.

= subject + ***was / were*** + ***not*** (wasn't / weren't) + past participle

Questions	**Short answers**
Were the correct procedures **followed**?	Yes, they **were**. No, they **weren't**.

= ***Was / Were*** + subject + past participle

We use the Past Passive to talk about procedures that happened at a specific point in the past. As with the Present Passive, we use the Past Passive when the action is more important than the agent, or where the agent is not known.

Active or Passive

It is often possible to use an Active form of the Present Simple or Past Simple instead of a Passive form, with little difference in meaning. However, with an Active verb it is necessary to say who performed the action.

Passive	*The ventilator is monitored.*
Active	***Someone*** *monitors the ventilator.*

If we want to say who performs an action in a Passive sentence, we can use *by*.

The ventilator **is monitored by** *the anaesthetist.*

14 *be going to* v Present Continuous for future

be going to

Positive

I **am going to** change my clothes.

= subject + ***am / is / are going to*** + infinitive

Negative

He **is not (isn't) going to** change his mind.

= subject + ***am / is / are*** + ***not going to*** + infinitive

Questions	**Short answers**
Is the operation **going to** be cancelled?	Yes, it **is**.
	No, it **isn't**.

= ***Am / Is / Are*** + subject + ***going to*** + infinitive

We use *be going to* + infinitive to talk about general intentions and plans.

*She **isn't going to** apply for that job.*

We use *be going to* + infinitive to predict the future based on information that we have now.

*That's a big needle. The injection**'s going to hurt**, isn't it?*

We use ***be going to*** + infinitive to talk about actions that we are about to perform.

***I'm going to check** your blood pressure now, so try to relax.*

We often use future time expressions with *be going to*. These include *tomorrow, this afternoon / week, next Friday / month / year, on Thursday, at* 3.00.

***Are** you **going** to visit the hospital **tomorrow**?*

Present Continuous

For information on how to form the Present Continuous, see p.116.

As well as using the Present Continuous for current actions, we can also use the Present Continuous to talk about future arrangements and schedules.

To avoid confusion, it is common to use future time expressions, such as *tomorrow, next week, in two hours, at three o'clock, later today.*

*I'**m seeing** the consultant **this afternoon**.*

Because the Present Continuous relates to appointments, it is generally used for the near future.

15 Giving reasons

There are several ways of giving a reason for something, for example *for, to, so that, because, so, that's why.*

We use *for* and *to* to talk about the purpose of an object, i.e. to say what we use it for.

for + noun	*Plants are often used **for pain relief**.*
for + *-ing*	*Plants are often used **for relieving** pain.*
to + infinitive	*Plants are often used **to relieve** pain.*

We use *so that* to talk about the purpose of an action.

so that + clause	*Many people take vitamins **so that** they can stay healthy.*

We use *so* to talk about the result of an action or decision.

so + clause	*I felt tired, **so I bought** some vitamins.*

We use *because* to introduce a reason for an action.

because + clause	*I'm in London **because I've got an appointment** with my chiropracter.*

We use *that's why* at the beginning of a sentence or clause, after a dash, full stop, or semicolon, to explain the result of an action or decision. It has a similar meaning to *so*.

that's why + clause	*I've got an appointment with my chiropractor – **that's why** I'm in London.*

Listening scripts

Unit 1

Scrub up

1 scrub nurse
2 cardiologist
3 receptionist
4 surgeon
5 physiotherapist
6 radiologist
7 consultant
8 anaesthetist
9 paediatrician
10 porter

Listening 1 – An admission

1

P=paramedic, B=Mrs Benson

P Can you hear me? Mrs Benson?
B Yes. Where am I? What happened?
P You're in my ambulance. You've had a fall and we're taking you to hospital.
B Yes, now I remember.

2

R=radiologist, B=Mrs Benson

R Right, Mrs Benson. We're going to have a closer look at your heart. Have you had an x-ray before?
B Yes, I broke my leg once.

3

S=sister, B=Mrs Benson

S Hello, Mrs Benson. How do you feel?
B Terrible. I've got a terrible headache and I need to use the toilet.
S OK. I'll draw the curtains and you can use a bedpan. Doctor Bright is coming to have a look at you in a moment.

4

C=consultant, B=Mrs Benson

C Mrs Benson. We've been worried about you but I've got good news. The x-ray shows your heart is clear and Sister says your blood pressure is back to normal. How are you feeling?
B I feel fine now.
C Good. I'm going to prescribe some medicine and I'm discharging you.

5

R=receptionist, B=Mrs Benson

R Right, Mrs Benson, so you want to make an outpatient's appointment for next week?
B Yes, please.
R Thursday at four?
B Fine.
R Good. Next Thursday at four o'clock to see Doctor Lee in Outpatients.

Listening 2 – A job interview

I=Interviewer, R=Rachel

I OK Rachel, let's start the interview with a few questions. Your CV says that you're working at City Hospital.
R Yes, in the operating theatres.
I Are you a fully-qualified scrub nurse?
R Not yet. At the moment I'm doing a part-time course and working at the same time. I'm preparing for the exams, which are next month. It's hard, especially when I'm working a night shift and going to lectures next day.
I Tell us about your job. What do you do every day?
R Well, I assist the surgeons. I prepare the instruments for surgery and I help with the operations.
I What do you like best about being a scrub nurse?
R Well, I like watching operations, but it's the contact with the patients that's most rewarding.
I So, why are you applying for a new job?
R Well I'm very happy in my job, but I want more responsibility.

Unit 2

Pronunciation

1 Cardiology
2 Pharmacy
3 Gynaecology
4 Neurology
5 Obstetrics
6 Orthopaedics
7 Paediatrics
8 Pathology
9 Dermatology
10 Physiotherapy
11 Renal Unit
12 Surgery

Listening 1 – Directions

1

P=physiotherapist, M=man

P Go out of here and the door you want is just opposite. Go in through the door and give your prescription to the man behind the counter.
M So it's just outside here?
P Yes, just across the corridor.

2

P=porter, M=man

P Go into the hospital through these swing doors. Go along the corridor, take the first right, and it's the second door on your left.
M Through the swing doors, down the corridor, first right, second left.
P That's it.
M Thanks.

3

R=receptionist, V=visitor

R Go along this corridor and turn left at the end. Go along the next corridor, take the second left and go all the way along that corridor. The ward you want is right at the end, straight in front of you.
V Thank you.

Listening 2 – The porter's office

H=head porter, W=porter Wahid, B=porter Brian

H Sure, right away. Hello, Wahid? Are you there?
W Yes.
H Where are you?
W I'm at the top of the stairs outside Physiotherapy.
H OK. Can you go across the hospital to the stores and collect a box of disposable syringes and take them to the Path lab? And also, a wheelchair.
W Box of syringes and a wheelchair. OK.
H Porters' office … Yes, Doctor Sayed, I'll do that … Hello. Brian?
B I'm here.
H Doctor Sayed from Cardiology wants a porter. They've got a lot of empty bottles – can you take them to the bins?
B Where are they?
H Outside Cardiology near the swing doors on the main corridor … and then take a stretcher to Ward four, collect a patient, and take him to Radiology … Hello. Porter's office …

Unit 3

Scrub up

1 I was at a party, and one of my friends gave me a little white tablet. I'd had a few drinks and I was feeling good, and I took it, even though I didn't know what it was. It made me feel, like, really weird. I could see and hear really strange things, and it scared me. I still don't feel normal today, and I'm very worried.
2 It's not due until next month, but when I was washing up this morning there

was a little blood. It worried me. Then I got these pains.

3 I was working high up on a ladder. My foot slipped and I fell. I hit my head but there's no blood and I don't feel too bad.

4 I was walking by the river, and I think I stepped on it and it bit me. I don't know what type it was but it was long and silver with a black head.

5 I was looking in the mirror and I saw this big spot on my face. I checked it on the Internet and I'm sure I've got cancer. Do you think I'm going to die?

Listening – A patient record form

M=Mustapha, N=nurse

1

N Mustapha, isn't it?
M Yes, that's right.
N So, what happened to you?
M I was working on a ladder. It was raining and I slipped and fell.
N Did you hit your head?
M Yes. I saw stars and felt sick at first. But now it's OK.
N I see. You may have concussion. First, I'll take down your details and fill in this form. So, what's your surname?
M It's Hussein.
N Can you spell that for me?
M H-U-double S-E-I-N.
N What's your occupation?
M I'm a painter.
N Right. What's your date of birth?
M First of the ninth, eighty-two.
N One, nine, eighty-two ... and where were you born?
M Karachi, Pakistan.
N What's your marital status?
M Sorry?
N Are you married?
M No, I'm single.
N And do you have a contact telephone number for your next of kin?
M 07709-401229 – it's my brother, Yusuf.
N Do you smoke?
M Yes.
N How many do you smoke a day?
M Twenty a day.
N Uh huh. Do you drink?
M No.
N Right. Are you allergic to anything?
M No.
N Now, family history. Do any of your close family suffer from any of the following – mental illness?
M No.
N Diabetes?
M My mother's parents are both diabetic.
N Maternal grandparents ... diabetes. Tuberculosis?
M No.
N HIV / AIDS?
M No.

Unit 4

Listening – Instructions

P=paramedic, N=nurse

P Roger, Oscar Lima Charlie, we're with the patient now. Possible cardiac arrest. Stand by, over. Nurse, check his pulse.
N There's no pulse.
P OK.
N He's not breathing.
P It is cardiac arrest. Give him CPR. I'll talk you through it, OK?
N OK.
P Give him mouth-to-mouth first. Support his head. That's it, lift it back. Right, hold his nose closed, then open his mouth and breathe strongly into it. Give two full breaths into his mouth. OK?
N Right.
P Let his chest fall again. Nothing?
N Nothing.
P Turn his head. That's right. Put your hand on his chest. Now put your other hand on top of your first hand. OK?
N OK.
P Push down a little ... and release ... Do it again. One ... two ... three ... four.
N How many times should I do it?
P Repeat the procedure fifteen times ... OK. Check his pulse again. Anything?
N No. Still no pulse.
P OK. Don't wait. Use the AED. Set it at a charge of two hundred.
N Right. It's two hundred.
P Apply the pads to his chest.
N Where do I put them?
P Put one above the heart and one below. Stand clear of his body. Make sure you don't touch him. Call 'everybody clear' and then press the buttons and hold for two seconds. OK?
N OK. Everybody clear!
P Check his pulse again.
N Nothing.
P Are you sure?
N Yes. There's no pulse.
P OK– repeat the procedure. Same charge – two hundred.
N Right. Everybody clear! Ah hah! There's a pulse.
P Good. Well done. Now set up an IV and give him Lidocaine.
N How much shall I give him?
P One hundred mil over two minutes.

Unit 5

Listening 1 – A pain chart

N=nurse, P=patient

1

N How are you today, Kath? Are you still in pain?
P Well, there's pain around my stomach. It's quite bad.
N What kind of pain is it?
P It's a burning pain.
N Do you always have it?
P It never goes away. Never.
N Is it getting worse?
P No, it's staying about the same.

2

N How's the pain today, Emir?
P It's much better, thanks. I have a slight pain, just here in my right side, but it's a lot less painful than yesterday.
N How often do you get the pain?
P Only every now and again – it comes and goes.

3

N Do you still have a headache?
P Yes, I've got this throbbing pain in my head.
N Whereabouts?
P In the forehead, right between my eyes.
N Does it feel the same all the time?
P No, it changes. Sometimes it's not too bad, but it gets a bit worse at night.
N And it's getting more severe now, is it?
P A little bit, yes.
N I'll get you some painkillers.

4

N So, you're having pains in your arm.
P Yes, I keep getting this terrible pain down my left arm. It starts at the shoulder and shoots down to my hand.
N Is this all the time?
P No, but most of the time, but it's agonizing when it happens.

N When did this start?
P It started yesterday, but it's much more severe today.
N Mm, we'd better take a look …

Listening 2 – Pain relief

J=Janice, K=Karen

J Hello, my name's Janice.
K Hello, Janice. I'm Karen.
J Hi, Karen. Boy or girl?
K A boy. And yours?
J A girl.
K Lovely. I think we gave birth at the same time last night, didn't we?
J Yes. I heard you.
K Was I making so much noise? Well, it was the pain.
J Didn't you have any pain relief?
K Oh, yes. I had just gas and air at first. It does relieve the pain a bit, but the effect wears off very quickly. It makes you feel so light-headed if you have too much. It made me feel sick too. Anyway, when the pain became unbearable, I had an epidural.
J Did that help you cope with the pain?
K It took away the pain completely! My whole lower half went numb! It was great. How about you?
J This was my third, so the pain was easier to bear. I did breathing exercises. I decided to have gas and air if the pain got worse, but I didn't need it. I had an epidural last time, but I didn't like losing all sensation. This time I wanted to feel the birth.
K I'm sorry, Janice – I think you must be mad.

Pronunciation

air	hurt	doctor
care	nurse	appointment
first	hair	tumour
ulcer	worse	where

Unit 6

Scrub up

diarrhoea	numbness	bruising
nausea	aching	tiredness
cough		

Listening 1 – Symptoms

1

N=nurse, P=patient

N How does it feel? A little deformed, isn't it?
P Yes, there's a huge lump just above the ankle. And there's quite a lot of bruising. And just here, it's very swollen.
N Is it painful when you move it?
P Yes, *very*.
N Can you move your toes?
P It's difficult, they're numb – I can't feel them at all.

2

N How are you feeling?
P I feel so hot. What does the thermometer say?
N Yes, you do have fever. Your temperature is a little over 38. Have you got a sore throat?
P Yes, it hurts when I talk.
N I can see you have spots. Any redness?
P Yes, my chest and back are all red.
N And do you feel tired?
P Yes, constant tiredness. And my legs feel achy, too.

3

N How's it going?
P I'll be glad when this is over. Doing anything is really tiring.
N Oh dear. Do you feel dizzy at all?
P Yes, some days I feel dizzy and sometimes sick.
N When do you feel sick, mostly?
P In the mornings. And I'm very constipated – haven't been to the toilet for three days. Sorry to moan.
N That's all right. We all need a good moan sometimes. What about pain?
P No. No pain.

Language spot

N=nurse, P=patient

1

N OK, Mrs Hales?
P Not too bad, thanks.
N What happened to you?
P I had a fall.
N Where does it hurt?
P From my wrist to my elbow.
N What about your shoulder?
P That's fine.
N Let's have a look – swollen, isn't it!
P Yes, it is, isn't it.
N You've had an x-ray, haven't you?
P Yes, I have.
N Anything broken?
P No, just bruising.
N You aren't on any other medication, are you?
P No, I'm not.

2

N How are you feeling?
P Not bad, thanks – a bit sore.
N What happened to you?
P I fell off my bike.
N Where does it hurt?
P Here, around my wrist.
N Can you move your fingers?
P Yes, I can, slowly.
N Is it painful?
P Yes, *very*! I've also got a cut on my leg – look.
N Oh, that's deep, isn't it!
P Yes, it *is* deep. Will I need stitches?
N Maybe. Have you had stitches before?
P No, never – and I don't want any!
N You've seen the doctor, haven't you?
P No, I haven't seen him yet.

Listening 2 – A helpline call

N=nurse, M=mother of child

N National Health line. How can I help?
M Oh, hello. It's my little boy – he's seven. I'm worried because he's got a terrible cough.
N OK. So, can you describe the cough? I mean, does he wheeze when he coughs?
M Yes, he does.
N Does he wheeze when he breathes in or when he breathes out?
M Mm … when he breathes in. Yes, not when he breathes out.
N When he coughs, does he cough up any blood?
M No, but sometimes when he coughs, he vomits.
N I see. Does he have any allergies?
M No. I don't think so.
N Right. Does he have a fever? Have you taken his temperature?
M Yes, he's burning. The thermometer says 37 degrees.

Unit 7

Listening 1 – A care home

E=Edith, B=Betty

E ... and that nurse – Barbara– I don't like her.

B Sssh, Edith, she'll hear you!

E I don't care if she hears me, Betty. She speaks to me like a child –'That's a lovely jumper you're wearing, Edith. Don't you look pretty!' She should call me 'Mrs Taylor', thank you very much! No respect, you see! And she comes into my room *without* knocking. You've got no privacy, no self-respect.

B Oh, cheer up. Let's go over and play some bingo.

E Bingo? I'm not interested in playing bingo with a group of old ladies! It's not very stimulating, is it! They're all so slow because they've got nothing to keep their minds busy, and their medication slows them up some more. They just sit in front of the television all day.

B Are you coming on the trip to the seaside next week?

E No, I don't like coach trips. I just want to go home. I miss my independence. I miss my kitchen. And that's another thing – I don't like the food here.

B Yes, but we don't have to cook or do the washing ourselves. I like this care home. It's clean. The staff are very professional, and it's nice to know there's someone near in an emergency. And there's always someone to talk to. I'm never lonely.

E Well, I don't want some young nurse telling me what I can and cannot do. I want children around me. It's not natural living like this – everybody here is old!

Language spot

2

A Will you pass me my glasses? Then I'll be able to see the television.

B Here you are.

A Thanks. Oh, and will you do me another favour?

B What now?

A Will you help me stand up? I want to switch it on.

B You'll probably fall over. I'll do it.

A Thank you. I won't trouble you again.

Listening 2 – Assessing a patient

N=nurse, D=daughter of elderly patient

N Your mum is going to be fine. There are no bones broken.

D Oh, that's good news. I was worried because she's a bit frail.

N Is that the first time she's had a fall?

D Yes, it is.

N I'm doing an assessment of her, so I've got some questions. Can you help me with them?

D Of course, go ahead.

N Right. Number one. How's your mother's hearing? Does she wear a hearing aid?

D Yes, she is very deaf. Without her hearing aid she hears nothing at all.

N OK. Can she see OK?

D With glasses, yes – very well for her age.

N Right. Mobility? Are her movements very restricted?

D Well, she needs help getting dressed and getting in and out of the bath. She has a walking stick and she's very independent. But some days she gets dizzy and can be unsteady on her feet. She uses a scooter for shopping.

N The next question is about sleeping habits. Does she have any sleep disorders?

D She has a lot of problems. She often wakes up in the middle of the night. Sometimes she can't sleep at all. She takes sleeping pills, and of course she has a nap every now and then during the day.

N OK. Any problems eating? Can your mother feed herself?

D Oh yes, she's fine at the table.

N Right. Continence is next. Does she ever wet herself?

D Well, that happens quite often. Probably because she doesn't like using a bedpan and she can't get to the bathroom. We have to make sure she has an incontinence pad.

N Does she ever show signs of confusion?

D Occasionally, yes. Sometimes she thinks I'm her sister. Last night I heard someone moving around downstairs, and when I went down, I found Mum in the kitchen. She didn't know where she was. We laughed about it afterwards.

N Does this often happen?

D No. Very rarely.

Unit 8

Listening 1 – A diabetic patient

S=student nurse, N=nutritionist

S The new patient has had diabetes since childhood, his notes say.

N Uh huh. He has type one, then?

S What's that?

N There's type one diabetes and there's type two. Type one usually appears before the age of eighteen. Does he inject himself with insulin?

S Yes, daily.

N Uh huh, OK. He's on a special diet, is he?

S Yes, but he's not overweight.

N No. Type one diabetes is not linked to obesity.

S So obesity is linked to type two, is it?

N Yes. Type two is the common one.

S This patient has a special machine to check levels of glucose in his blood. And he shouldn't eat sugar, right?

N Well, no, it's not true that diabetics shouldn't eat sweet things. Actually, what's important is balance. A diabetic like your patient should eat the same amount of food at the same time of day. He needs to count the calories in his meals, and he should have snacks, not big meals – especially before bed.

S Oh, why is that?

N To avoid hypoglycaemia.

S Hypoglycaemia – not enough glucose in the blood, right?

N Right.

Speaking

1 one metre eighty
2 ninety-five point seven kilos
3 five feet eleven
4 two hundred and eleven pounds
5 one point eight times one point eight equals three point two four
6 ninety-five point seven divided by three point two four equals twenty-nine point five four

Listening 2 – An eating disorder

S=staff nurse, N=nurse

S The new patient's name is Anita Josephs. Anita is sixteen. She fainted and an ambulance brought her in, so we are keeping her in for a forty-eight-hour observation. Anita is very underweight. She weighs 38.8 kilos.

N1 That puts her BMI in the danger zone.

S Yes, her mother believes she has anorexia. She told me about Anita's personality changes and mood swings ...

N2 A typical teenager?

S To a point, yes. But Anita is obsessed with dieting. She doesn't eat, so she gets stomach pains, frequent constipation, and attacks of dizziness.

N1 What does Anita say?

S She says she feels miserable all the time, but she doesn't know why. However, she doesn't believe she has a weight problem. She told *me* that she eats the same as everyone else, and she doesn't think her weight loss is abnormal. However, she *does* say she has difficulty sleeping, and is losing her hair, and she has also stopped having periods.

Unit 9

Listening 1 – Blood types

I=instructor, S1 / S2= students 1 and 2

I I want to show you what happens if you mix the wrong types of blood. Now, in front of you, you've got test tubes with different types of blood in them. The blood in one test tube is type A. Now who can receive blood type A?

S1 A patient with blood type AB.

I Right. So AB can receive type A. But can B receive A? What happens if you give type A to type B? Now there's some type B blood in the second test tube. If you add a drop of type A, you'll see how they react together. Now put a drop of the blood on a slide and look at it through the microscope.

S2 The red blood cells are joining together.

I Yes, that's right. We call that 'clumping'. Now the blood stops moving if the red cells clump. And of course, if the blood stops moving, the patient dies. Now, if we put a little of blood type O into more type A, we'll see the difference ... And what do you see now?

S1 The red blood cells are moving. The blood looks OK.

I Right. You can give type O blood to all the other blood types. So, if we have an emergency, we usually use type O. It's the universal donor.

Listening 2 – A blood test

N=nurse, P=patient

N How do you feel?

P Tired all the time, really – I never have any energy.

N Have you had a blood test before?

P No, I haven't, no. How much blood will you take?

N Oh, just enough to fill the syringe – just five millilitres ... Well, we've got the results of your blood test. As I thought, you're a little bit anaemic.

P Is that bad?

N No, not necessarily. It just means that your red blood cell count is a little on the low side. A normal count is about 4.2 to 5.4 million red blood cells per microlitre of blood, and yours was 3.9.

P Oh dear – what does that mean?

N Don't worry – anaemia's very common in women. If you take iron supplements, your red cell count should soon go up. The cells are normal in size and shape, so that looks good. Your white cells are a little high, but you've just had a sore throat, haven't you?

P Yes.

N Well, that's just a sign that your body's been fighting the infection, so that's fine. And platelets were normal.

Unit 10

Listening – Report of a death

N=nurse, S=supervisor

N When I visited Mr Jacobs on Monday, he was going downhill fast. He was conscious most of the time. His hands and feet were cool. His arms were pale grey. He spoke, but not to us – to people we couldn't see. At about four o'clock he tried to get out of bed and fell to the floor. His breathing was restricted and noisy, so I gave him oxygen to help him breathe.

S And you saw him on Tuesday, too, didn't you?

N Yes. By Tuesday he was unconscious all the time. Irregular breathing – sometimes a pause of a minute or more. He took no fluids and no food, so there was no urine. Mrs Jacobs and I turned him regularly.

S And when did the end come?

N The end came on Wednesday morning. Mr Jacobs was no longer breathing. I called Doctor Simpson and he pronounced Mr Jacobs dead at ten o'clock, the seventh of July.

Writing

A Did you hear Mr Webb died last night?

B Did he? Oh dear. He got a lung infection, didn't he?

A Yes, two weeks ago. He was receiving treatment for that, but he actually died of a heart attack.

B Really? What caused it?

A A blood clot.

B Right. He had AIDS, of course, didn't he. When was he diagnosed with that?

A Six months ago. And he was HIV-positive for five years. He started suffering from depression at about the same time.

Unit 11

Listening 1 – A hygiene report

H=hospital administrator, S=sister

H Ah, Sister, I need to talk to you about the hygiene inspection.

S OK. How was our score?

H Mm. Three out of ten.

S Oh dear. Well, they came at a very bad time. Mid-morning.

H I have their report here. Er ... I'll just run through the *important* things ... under 'Ward hygiene' – 'Door handles are not regularly cleaned. Beds are not always cleaned between patients. Toilets must be cleaned three times a day but they are only cleaned once a day. Floors must be cleaned four times a day but they are only cleaned once a day.'
Under 'Spillages of bodily fluids', the report says that the average time was

thirty-five minutes to clean up a spillage of urine. And it says 'Nurses' knowledge of MRSA is good, but ...'

S They always wear gloves.

H Not good enough. It says here, 'Nurses must wash hands before putting on gloves and after removing gloves.'

S Well. We certainly need to improve, but we *are* very short staffed.

H Mm.

Listening 2 – Test results

W=ward nurse, P=Path lab technician

W Hello. Ward 5.

P Hello, this is Peter Forbes from the Path lab. I'm phoning with Sandra Browning's results.

W Hi, Peter. Good news?

P I'm afraid not. I can confirm it is MRSA. We have identified the bacterium – it's MRSA clone 15. OK. Now, Mrs Browning has an infection in her right hip. Correct?

W Yes.

P Well, we tested her urine and blood, and took throat and nasal swabs. First things first. Blood – high white cell count.

W OK.

P Negative for E. coli. But positive for Staphylococcus aureus. We tested this Staphylococcus for resistance to antibiotics. These are the results. It is resistant to: Cefazolin, Penicillin, and Methicillin. We also tested for resistance to Erythromycin, Clindamycin, and Tetracycline – all positive. However, tests show the bacterium has a susceptibility to Mupirocin. Also, the bacterium is *not* resistant to Vancomycin and Oxacyllin.

W OK, I've got that, Peter – thanks very much.

Unit 12

Pronunciation

posture	disoriented
unemotional	uncommunicative
hallucinations	delusions
manic	irrational
paranoia	depression

Language spot

J=Jack, P=Paula

J Have you changed the patients' dressings? That's the first thing on my list.

P No, I haven't done them yet.

J Mrs Eriksson's blood pressure needs to be taken. Have you done that yet?

P Yes, that was the first thing I did.

J What about Mr Sissoko's temperature? Have you taken it?

P Yes, I've done that. It's lower than it was.

J It says here that somebody spilt their orange juice. Have you cleaned the floor?

P That's the next thing on my list, so no, I haven't done that yet.

J And Mrs Wong needs some tests. Have you taken a urine specimen from her?

P She's having a shower at the moment, so I haven't had a chance yet.

Listening – A case conference

P=psychiatrist, N=nurse therapist

P ... so let's move on. Next on the list is new patient Delroy Moseki. For those of you who don't know him, he is 51, admitted on Tuesday. Who is Mr Moseki's nurse therapist?

N It's me, doctor.

P Paul. Thank you. Can you take over?

N Yes. Er ... Delroy ... The notes say that when he was admitted last Tuesday he er ... appeared normal in his movements and posture. However, he didn't know where he was and what was happening. He avoids eye contact, and has spoken to none of the other patients, as far as I know. The night staff report that he has some sleepless nights. He shouts out in the night and wakes other patients. I think he has auditory hallucinations.

P Yes, that's in the notes. He hears voices. Have you done any tests?

N Yes, the charge nurse on night shift has tested him. He names objects correctly, but forgets them almost immediately. He gets frustrated easily, and often cries. It's also very hard to understand what he says.

P Thank you Paul. Now I'd like to ask some questions ...

Unit 13

Scrub up

1 Your temperature is ... let's see ... thirty-eight point five.

2 Now relax while I measure your heart rate ... that's one hundred and twenty bpm.

3 Your blood pressure is a hundred and fifty over ninety.

4 The patient's respiratory rate is around eighteen bpm.

Pronunciation

1 heart rate	4 respiratory rate
2 temperature	5 blood pressure
3 pulse	6 vital sign

Patient care

1 Just pop this under your tongue.
2 Can you roll up your sleeve?
3 This may feel a bit cold on your chest.
4 Just breathe in and out normally.
5 Relax your arm for me.
6 Could you undo your shirt for me, please?

Listening 1 – A coma patient

I=ICU nurse, D=doctor

I ICU?

D Hi. Doctor Michaels here.

I Good evening, doctor.

D Good evening. How's our TBI patient?

I Mr Forrester? Mm. It's not looking good. He's still unconscious, doctor.

D What's the blood pressure reading?

I BP is one seventy over one twenty.

D Mmm. Much too high. And what was it at twenty hundred hours ?

I One fifty over ninety. It started rising an hour later – at twenty-two hundred hours it was one sixty over one ten.

D So, rising all the time. What about his ICP?

I ICP was stable at twenty at twenty hundred hours. But it rose to twenty five at twenty-one hundred. At twenty-two hundred it was twenty six. Now it's twenty seven.

D Right. We must get his ICP back to below twenty. Twenty and over is too high. OK. I'll be there in ten minutes.

Listening 2 – A scan

N=nurse, M=Mrs Murphy

N OK, Mrs Murphy, just lie back on this examination table. Are you comfortable?
M Yes, thank you.
N Have you had plenty of water to drink?
M Yes – three glasses.
N Good, we need your bladder full. I'm putting some gel onto your abdomen. That helps the ultrasound work well.
M OK.
N Your notes say the baby has stopped moving. Is that right?
M Yes, I'm a bit worried.
N And you're in the twenty-second week of your pregnancy?
M Yes.
N Right. Well the ultrasound scan is very simple. When I pass the transducer over your abdomen, it bounces sound waves off the baby's body and it makes a picture here on the monitor. Then we can see if there is anything wrong. It shows up any abnormalities. A scan can usually show if the baby is a boy or a girl. Do you want to know the baby's sex?
M Yes, please.
N OK. I'm passing the transducer over your abdomen now. Ah, here we are. There's the baby. Can you see it?
M It's not very clear.
N Well, here's the head. Can you see that?
M Oh, yes.
N And there's a hand. Five fingers. And there's a foot – can you see?
M Yes.
N Can you see the heart beating? The baby's alive and looks good. Yes, everything is normal. And look – a penis. It's a boy.
M Really? I wanted a girl.
N You did? Just a moment! Well you're not going to be disappointed – you're going to have twins – a boy and a girl.

Unit 14

Listening – Patient medication

1 Let's start with Mr Gupta. He's had pain all night in the lower abdomen. The doctor says he needs stronger pain relief, so he has prescribed thirty milligrams of Morphine every four hours.
2 We've moved Mr Gill to an isolation room, as he has an infection in his respiratory tract. A new antibiotic may work, so we are giving him a 600 milligram infusion of Clindamycin over a period of four hours.
3 Now, Mr Sawyer. We have to encourage bowel movement, so a laxative could be useful. He has one tablespoon of Metamucil – that's 15 milligrams – three times a day.
4 Right. Mr Thomas is on antibiotics for his skin infection. Cephalexin is in tablet form, to be taken with food. 250 milligrams every six hours.
5 Lastly, Mr Cheong. Mr Cheong receives an injection of an antihistamine every eight hours – 10 milligrams of Dimotane each time. Maybe this will control his allergies.

Patient care

1 She needs to take two tablets twice a day for a week.
2 What dosage of Penicillin is Mr Oliver on?
3 How often does he need his medicine?
4 Give Mrs Muben one 0.5 mil eye drop in each eye every four hours.
5 He's on two tablets three times a day with water at mealtimes.

Unit 15

Listening 1 – *Qigong*

I=interviewer, A=Amber, P=Professor Silver

I Can you cure illness without medicine or surgery? Energy healers say yes. Energy healers say they can heal without touching the patient. In the studio, to tell us about energy healing, is Amber Chesterman, who is a *qigong* healer.
A Hello.
I Also with us is Professor Julius Silver who is sceptical about *qigong*.
P Hello.
I But to start us off, Amber. Can you tell us about *qigong* healing?
A *Qigong* is holistic. It sees illness as a problem of mind, spirit, *and* body, so the whole person is treated, not just the illness.
I Right. And *qi* is important, isn't it? What exactly is *qi*?
A *Qi* is energy. *Qi* is part of everything that exists. Illness, you see, is caused by an imbalance of *qi*, and a *qigong* healer restores energy balance so that healing can happen.
I And you heal from a distance, don't you? Over the telephone?
A That's correct. I practice external *qi* healing. I speak to my patients by telephone.
I And you unblock their *qi*?
A Put simply, yes.
I Thank you. Professor Silver – you don't believe in *qi*, do you?
P No. I have found no evidence for *qi*, no.
I And yet energy healing *does* work, don't you agree?
P It does work, *sometimes*, yes.
I So how do you explain it?
P We find a lot of evidence for a placebo effect. Belief is seventy per cent of any treatment. In other words, my hands can't heal you, but if you *believe* I have healing hands, then I can heal you by moving my hands over you.
I So, what's really going on here?
P Well, we do know that being completely relaxed helps us recover more quickly.
I So, you are saying that all I need is to relax and *believe* that you have the power to heal me?
P Exactly. My explanation is not as interesting as Amber's, but we live in the twenty first century and …

Glossary

Vowels

iː	tw**ee**zers	ʊ	f**u**lly-qualified	aɪ	s**i**de effects
i	arter**y**	uː	junk f**oo**d	aʊ	ultras**ou**nd
ɪ	b**i**n	u	us**u**al	ɔɪ	app**oi**ntment
e	dr**e**ssing	ʌ	l**u**mp	ɪə	bact**er**ia
æ	sc**a**n	ɜː	f**ir**st aid	eə	c**are** home
ɑː	c**ar**diac arrest	ə	disord**er**	ʊə	c**ure**
ɒ	b**o**dy	eɪ	f**a**tal		
ɔː	s**or**e	əʊ	diagn**o**sis		

Consonants

p	dro**p**	f	**f**ee	h	**h**ealer
b	o**b**ese	v	**v**ein	m	**m**icroscope
t	**t**ic	θ	**th**erapy	n	**n**ap
d	**d**ose	ð	**th**e immune system	ŋ	swelli**ng**
k	**c**lot	s	**s**ample	l	**l**abour
g	**g**ait	z	sterili**z**e	r	**r**ash
tʃ	stret**ch**er	ʃ	**sh**ift	j	**y**ear
dʒ	aller**g**ic	ʒ	infu**s**ion	w	**w**ard

abnormality /ˌæbnɔːˈmæləti/ *n* something that is not normal

accounts /əˈkaʊnts/ *n* a record of money received and spent

aching /ˈeɪkɪŋ/ *n* a continuous, steady pain

addicted /əˈdɪktɪd/ *adj* having a physical and mental need to consume a substance, especially a harmful drug

agonizing /ˈægənaɪzɪŋ/ *adj* extremely painful

allergic /əˈlɜːdʒɪk/ *adj* having a condition that causes a bad reaction on contact with a certain substance

antimicrobial agent /ˌæntimaɪˈkrəʊbiəl ˈeɪdʒənt/ *n* a substance that kills bacteria and other micro-organisms

antiviral /ˌantiˈvaɪrəl/ *adj* used to describe a drug that stops a virus from copying itself, and therefore prevents infection from spreading

apply for a job /əˌplaɪ fər ə ˈdʒɒb/ *v* to make a formal written request for a job

appointment /əˈpɔɪntmənt/ *n* a formal arrangement to see a doctor, etc. at a particular time

artery /ˈɑːtəri/ *n* any of the blood vessels which carry blood away from the heart

auxiliary nurse /ɒgˈzɪliəri nɜːs/ *n* a nurse with basic qualifications who helps with the care of patients

bacteria /bækˈtɪəriə/ *n* small organisms without a nucleus, that can sometimes cause infection

bereavement /bɪˈriːvmənt/ *n* the death of a loved one

bin /bɪn/ *n* a container for throwing waste into

bipolar disorder /baɪˌpəʊlə dɪsˈɔːdə(r)/ *n* a mental illness that causes somebody to change suddenly from being very happy to very sad

blister /ˈblɪstə(r)/ *n* a closed shell of skin containing liquid, that is caused, for example, by a burn or other injury

bodily fluids /ˌbɒdɪli ˈfluːɪdz/ *n* the liquids inside the body that allow it to function

body /ˈbɒdi/ *n* a dead person

bowel movement /ˈbaʊl ˌmuːvmənt/ *n* the release of solid waste matter from the body

bpm /ˌbiː piː ˈem/ *n* **1 beats per minute** used to measure heart rate
2 breaths per minute used to measure respiratory rate

brain waves /ˈbreɪn weɪvz/ *n* electrical signals in the brain

bruising /ˈbruːzɪŋ/ *n* blue or purple marks on the body, caused by bleeding under the skin

burial /ˈberiəl/ *n* a ceremony where a dead person is put in a box under the ground

calorie /ˈkæləri/ *n* a unit for measuring how much energy food will produce

cardiac arrest /ˌkɑːdiæk əˈrest/ *n* an occasion where somebody's heart stops beating

care home /ˈkeə həʊm/ *n* a home that provides accommodation, food, and care for elderly people

carer /ˈkeərə(r)/ *n* a person who is trained to take care of ill or elderly people

catering /ˈkeɪtərɪŋ/ *n* the work of preparing food for a hospital, school, etc.

cell /sel/ *n* the smallest unit of living matter

circulation /ˌsɜːkjəˈleɪʃn/ *n* the movement of the blood through the heart and blood vessels

clot /klɒt/ *n* (of blood) to form thick lumps

cognitive function /ˌkɒgnɪtɪv ˈfʌŋkʃən/ *n* the ability to use your brain effectively to think, recognize, remember, etc.

concentrate /ˈkɒnsəntreɪt/ *v* to focus attention on one thing

confinement /kənˈfaɪnmənt/ *n* the condition of being unable to leave your bed, a room, etc.

confusion /kənˈfjuːʒn/ *n* a state of not being certain about what is happening, what you should do, what something means, etc.

constipation /ˌkɒnstɪˈpeɪʃn/ *n* the condition of being unable to have a bowel movement easily
consultant /kənˈsʌltənt/ *n* a hospital doctor of high rank who has special knowledge in a particular area of medicine and advises the patient's doctor
consultation /ˌkɒnsəlˈteɪʃn/ *n* a meeting with an expert, especially a doctor, to get advice or treatment
contamination /kənˌtæmɪˈneɪʃn/ *n* the process by which a place, substance, etc. is affected by a substance that is dangerous or carries disease
conventional medicine /kənˌvenʃənl ˈmedsɪn/ *n* the usual, traditional form of medical treatment used in the West
co-ordination /kəʊˌɔːdɪˈneɪʃn/ *n* the ability to control your movements well
corridor /ˈkɒrɪdɔː(r)/ *n* a long narrow passage in a building, with doors that open into rooms on either side
cough /kɒf/ *n* a sudden noise produced when air is suddenly forced out of the throat, for example when you have a cold
CPR (cardiopulmonary resuscitation) /ˌsiː piː ˈɑː(r)/ *n* an emergency procedure used to keep a person alive who has stopped breathing or whose heart has stopped beating
cramp /kræmp/ *n* a squeezing pain in a muscle
craving /ˈkreɪvɪŋ/ *n* a sudden strong desire for something
cremation /crɪˈmeɪʃn/ *n* a ceremony where the body of a dead person is burnt in a special building
cubicle /ˈkjuːbɪkl/ *n* a small room that is made by separating off part of a larger room
deaf /def/ *adj* unable to hear
deficiency /dɪˈfɪʃənsi/ *n* the state of not having, or not having enough of, something that is essential
deformity /dɪˈfɔːmɪti/ *n* a condition in which a part of the body is not the normal shape
degenerative /dɪˈdʒenərətɪv/ *adj* (of an illness) getting or likely to get worse as time passes
dementia /dɪˈmenʃə/ *adj* a mental disorder caused by brain disease or injury that affects the ability to think and behave normally
diabetic /ˌdaɪəˈbetɪk/ *adj* being unable to produce enough insulin
diagnose /ˌdaɪəgˈnəʊz/ *v* to say what disease or condition a person is suffering from, based on tests, examinations, and symptoms
diet /ˈdaɪət/ *n* **1** the food that you eat and drink regularly **2** a limited variety or amount of food that you eat for medical reasons or because you want to lose weight; a time when you only eat this limited variety or amount
disabled /dɪsˈeɪbld/ *adj* having a physical or mental problem which means you are unable to do some things
disinfectant /ˌdɪsɪnˈfektənt/ *n* a substance that kills bacteria
disorder /dɪsˈɔːdə(r)/ *n* an illness that causes a part of the body to stop functioning correctly
dispense /dɪsˈpens/ *v* to prepare medicine and give it to people
disposable /dɪsˈpəʊzəbl/ *adj* made to be thrown away after use
dispose of /dɪsˈpəʊz əv/ *v* to throw away something that is no longer needed
distressing /dɪsˈtresɪŋ/ *adj* something that makes people feel extremely upset
dizziness /ˈdɪzinəs/ *n* a confused feeling that you are turning or spinning, or that everything else is
dose /dəʊs/ *n* the amount of a drug that is given at one time
dressing /ˈdresɪŋ/ *n* a piece of soft material placed over a wound in order to protect it
drip /drɪp/ *v* (of a liquid) to fall in small drops
drop /drɒp/ *n* a very small amount of liquid that forms a round shape
droplet /ˈdrɒplət/ *n* an extremely small drop of a liquid
ECG (electrocardiogram) /ˌiː siː ˈdʒiː/ *n* a medical test used to measure electrical activity in the heart to diagnose heart disorders or blockages in the arteries
eczema /ˈeksmə/ *n* a skin condition that causes redness and itching, and sores that secrete fluid and become dry and scaly
fatal /ˈfeɪtl/ *adj* causing, or capable of causing, death
fee /fiː/ *n* an amount of money that you pay for professional advice or services
first aid /ˌfɜːst ˈeɪd/ *n* emergency treatment that is given to somebody before professional medical help is available
floor /flɔː(r)/ *n* **1** one level of a building **2** the bottom surface of a room
foreign body /ˌfɒrən ˈbɒdi/ *n* a substance or object that is found in the body, but should not be there
forensic analysis /fəˌrenzɪk əˈnæləsɪs/ *n* scientific study that is done to try to help police solve a crime
frail /freɪl/ *adj* physically weak and easily injured
fully-qualified /ˌfʊli ˈkwɒlɪfaɪd/ *adj* having passed all necessary exams in order to do a particular job
funeral /ˈfjuːnrəl/ *n* a ceremony at which a dead person is buried or cremated
gait /geɪt/ n the way in which a person walks
gas and air /ˌgæs ənd ˈeə(r)/ *n* a gas that is given to patients to relieve pain, that is made up of 50% oxygen and 50% nitrous oxide
germ /dʒɜːm/ *n* a micro-organism that can cause infection and disease
grieving /ˈgriːvɪŋ/ *adj* feeling great sadness after a loved one has died
haemoglobin /ˌhiːməˈgləʊbɪn/ *n* a substance in red blood cells that carries oxygen around the body
healer /ˈhiːlə(r)/ *n* a person who cures people of illnesses and disease using natural powers rather than medicine
heart rate /ˈhɑːt reɪt/ *n* the speed at which the heart beats
herbalist /ˈhɜːbəlɪst/ *n* a person who uses herbs (=plants) to treat patients
holistic /həˈlɪstɪk/ *adj* used to describe medical care that looks at all aspects of a person's body, mind, and environment
hypodermic needle /ˌhaɪpədɜːmɪk ˈniːdl/ *n* a device with a sharp point used for injecting a substance through the skin
immobile /ɪˈməʊbaɪl/ *adj* unable to walk around
immune system /ɪˈmjuːn ˌsɪstəm/ *n* the system in the body that produces substances to help it fight against infection and disease
immune /ɪˈmjuːn/ *adj* not affected by and not able to catch a particular disease or illness
incontinent /ɪnˈkɒntɪnənt/ *adj* unable to control the release of urine and faeces
independence /ˌɪndɪˈpendəns/ *n* freedom to do what you want to do, without being controlled by others
infection /ɪnˈfekʃn/ *n* a condition caused by bacteria invading and multiplying in a bodily part or tissue, resulting in disease
infusion /ɪnˈfjuːʒn/ *n* a method for slowly putting a drug or other substance into a person's vein; the drug that is used in this way
initial assessment /ɪˌnɪʃl əˈsesmənt/ *n* a judgement made about how serious a patient's condition is when they first arrive at hospital
intake /ˈɪnteɪk/ *n* the amount of something that a person eats, drinks, takes, etc., in a particular period of time
itching /ˈɪtʃɪŋ/ *n* an irritating feeling on the skin that causes a desire to scratch
junk food /ˈdʒʌŋk fuːd/ *n* food, for example burgers and fries, that is quick and easy to prepare and eat, but is bad for your health

labour /ˈleɪbə(r)/ *n* the process of childbirth, from the start of contractions of the uterus to the birth of the baby
lecture /ˈlektʃə(r)/ *n* a talk that is given to a group of people to teach them about a particular subject, often as part of a college course
life-limiting condition /ˌlaɪf lɪmɪtɪŋ kənˈdɪʃn/ *n* an illness that prevents a person from living a normal life
life-threatening condition /ˌlaɪf θretənɪŋ kənˈdɪʃn/ *n* an illness that could kill the person that has it
lift /lɪft/ *n* a machine that carries people or goods up and down to different levels in a building
limb /lɪm/ *n* an arm or a leg
local anaesthetic /ˌləʊkl ænəsˈθetɪk/ *n* a drug that makes you unable to feel anything in one part of the body
long-term /ˌlɒŋ ˈtɜːm/ *adj* lasting for a long time, often many years
lose consciousness /ˌluːz ˈkɒnʃəsnəs/ *v* to become unconscious
lump /lʌmp/ *n* any kind of abnormal mass that can be felt in or on the body
medicinal /məˈdɪsɪnl/ *adj* helpful in the process of healing illness or infection
microscope /ˈmaɪkrəskəʊp/ *n* an instrument used in scientific study for making very small things look larger so that you can examine them carefully
migraine /ˈmaɪgreɪn/ *n* a severe headache that may be accompanied by nausea, vomiting, or sensitivity to light
mild /maɪld/ *adj* not strong
mineral /ˈmɪnrəl/ *n* a substance that is naturally present in the earth and in the human body, and is essential for good health
mobility /məˈbɪləti/ *n* used to describe how easy or difficult it is for a person to walk around
mood swings /ˈmuːd swɪŋgz/ *n* periods during which a person changes quickly from feeling very happy to feeling very unhappy
mortuary /ˈmɔːrtʃəri/ *n* a room in a hospital where dead bodies are taken
multi-sensory /ˌmʌlti ˈsensəri/ *adj* involving all or several of the senses of touch, sight, hearing, and smell
mutate /mjuːˈteɪt/ *v* to develop into a new form because of a genetic change
nap /næp/ *n* a short sleep taken during the day
nasal /ˈneɪzl/ *adj* of or relating to the nose
nausea /ˈnɔːziə/ *n* the unpleasant feeling that you are going to vomit
nervous system /ˈnɜːvəs ˌsɪstəm/ *n* the system of all the nerves in the body
night shift /ˈnaɪt ʃɪft/ *n* the period of work that takes place during the night
numbness /ˈnʌmnəs/ *n* a lack of feeling in a part of the body
nursing officer /ˈnɜːsɪŋ ˌɒfɪsə(r)/ *n* a senior nurse who is responsible for managing a ward and the people who work on it
nutritionist /njuːˈtrɪʃənɪst/ *n* a person who studies the effects of food on the body
obese /əʊˈbiːs/ *adj* very fat, in a way that is not healthy
onset /ˈɒnset/ *n* the time when a disease or condition starts to affect a person
overweight /ˌəʊvəˈweɪt/ *adj* too heavy and fat
oximeter /ɒksˈɪmiːtə(r)/ *n* a machine for measuring the amount of oxygen in the blood
pain relief /ˈpeɪn rɪˌliːf/ *n* drugs or treatment given to a patient to take away pain
paralyse /ˈpærəlaɪz/ *v* to make all or a part of the body unable to move
part-time /ˌpɑːt ˈtaɪm/ *adj* (of a job, course of study, etc.) occupying only part of the normal week
pathogen /ˈpæθədʒən/ *n* a harmful micro-organism capable of causing disease, such as a virus, bacterium, or fungus
physiotherapist /ˌfɪziəʊˈθerəpɪst/ *n* a person who is trained to treat disease, injury, or weakness in the joints or muscles by exercises, massage, and the use of light and heat
pipette /pɪˈpet/ *n* a narrow tube used in a laboratory for measuring or transferring small amounts of liquids
placement /ˈpleɪsmənt/ *n* a job, often as part of a course of study, where you get some experience of a particular kind of work
platelets /ˈpleɪtləts/ *n* small discs in the blood, that help to clot the blood from a cut or wound
practitioner /prækˈtɪʃənə(r)/ *n* a medical professional who is licensed to treat patients
pre-med /ˈpriː med/ *n* drugs given to somebody in preparation for an operation or other medical treatment
prescribe /prəˈskraɪb/ *v* (of a doctor) to authorize a patient to receive a particular drug or treatment
prescription /prəˈskrɪpʃn/ *n* a medicine or treatment authorized by a doctor; the written order that authorizes this treatment
priority /praɪˈɒrɪti/ *n* a thing or person that you think you need to deal with first
procedure /prəˈsiːdʒə(r)/ *n* the usual or correct way of doing something
progress notes /ˈprəʊgres nəʊts/ *n* a written record of a patient's condition over a period of time
promotion /prəˈməʊʃn/ *n* a move to a more important job or rank
protein /ˈprəʊtiːn/ *n* a natural substance found in meat, eggs, fish, some vegetables, etc., which we need in order to grow and stay healthy
psychiatric /ˌsaɪkiˈætrɪk/ *adj* relating to mental illness or to the treatment of it
psychotic /saɪˈkɒtɪk/ *adj* relating to severe mental illness
qualifications /ˌkwɒlɪfɪˈkeɪʃnz/ *n* exams that you have taken and courses of study that you have completed
qualified /ˈkwɒlɪfaɪd/ *adj* having passed the exams necessary to do a particular job
rank /ræŋk/ *n* the level of job that a person has in a particular area of work, such as nursing
rash /ræʃ/ *n* an area of red spots on a person's skin, caused by an illness or a reaction to something
reception /rɪˈsepʃn/ *n* the area inside the entrance of a hospital, where patients and visitors go when they first arrive
registration /ˌredʒɪˈstreɪʃn/ *n* the official recording of something in writing
resistant /rɪˈzɪstənt/ *adj* not affected by something; able to resist something
responsibility /rɪsˌpɒnsəˈbɪləti/ *n* duty to do something important
rewarding /rɪˈwɔːdɪŋ/ *adj* (of a job or activity) that makes you happy because it is useful or important
root /ruːt/ *n* the part of a plant that grows under the ground
saliva /səˈlaɪvə/ *n* the liquid that is produced in your mouth that helps you swallow food
sample /ˈsɑːmpl/ *n* a small amount of a substance, for example blood or body tissue, that is tested in order to obtain information
scan /skæn/ *n* a medical test for pregnant women in which a machine uses ultrasound to produce a picture of a baby inside its mother's body
sceptical /ˈskeptɪkl/ *adj* not believing completely in something
severe /sɪˈviə(r)/ *adj* (of an illness, injury, etc.) serious; very bad
severed /ˈsevəd/ *adj* (of part of the body) cut off in an accident
shivering /ˈʃɪvərɪŋ/ *n* slight shaking of the body caused by cold, illness, etc.
shuffling /ˈʃʌflɪŋ/ *adj* used to describe a way of walking with short steps, with the feet not leaving the floor

siblings /ˈsɪblɪŋz/ *n* brothers and sisters
side effects /ˈsaɪd ɪˌfekts/ *n* an extra and usually bad effect that a drug has on you, as well as curing illness or pain
slide /slaɪd/ n a small piece of glass that something is placed on so that it can be looked at under a microscope
slight /slaɪt/ adj not great; a small degree of
snack /snæk/ *n* a small meal or amount of food
sore /sɔ:(r)/ *adj* (of part of the body) painful and possibly swollen, for example because of infection or being used too much
sore /sɔ:(r)/ *n* a painful, often red, place on your body where there is a wound or an infection
source /sɔ:s/ *n* a place or thing that you can get something from
specialize /ˈspeʃəlaɪz/ *v* to become an expert in a particular area of work
specimen /ˈspesɪmən/ *n* a sample of blood, urine, tissue, etc., collected for laboratory analysis
spillage /ˈspɪlɪdʒ/ *n* an occasion when liquid is dropped by accident; the liquid that is dropped
spot /spɒt/ *n* a small, often red, mark or lump on a person's skin, sometimes with a yellow head to it
spotless /ˈspɒtləs/ *adj* completely clean
spread /spred/ *v* (of a disease, an infection, etc.) to move from one person or place to cover a wider area
sterile /ˈsteraɪl/ *adj* that has been heated to kill micro-organisms
sterilize /ˈsterɪlaɪz/ *v* to heat something in order to kill micro-organisms on it
stimulant /ˈstɪmjələnt/ *n* a drug that makes you feel more awake, and that makes the body work faster
stimulation /ˌstɪmjəˈleɪʃn/ *n* activity that makes the mind more active
stitches /ˈstɪtʃɪz/ *n* short pieces of thread, etc. that doctors use to sew the edges of a wound together
stomach ulcer /ˈstʌmək ˌʌlsə(r)/ *n* a sore area on the outside of the body or on the surface of an organ inside the body which is painful and may bleed or produce a poisonous substance
stretcher /ˈstretʃə(r)/ *n* a piece of equipment that allows two people to carry a sick or injured person who is lying down
stroke /strəʊk/ *n* damage to part of the brain caused by a blocked or broken blood vessel, that can cause loss of muscle control, speech difficulties, etc.
suicide /ˈsu:ɪsaɪd/ *n* the act of killing yourself
superstition /ˌsu:pəˈstɪʃn/ *n* a belief that cannot be explained by reason or science
supplement /ˈsʌplɪmənt/ *n* something that you eat in addition to your normal food to maintain or improve your health
suppository /səˈpɒzɪtri/ *n* a medication in tablet form which is inserted into the rectum, where it melts
susceptible /səˈseptɪbl/ *adj* likely to be affected by something
swab /swɒb/ *v* to clean something using a piece of soft material
swear /sweə(r)/ *v* to say bad words
swelling /ˈswelɪŋ/ *n* an increase in size of an injured or diseased area of the body as a result of fluid build-up
swollen /ˈswəʊlən/ *adj* (used about part of the body) increased in size as a result of fluid build-up
sympathy /ˈsɪmpəθi/ *n* a feeling of understanding and caring between people
syringe /sɪˈrɪndʒ/ *n* a medical instrument used to remove fluids from the body or inject them into it using a needle
test tube /ˈtest tju:b/ *n* a glass or clear plastic tube used in laboratories for holding a liquid or other substance to be tested
therapy /ˈθerəpi/ *n* the treatment of a physical problem or an illness
threat /θret/ *n* a bad thing that somebody says they will do to another person
tic /tɪk/ *n* a fast, uncontrollable muscle movement, often occurring in the face
transducer /trænzˈdju:sə(r)/ *n* a device that is passed over a patient in an ultrasound examination in order to produce an image
trauma /ˈtrɔ:mə/ *n* a serious shock to the body or mind, for example caused by a violent event
traumatic /trɔ:ˈmætɪk/ *adj* **1** extremely unpleasant and causing you to feel upset and / or anxious
2 (of an injury, etc.) sudden and violent
treatment /ˈtri:tmənt/ *n* the medication, surgery, therapy, etc. that is given or done in order to cure or improve a condition or injury
triage nurse /ˌtri:ɑ:ʒ nɜ:s/ *n* a person whose job is to decide how urgently patients need to be treated, according to how serious their condition is
tumour /ˈtju:mə(r)/ *n* an abnormal growth of tissue caused by an uncontrolled increase in cells
tweezers /ˈtwi:zəz/ *n* a metal tool for picking up or removing very small objects, consisting of two arms that you pinch together
ultrasound /ˈʌltrəsaʊnd/ *n* the use of high-frequency sound waves to make an image of a part inside the body; the image produced
unbearable /ʌnˈbeərəbl/ *adj* too bad or extreme to cope with
vein /veɪn/ *n* any of the blood vessels that carry blood back to the heart
ventilator /ˈventɪleɪtə(r)/ *n* a piece of medical equipment used to allow somebody to breathe who cannot do so without help
virus /ˈvaɪrəs/ *n* a micro-organism that causes infection and disease and that spreads by copying itself
vital signs /ˌvaɪtl ˈsaɪnz/ *n* a patient's pulse rate, temperature, respiratory (= breathing) rate, and blood pressure
vitamin /ˈvɪtəmɪn/ *n* any of a group of organic compounds that are needed in small amounts but cannot be made within the body
ward /wɔ:d/ *n* any of the rooms in a hospital which has beds for patients
waste /weɪst/ *n* materials that are no longer needed and are thrown away
worms /wɜ:mz/ *n* long thin creatures that live inside the body and can cause illness
wound /wu:nd/ *n* an injury that involves the skin being cut or broken

OXFORD
UNIVERSITY PRESS

Great Clarendon Street, Oxford OX2 6DP

Oxford University Press is a department of the University of Oxford. It furthers the University's objective of excellence in research, scholarship, and education by publishing worldwide in

Oxford New York

Auckland Cape Town Dar es Salaam Hong Kong Karachi Kuala Lumpur Madrid Melbourne Mexico City Nairobi New Delhi Shanghai Taipei Toronto

With offices in

Argentina Austria Brazil Chile Czech Republic France Greece Guatemala Hungary Italy Japan Poland Portugal Singapore South Korea Switzerland Thailand Turkey Ukraine Vietnam

OXFORD and OXFORD ENGLISH are registered trade marks of Oxford University Press in the UK and in certain other countries

First published 2007
2016 2015 2014 2013 2012
20 19 18 17 16 15 14 13 12

ISBN: 978 0 19 456977 4

Printed in China

This book is printed on paper from certified and well- managed sources.

ACKNOWLEDGEMENTS

Art and photo editing by: Pictureresearch.co.uk

The authors and publisher are grateful to those who have given permission to reproduce the following extracts and adaptations of copyright material: p.52 *Pets come to visit* by Juliet Farmer, Copyright (2005). Nursing Spectrum Nurse Wire (www.nursingspectrum.com). All rights reserved. Used with permission. p.53 *Mobile hospital found* at www.normeca.com. Reproduced by kind permission of Normeca. p.54 *Inquest told of hospital bungle* article reproduced by courtesy of The Press, York.

The author and publisher are grateful to the following for their permission to reproduce photographs and illustrative material: Alamy pp.8 (Florence Nightingale/Pictorial Press), 13 (trolley/Photofusion Picture Library), 18 (moon/nagelestock.com), 19 (Reimar Gaertner), 20 (barcoding/Phototake), 23 (Photostock/Chris Müller), 30 (mother/Tom Tracy Photography), 35 (Mr T), 44 (scooter/Geldi), 46 (mushrooms/foodfolio), (olives/foodfolio), (tuna/Sue Wilson), 47 (cereals/ bildagentur-online.com/th-foto), (cheese/Purple Marbles), (sun/skin/Enigma), (meat/TastyPix), (shellfish/foodfolio), (oily fish/Peter Szekely), (nuts/Chris Stock), 48 (Clark Brennan), 50 (feet/Darren Matthews), 51 (Janine Wiedel Photolibrary), 55 (Shout), 57 (Phototake Inc.), 59 (Craig Holmes), 72 (sickle/ Ingram Publishing), (bloodstains/plainpicture GmbH & Co. KG), 73 (accident/ Andrew Sadler), 76 (massage/wonderlandstock), 80 (washing hands/Bubbles Photolibrary), 84 (tree/Fabio Pili), 85 (child/Janine Wiedel Photolibrary), 86 (woman at window/Gary Roebuck), 88 (Virginia Woolf/Lebrecht Music and Arts Photo Library), 92 (pulse/Paddy McGuinness), 96 (19th-century mother/ Mary Evans Picture Library); Anthony Blake Photo Library p.46 (steak); The Bridgeman Art Library p.103 (Cowpox cartoon/The Cow Pock or the Wonderful Effects of the New Inoculation, 1809 (coloured engraving) by Gillray, James (1757–1815) © Private Collection); Corbis pp.20 (dispensary/Tom Stewart), 25 (Bangkok/Macduff Everton), 34 (Steve Prezant), 40 (two women/Poppy Berry/ zefa), 47 (fruit/J.Garcia/photocuisine), 49 (Robert Wadlow/Bettmann), 52 (Jose Luis Pelaez, Inc.), 77 (Franco Vogt), 80 (Florence Nightingale/Robert Riggs), 88 (André Malraux/Bettmann), 99 (JLP/Sylvia Torres), 101 (1918 ward), 104 (faith healer/Roger Ressmeyer), (cups/Stephanie Maze), 106 (woman/Henry Diltz); Empics pp.49 (George Clooney/Jennifer Graylock/AP), 53 (David Longstreath/ AP), 86 (Andy Park/Barry Batchelor/PA); Fabfoodpix p.46 (beans); Getty Images pp.6 (interview/Sean Justice), 8 (1950s nurses/Kurt Hutton), 13 (O'Neill/Ranald Mackechnie), 15 (wooden wheelchair/Reg Speller/Fox Photos), (iBOT/ Independence Technology), 18 (football fan/Christof Koepsel/Bongarts), 20 (Elena Kneip/Trevor Lush), 24 (Henrik Sorensen), 25 (mother/Sean Justice), 26 (Jeff Oliver/Karen Moskowitz), 36 (ill man/Bruce Ayres), (Sandy McGuire/ B.Busco), 40 (hands/Elyse Lewin), 41 (crossword/K-P.Wolf), 42 (Alex Wong), 47 (rice/David McGlynn), 50 (Lillian Russell/Time Life Pictures), 66 (Photosindia/ Jack Hollingsworth), 71 (Stock Illustration Source/Christopher Creek), 73 (Howard Kingsnorth), 74 (grave/Alan Thornton), (cremation/Indranil Mukherjee/ AFP), (burial at sea/Rob Gaston/US Navy), 76 (wheelchair/Workbook Stock/ Ann Cutting), 81 (Peter Dazeley), 84 (tie/Peter Dazeley), 86 (Stephen Gough/ Peter Macdiarmid), (teen boy/Denis Boissavy), 88 (case conference/Photographer's Choice RF/Manchan), 89 (schizophrenia/Ian Jackson), 90 (Romilly Lockyer), 95 (tunnel/Nicholas Eveleigh), 97 (Taxi/Getty Images), 101 (people wearing masks/ Alex Hofford/AFP), 104 (Chinese medicine/Ken Chernus); © Jedrzej Jaxa-Rozen p.14; Mary Evans Picture Library p.62 (New York American, 20/6/1909); Royalty-free p.46 (eggs & tofu); © Philip Game p.107 (bomoh); Photolibrary.com p.28 (Dennis Macdonald); Punchstock pp.6 (student with laptop/Image Source), 17 (Brand X Pictures), 20 (prescription pad/SuperStock), 25 (taxi driver), 36 (sick child/rubberball), 38 (Dave Harries/PhotoDisc Red/Anna Moller), 38 (shadowy figure/Blend Images), 45 (Image Source), 46 (beansprouts/Image Source), (broccoli/Medioimages), (lentils/Image Source), (noodles/Image Source), (chops/ Foodcollection.com), (soy sauce/Foodcollection.com), 73 (The Cooks/Jack Hollingsworth), 84 (technician/PhotoDisc Green/John A. Rizzo), 85 (nurse/ Blend Images/Jose Luis Pelaez, Inc.), 86 (hand washing/Stockbyte Platinum), (angry driver), 89 (woman/PhotoAlto), 92 (blood presssure/Thinkstock), (temperature/Dynamic Graphics Group/Creatas), 93 (BananaStock), 105 (Corbis Royalty-free), 106 (man/Rayman), 107 (Christian woman), 108 (Digital Vision/ Louis Fox); Rex Features pp.15 (Hawking/Geoff Robinson), 26 (accident/ Alisdair Macdonald), 31 (Sipa Press), 44 (Adolph Zukor/Everett Collection), 49 (Morgan Spurlock), (Heidi Klum/Matt Baron/BEI), (Walter Hudson/Sipa Press), 70 (Alix/Phanie), 76 (hospice), 78 (Sipa Press), 94 (Philippe Hays), 95 (curare/Paul Raffaele); Science Photo Library pp.8 (modern nurses/John Cole), 39 (Tek Image), 41 (scan/Sovereign, ISM), 58 (Peter Menzel), 60 (Astrid & Hanns-Frieder Michler), 64 (Tim Beddow), 69 (blood letting), 80 (bacterium/Dr Kari Lounatmaa), 82 (John Daugherty), 83 (Dr P. Marazzi), 96 (Sir Humphrey Davy/Sheila Terry), 101 (sneeze/Kent Wood), 103 (smallpox bacterium/Chris Bjornberg), 104 (acupuncture/Andew McClenaghan), 109 (Chris Knapton); Topfoto p.79

Front cover images by Getty Images (nurse behind desk/The Image Bank/Peter Dazely); PunchStock (watch/Digital Archive Japan)

Illustrations by: Emma Dodd pp.14, 68 (women), 83, 96, 111 (figures), 112, 114; Mark Duffin pp.10, 30, 43, 80, 99, 102; Andy Hammond/Illustration pp.16, 18, 19, 34, 98; Annabelle Hartmann p.22; Paul Oakley pp.26–27, 33, 75; Oxford Designers and Illustrators/Elaine Leggett p.68 (blood types), 69 (blood cells), 70; John See pp.24, 28 (paperclip test & faces), 29, 32, 111 (outline); Tony Sigley pp.4–5, 12

The author and publisher would like to thank the many institutions who assisted in the development of this title, in particular: Dr D Dewhurst and Sheffield Bioscience Programs; The Fund for the Replacement of Animals in Medical Experiments (FRAME); Staff and patients at Broadgreen hospital, Liverpool; Taiping hospital, Taiping, Malaysia; Calderdale Royal Hospital, Halifax; Faculty of Health and Wellbeing, Sheffield Hallam University

Special thanks are also due to: Suraya Grice, James Greenan, Suzanne Williams, Geoff Holdsworth, Anna Cowper